# Valuation and Financial Forecasting

## A Handbook for Academics and Practitioners

**World Scientific Series in Modern Finance: Advanced Topics in Finance for the Academician and Practitioner**

Series Editor: Ivan E Brick (*Rutgers University, USA*)

---

*Published:*

Vol. 2 *Valuation and Financial Forecasting: A Handbook for Academics and Practitioners*
by Ben Sopranzetti & Braun Kiess

Vol. 1 *Cases in Financial Management: Applications for Financial Analysis*
edited by Ivan E Brick & Harvey Poniachek

World Scientific Series in Modern Finance:
Advanced Topics in Finance for the Academician and Practitioner
**Volume 2**

# Valuation and Financial Forecasting

## A Handbook for Academics and Practitioners

**Ben Sopranzetti**, Ph.D • **Braun Kiess**, M.B.A.

*Rutgers Business School at Newark and New Brunswick, USA*

World Scientific

NEW JERSEY • LONDON • SINGAPORE • BEIJING • SHANGHAI • HONG KONG • TAIPEI • CHENNAI • TOKYO

*Published by*

World Scientific Publishing Co. Pte. Ltd.
5 Toh Tuck Link, Singapore 596224
*USA office:* 27 Warren Street, Suite 401-402, Hackensack, NJ 07601
*UK office:* 57 Shelton Street, Covent Garden, London WC2H 9HE

**Library of Congress Cataloging-in-Publication Data**
Names: Sopranzetti, Ben, author. | Kiess, Braun, author.
Title: Valuation and financial forecasting : a handbook for academics and practitioners /
Ben Sopranzetti, Ph.D, Braun Kiess, M.B.A.,
Rutgers Business School at Newark and New Brunswick, USA.
Description: New Jersey : World Scientific, [2024] | Series: World Scientific series in modern finance: advanced topics in finance for the academician and practitioner ; Volume 2 | Includes index.
Identifiers: LCCN 2022048781 | ISBN 9789811218774 (hardcover) |
ISBN 9789811218781 (ebook) | ISBN 9789811218798 (ebook other)
Subjects: LCSH: Financial statements. | Capital investments. | Business enterprises--Finance. |
Finance--Forecasting.
Classification: LCC HG4028.B2 S677 2024 | DDC 657/.3--dc23/eng/20221228
LC record available at https://lccn.loc.gov/2022048781

**British Library Cataloguing-in-Publication Data**
A catalogue record for this book is available from the British Library.



For any available supplementary material, please visit
https://www.worldscientific.com/worldscibooks/10.1142/11782#t=suppl

Desk Editors: Balasubramanian Shanmugam/Nicole Ong

Typeset by Stallion Press
Email: enquiries@stallionpress.com

*To our families, without whose love, patience, and support this book would never have been possible. Of all the things we value, we value you the most.*

# About the Authors

**Ben Sopranzetti** holds the title of RBS Dean's Professor of Business. He earned his Ph.D. in Finance from the University of Illinois at Urbana-Champaign in 1995 and is a recognized expert in the areas of Business Valuation, Financial Strategy, and Investment Banking. He has published in the *Journal of Business*, *Journal of Finance*, *Journal of Financial and Quantitative Analysis*, and *Manufacturing & Service Operations Management*, among others. Professor Sopranzetti has deep ties to industry and has placed over 600 students on Wall Street. He is widely recognized as a master teacher and is the recipient of more than 20 awards for excellence in teaching. In 2008, he was honored by *Business Week* as one of their twenty-one "Favorite Professors" and in 2021 by *Poets & Quants* as one of the top 50 business professors in the world.

Professor Sopranzetti was a founding managing director of the Rutgers Business, Engineering, Science and Technology Institute (BEST), a university-wide organization that did due diligence for and commercialized early-stage technologies. Most recently, he has taken the responsibility of Vice Chairman of the Department of Finance and Economics at Rutgers Business School. He sits on the board of three companies and is an active advisor and valuation consultant to several bulge-bracket investment banks. Professor Sopranzetti is a founding principal at Piermont Valuation Group, Kebo's Bass Works, and Sopranzetti/Under One. He is responsible for bringing the Road to Wall Street program into the business school, for pioneering the Rutgers 24/7 Omni-channel Teaching Initiative, and for spearheading the business school's mission critical Road to Rutgers diversity initiative.

**Braun C. Kiess** is a successful financial executive, serial entrepreneur, educator, and investor. With decades of experience in a diverse range of industries, Mr. Kiess's professional roles have included: Chief Executive Officer, Chief Financial Officer, Senior Vice President of Sales & Marketing, and Director of Business Development. Mr. Kiess has been a founder, executive, and investor in dozens of startups and middle market companies. He sits on multiple corporate boards and is an Adjunct Professor of Finance and Entrepreneurship at Rutgers Business School.

In addition to being a member of the Rutgers faculty, Mr. Kiess is a widely recognized expert on financial statement analysis, valuation, and financial strategy. He regularly instructs for Rutgers Executive Education and consults Fortune 500 companies and intellectual property-based startups on valuation. As a Principal of the Piermont Valuation Group, Mr. Kiess has testified as an expert witness in forensic valuation and litigation support cases in the Federal Court. He holds a Bachelor's of Science (BS) degree in Finance, Summa Cum Laude, from Rutgers University and holds Master's of Business Administration (MBA) degrees from both Columbia Business School and London Business School.

# Acknowledgments

We would like to thank all of those who have helped us on this journey. First and foremost, we would like to thank our brilliant editor, Ivan Brick, Ph.D., whose insights, knowledge, and guidance have had an immeasurable impact on this book. We would also like to thank Andrew Kim, J.D., M.B.A., Chirag (Chris) Rana, M.FinA, and Silu (Arya) Zhang, M.FinA, for their friendship and exceptional research assistance.

# Declaration

Please note that our financial models may contain calculations using machine precision; thus, if you are following along, and your answers are slightly off, it is likely because of rounding.

# Contents

# Chapter 1

# Introduction

Welcome to *Valuation and Financial Forecasting: A Handbook for Academics and Practitioners*. This book is intended for a very wide audience, ranging from novices to seasoned professional valuation experts. Don't worry if you don't have a strong accounting or finance background. We will build a strong foundation for you before diving into the more advanced concepts.

The goal of financial forecasting and business valuation is to determine forecasted future cash flows that are accurate, fair, and defensible: forecasts upon which we will rely to determine a valuation that is reasonable and that will be accepted by our counterparty. So, what actually *is* value? That is, what is something really worth? Some people say that things are worth what the highest bidder is willing to pay for them. As long as there is someone willing to pay a given price for an asset — even if that price seems extremely high to most people — then that must be what the asset is worth, right? Well, not really! What if that individual that paid the high price for the asset got tired of owning the asset and wanted to turn around and sell it? Could the seller be sure that the asset would be worth the same high amount to someone else? For example, my father's wedding ring is worth a lot more to me than it is to anyone else. So, does it make sense to say that the inflated price that I would be willing to pay for my dad's wedding ring — because of my emotional attachment to it — should be considered the fair market price for the ring when there is no one else in the world that would ever be willing to buy it for that price? That sounds kind of silly, doesn't it?

So, maybe a better question is what "should" something be worth to a rational, arm's length buyer (that is, a buyer that has no emotional attachment to the asset and no significant relationship with the seller)? OK, that question is a little better. But, when we determine what something "should" be the worth in an arm's length transaction, upon what criteria should we base our valuation? What are the factors that drive what something should be worth? And once we know and agree upon those factors, how do we actually go about pricing them? These are important questions, and they lie at the heart of valuation and of this book.

We invest in assets, and in return they generate cash flows. So, when we are valuing a business, it makes sense that what we are valuing is the firm's stream of future expected cash flows. Intuitively, all other things equal, if two firms have the same cash flows, then they should be worth the same amount. When we say, "all other things equal," what do we really mean? You will see later in this book what we really mean is that if the risk is the same, and the cash flows and their timing are the same, then the value should be the same.

The book begins with an overview of financial accounting and a discussion of the basics of financial statement analysis. Readers who already have a deep understanding of financial accounting might want to skip over this section, but there are likely to be a few tidbits of information in that section that even experienced valuation experts will find to be useful. We will explain the three principal financial statements (The Balance Sheet, Income Statement, and Cash Flow Statement) and the line items that are typically found on those statements. We will also explore Financial Statement Analysis, specifically as it refers to measuring Profitability, Efficiency, Leverage, and Liquidity to (1) better understand the strengths and weaknesses of the firm so that we can form better expectations about its future and (2) to protect ourselves from falling prey to accounting fraud and misdirection.

Next, we will explore the time value of money — which is based on the notion that a dollar today is worth more than a dollar tomorrow — and how the time value of money is used to value future cash flows. This is the kind of foundational information that a student would learn in a good introductory finance course, but distilled down to its essentials. We will discuss discounting and compounding, which involve taking the present value and future value of cash flows, respectively. For example, if we get

$100k in 5 years and we require a 10% return on our investments, then what would that $100k be worth today? Or, if I were to invest $100k today for 5 years at a rate of 10%, what would it be worth at the end of the 5 years?

Once we have command of the basics of the time value of money, then we will explore some important tools for financial decision-making, namely Net Present Value, Internal Rate of Return, and Payback Period. To this end, we will also learn about the cost for bearing risk; specifically, the Weighted Average Cost of Capital. These tools are used ubiquitously in the business world to evaluate investments, so it is important that we have a solid understanding of them.

The next part of the book is focused on the three principal valuation methodologies that we are likely to encounter when doing a business valuation: The Income Approach, The Market Approach, and The Asset Approach (both Adjusted Net Asset Value and the Cumulative Excess Earnings methods). Each of these important valuation methodologies takes a somewhat different approach to estimating the value of a business enterprise. They each have their own pros and cons and are more appropriate for use in some cases than in others, but they are all encountered fairly often (albeit, some more than others), so we will explore all three in significant detail.

Next, we will explore financial forecasting; in particular, how to forecast Unlevered Free Cash Flows. Don't worry if you don't know what this means right now; we will explain what Unlevered Free Cash Flows are in detail later in the book. We will also examine some special cases in valuation, such as cyclical firms and firms that are in financial distress. Once we know the different valuation methodologies and how to forecast the cash flows used in those methodologies, we will discuss how to arrive at a consensus price estimate, and how to stress test that estimate by conducting a sensitivity analysis to ensure its robustness to reasonable changes in our assumptions.

This is the book that we both wish we had access to when we were students first learning the ropes and then again as professionals when we started to get contracted to do more complicated valuations. We sincerely hope that you enjoy our handbook and find it to be a helpful reference tool for financial forecasting and valuation, irrespective of your current level of expertise.

## Key Takeaways

- The goal of valuation is to arrive at a value that is fair and defensible: an estimate around which you can develop agreement and consensus.
- We will be working with three principal financial statements — Balance Sheet, Income Statement, and Cash Flow Statement.
- The three principal valuation methodologies for doing a business valuation are: The Income Approach, The Market Approach, and The Asset Approach.

# Chapter 2

# The Balance Sheet

One of the first financial statements that many individuals encounter is the Balance Sheet. You may have heard that the Balance Sheet is used to assess the firm's financial condition, but what is a Balance Sheet exactly and what does it have to do with financial condition? The Balance Sheet is a reckoning, at a specific point in time, of what the firm owns (called *assets*) and what the claims are against what the firm owns (*liabilities and equity*). For example, if the firm has yet to pay for some of its assets or it borrowed money to pay for the assets, then the firm has an obligation (i.e., a *liability*) to pay these obligations back. Until these financial obligations are satisfied, that is, the firm pays back what it owes, the liability holders have a legitimate claim on the firm's assets.

OK, there are assets and liabilities, but what about the owners of the company? What do they get? The owners' claims are called *equity* (also referred to as shareholders' equity or owners' equity), and it is simply the difference between the value of the assets and the value of all the other claims against those assets. Another term that is used synonymously with equity is *net worth*. They both mean the difference between assets and liabilities. The difference between the two is that shareholders' equity usually refers to the value of the owners' investments in an enterprise, whereas net worth is typically used to talk about the company's book value. It is a fine line, and you don't have to worry too much about which word you use. That being said, when a shareholder invests in a corporation, the value of their investment is usually called equity.

The relationship between assets, liabilities, and equity can formally be delineated by the following balance sheet identity:

**Assets = Liabilities + Shareholders' Equity**

**Rule Number One: The balance sheet must balance.** There is no free lunch. If the firm has an asset, then someone must have a claim on it. If the balance sheet did not balance, say perhaps that Assets > Liabilities + Shareholders' Equity, then that means that something existed (an asset) but that no one had a claim to it. In this case, either the liabilities or the equity would be understated, or the assets would be overstated. Likewise, if Assets < Liabilities + Shareholders' Equity, then someone has a claim to an asset that doesn't exist, which is nonsense (at least to any rational person). In this case, either the liabilities or equity is overstated, or the assets are understated; either way, something definitely isn't right.

It is important to note that sometimes, from an accounting perspective, the Shareholders' Equity section isn't always reported as the simple difference between Assets and Liabilities. We can certainly calculate Shareholders' Equity in that way, but that isn't always the way an accounting ledger keeps track of it. From an accounting perspective, the Shareholders' Equity section is often reported as the sum of all the profits a firm has ever made, minus all its losses, plus any capital the owners have initially invested into the business (paid-in capital) and any additional capital that the Shareholders invest in the business over time (additional paid-in capital) minus any capital the owners have taken out of the business (referred to as *dividends*, which are cash disbursements from the firm to the owners). Thus, from an accounting perspective, we often see Owners' Equity being calculated as the following:

$$\begin{aligned}\text{Owners' equity} = {} & \text{Initial paid-in capital} \\ & + \sum_{t=1}^{\text{Today}} (\text{Profit}_t - \text{Losses}_t \\ & \qquad + \text{Additional paid-in capital}_t - \text{Dividends}_t)\end{aligned}$$

The following is a sample Balance Sheet for Alpha Brewing Company (AB), the hypothetical company that we will be studying throughout this handbook. Alpha Brewing Company is a small, craft micro-brewery that has been in business for a few years.

As you can see, all the numbers are in dollars. Using dollars makes it difficult to compare the balance sheets of firms of vastly different size and scale. To facilitate this comparison, we often scale the balance sheet values by Total Assets to get the percentage of Total Assets tied up in the firm's various accounts; this is called *common sizing*.

| **Year** | **2017** | **2018** | **2019** |
|---|---|---|---|
| **Assets** | | | |
| Cash | 93,466 | 213,709 | 266,507 |
| Accounts Receivable | 21,602 | 98,485 | 163,053 |
| Inventory | 15,632 | 17,843 | 20,173 |
| Total Current Assets | 130,700 | 330,037 | 449,733 |
| Security Deposit | 20,000 | 20,000 | 20,000 |
| PP&E, net | 921,994 | 847,488 | 814,982 |
| **Total Assets** | **1,072,694** | **1,197,526** | **1,284,715** |
| **Liabilities & Owners' Equity** | | | |
| A/P – Ingredient Suppliers | 3,829 | 7,749 | 12,819 |
| Current Portion Long-Term Debt | 50,224 | 53,455 | 56,893 |
| Total Current Liabilities | 54,053 | 61,204 | 69,712 |
| Long-Term Debt | 537,342 | 483,888 | 426,995 |
| Total Liabilities | 591,395 | 545,091 | 496,707 |
| Owners' Units — par value | 1,000 | 1,000 | 1,000 |
| Owners' Units — add'l paid-in capital | 422,170 | 422,170 | 422,170 |
| Retained Earnings | 58,129 | 229,264 | 364,838 |
| Total Owners' Equity | 481,299 | 652,434 | 788,008 |
| **Total Liabilities & Owners' Equity** | **1,072,694** | **1,197,526** | **1,284,715** |

## Common-Sized Balance Sheet (Example)

| Assets | 2018 | 2019 | 2020 |
|---|---|---|---|
| Current Assets | | | |
| Cash & Cash Equivalents | 15.3% | 20.1% | 8.9% |
| Short-Term Investments | 1.6% | 1.9% | 2.0% |
| Receivables | 19.7% | 18.9% | 18.9% |
| Inventories | 21.8% | 19.1% | 17.4% |
| Other Current Assets | 6.4% | 5.8% | 5.8% |
| Total Current Assets | 64.8% | 65.9% | 53.1% |
| Non-Current Assets | | | |
| Net PP&E | 10.9% | 10.6% | 12.0% |
| Intangible Assets | 19.6% | 19.7% | 31.5% |
| Deferred Income Taxes | 1.4% | 1.1% | 1.5% |
| Other Long-Term Assets | 3.3% | 2.8% | 1.9% |
| Total Non-Current Assets | 35.2% | 34.1% | 46.9% |
| Total Assets | 100.0% | 100.0% | 100.0% |
| **Liabilities & Owners' Equity** | **2018** | **2019** | **2020** |
| Current Liabilities | | | |
| Short-Term Debt | 1.1% | 6.3% | 2.1% |
| Capital Leases | 0.1% | 0.1% | 0.1% |
| Accounts Payable | 8.3% | 7.3% | 7.5% |
| Taxes Payable | 2.0% | 1.0% | 1.5% |
| Other Current Liabilities | 15.1% | 13.3% | 14.2% |
| Total Current Liabilities | 26.5% | 28.0% | 25.4% |
| Non-Current Liabilities | | | |
| Long-Term Debt | 24.7% | 22.6% | 20.9% |
| Capital Leases | 0.1% | 0.1% | 0.1% |
| Deferred Tax Liabilities | 2.3% | 1.2% | 1.1% |

*(continued)*

| | | | |
|---|---|---|---|
| Pensions & Other Benefits | 1.8% | 1.6% | 2.4% |
| Minority Interest | 0.1% | 0.2% | 0.2% |
| Other Long-Term Liabilities | 3.1% | 1.3% | 2.0% |
| Total Non-Current Liabilities | 32.1% | 26.9% | 26.6% |
| Total Liabilities | 58.6% | 54.9% | 52.0% |
| Owners' Equity | | | |
| Additional Paid-In Capital | 6.9% | 6.5% | 5.7% |
| Retained Earnings | 34.9% | 38.8% | 37.5% |
| Accumulated Other Income | (0.4%) | (0.2%) | 4.8% |
| Total Owners' Equity | 41.4% | 45.1% | 48.0% |
| Total Liabilities & Owners' Equity | 100.0% | 100.0% | 100.0% |

As we start our journey toward understanding the various entries on the balance sheet, it is important to realize that the numbers reported on the balance sheet are recorded at their *book* values. The rules for recording book values of balance sheet items are set forth in, for the US, Generally Accepted Accounting Principles (GAAP), and for many countries outside of the US, International Financial Reporting Standards (IFRS). Canada has its own version of GAAP. Note, there is no universal standard set of rules that govern financial reporting. Many countries have their own governing body that sets the rules for that country. In the US, the governing body that sets the accounting rules is called the Financial Accounting Standards Board (FASB). It is important to note that there are material differences in GAAP reporting versus IFRS reporting and that in most cases these differences need to be properly accounted for before an apples-to-apples comparison can be made between a US firm and a non-US firm.

It is also important to note that reported book values can differ substantially from the real, market values of the respective accounts. Because the way in which the rules are structured, some accounts on the balance sheet, specifically accounts on the Asset side of the balance sheet like Inventory, Property, Plant & Equipment (also commonly referred to as Fixed Assets or Tangible Assets) and Intangible Assets (like patents and copyrights) can differ substantially from their real world, or market, value. But more on that later. For now, let us turn our attention to understanding the most commonly encountered accounts on a balance sheet. In doing so, we will start by discussing the Asset accounts, followed by the Liabilities, and then the Shareholders' Equity account.

Before we begin our review of accounts, something else worth noting is that the date reported on the balance sheet is very important. A balance sheet provides us with the book value for every item the company owns and for every dollar the company owes as of a *particular date* in time. This date will be indicated on the balance sheet (usually at the top of it). In general, for valuation purposes, the older the date and the more dynamic the firm and its product market, the less relevant and useful will be the information on that particular balance sheet. For example, a balance sheet dated yesterday is probably more useful than one dated a month ago, which is more useful than one dated 6 months ago, etc.

It is helpful to think of the balance sheet as a snapshot of the firm: a picture of all the stuff that the firm owns and who has a claim on the stuff. Imagine a picture or snapshot of yourself when you were 2 years old. Chances are you look substantially different today. There is nothing wrong with the photo: it accurately shows what you looked like when you were two, but that was a very long time ago. The information provided by that photograph is stale and of limited use to us for making inferences about you today. A similar logic applies to a firm's balance sheet: its age and staleness matter, so be sure to note the date of the balance sheet before you begin your analysis. Also, it is important to note that, similar to a photographer who can photoshop a photograph in order to make it more appealing, an accountant has a tremendous amount of flexibility in how they interpret the accounting standards in order to present the firm in the best light that is legally and ethically permissible. Our goal, however, is to get to the truth. Remember that accountants are paid by their clients to prepare the financial statements. Don't be afraid to be skeptical and ask questions when you see something that doesn't seem quite right.

While we are on the topic, please always check to make sure that the balance sheet you are looking at balances; that is, that the firm's assets do indeed equal the firm's liabilities + shareholders' equity. If the balance sheet does not balance, then simply hand it back to whomever gave it to you and ask them to correct their accounting before giving it to you to review. Note, they shouldn't be delivering such an erroneous product to you in the first place; that, in and of itself, is a massive red flag.

When looking at a balance sheet, it is also always worth noting in which currency denomination the balance sheet is being presented.

This information is usually indicated at the top of the page. What currency is used to record the balance sheet items? Is it in USD, or CAD, or EUR, or YEN? Are the numbers being shown in thousands ($000), or millions ($000,000), or neither? If the numbers on the balance sheet are being reported in thousands, then be sure to add three zeros on to every number you see. For example, if the numbers are being reported in thousands, and you see ten thousand (10,000), that is really ten million (10,000,000); if the numbers are being reported in millions, then add six zeros on to every number you see, etc.

Turning our attention back to the accounts on the balance sheet, we should note that the accounts are generally presented in order of decreasing liquidity (at least in the US, the opposite is true in Europe). An asset's liquidity can be thought of as its ability to be monetized (turned into cash) on demand (typically in one business day). There are two factors that determine an asset's liquidity: (1) how long it takes us to monetize an asset, and (2) how expensive it is for us to monetize the asset (transaction costs). Imagine if it were the middle of the summer and we had $1MM in cash (say in a checking account) or $1MM in fur coats. There is a very large difference in the liquidity of these two assets. We can immediately monetize our cash. We don't bear any risk in monetizing it. The same cannot be said for our storeroom full of fur coats. It might take us a while to find buyers for all our inventory, that is, unless we want to blow it out at a huge discount, which leads us to the discussion of liquidity and transaction costs. We encounter no transaction costs for monetizing the funds in our cash account. There is no price risk, there is no liquidity risk, and there is no transaction cost associated with it; that is why cash is the most liquid asset — you don't have to do anything in order to spend it. The same cannot be said for our fur coats; thus, our fur coats are not as liquid as our cash account. The discount or "haircut" required to monetize an asset is to a large extent determined by the liquidity in the market for that asset. The more liquidity in the market, the more quickly and less expensively we can monetize the asset.

## *Historical cost*

GAAP accounting is very conservative with respect to asset value, because it protects against management's inclinations to overestimate the market value of the assets the firm owns. Thus, GAAP often sets the ceiling, or upper bound, on an asset's value as the price paid by the firm for the asset; that is, its *historical cost*, also known as its *cost basis*. This rule prevents the book value of the asset from rising above that cost basis; however, there is no limit set by GAAP as to the floor, or lower bound, on the value of the asset — besides zero. An asset cannot be worth less than zero, otherwise it would be abandoned.

The fact that, in general, the book value of a firm's assets, such as Buildings and Patents, cannot be increased but can only be decreased, most often by depreciation or amortization, can cause some significant distortions between the market value (what something is actually worth today) and book value of the firm's assets. Imagine a building the firm has owned for 40 years. The book value of this building would have depreciated to zero, assuming a useful life as determined by the IRS of less than 40 years, which is currently the case. However, the market value of the building is likely much greater than what was even originally paid for it. In this case, the firm may be in possession of an asset that, for accounting purposes, and hence investor reporting purposes, is worth zero, but has a real value (market value) of many millions of dollars.

The discrepancy between book value and market value is not lost on the savvy investor. Investors such as Eddie Lampert, the famous owner of Sears via his hedge fund firm, ESL Investments, purchased Sears partly because of the discrepancy in Sears's book value of real estate holdings versus the market value of its real estate holdings. When Mr. Lampert purchased Sears (circa 2008), he noted that he was able to purchase all of Sears, its assets, its brands (such as the Craftsman brand), and the business itself, for less than what he had calculated to be the market value of Sears' real estate holdings. That is to say that Eddie basically got the company, its brands, and its ongoing operations for "free" because the market had let the stock price of Sears get so low that the stock price no longer even accounted for the market value of Sears's real estate. Eddie saw an opportunity to take advantage of this market mispricing, which was partly attributable to the fact that Sears owned many of its properties for a long period of time: long enough that the book values of many of them were very low, and hence, Sears's balance sheet did not at all reflect the real market value of the firm's real estate holdings.

### *Vertical or horizontal*

Sometimes the balance sheet is laid out horizontally with assets on the left and liabilities and equity on the right; other times it is laid out vertically, with assets at the top and liabilities and equity on the bottom. Other than aesthetics, there is no real difference.

### *Cash versus accrual basis of accounting*

There are two ways in which a firm can report its financials: the Cash Basis or the Accrual Basis. If a firm chooses to use the Cash Basis of accounting, then the firm's Sales would be recorded when and only when the cash is actually received from the customer, and all of the firm's expenses would be recorded when they were actually physically paid by the firm. This is very different from what happens under the Accrual Basis of accounting. If a firm is using the Accrual Basis of accounting, then the firm's Revenues would be immediately recorded when the customer is invoiced (not when the customer actually pays) and the firm's expenses would be recorded when the bill was received from the vendor (and not when the bill is actually paid).

Fortunately, we have some guidance as to which basis is best for any given firm: the Matching Principle. The Matching Principle states that when choosing accounting methods, a firm should always choose whichever method most accurately matches the firm's costs of generating a dollar in sales to that actual dollar of sales. In other words, firms should always choose to do whatever allows them to most accurately match expenses incurred to revenues earned. The reason for this is that doing so gives a third party, for example, an investor, the most accurate picture of the economics, or earning power, of the business. For most firms, the Matching Principle means that they use the Accrual basis of accounting to most accurately match costs to sales. Note that all publicly traded firms in the US will use the Accrual Basis. Henceforth in this book, unless we explicitly say so, we will assume that the firm is using the accrual basis of accounting.

## Assets

The Asset section of the balance sheet is divided into two categories: Current Assets and Long-Term Assets. Current Assets are any assets that are expected to monetize during the normal course of business within the next year. Long-Term Assets are any assets the firm owns that are not expected to be converted into cash within the next year.

Let us start by reviewing the most commonly found Current Assets accounts: Cash, Marketable Securities (or Cash Equivalents), Accounts Receivable, Inventory, and Pre-paid Expenses. Under GAAP, we know that the first Current Assets account listed should be the most liquid asset: Cash.

## *Cash*

Cash is US dollars that are usually deposited in a firm's checking account, but it can be in other bank accounts, safes, cash registers, under your mattress, or even in a piggy bank. The Cash account is the sum total of all the cash the firm has anywhere it keeps its cash. The nice thing about cash is that it is safe and immediately monetizable; however, the disadvantage to holding cash is that it earns the firm little to no interest. Consequently, firms tend to keep just enough cash on their books in order to satisfy their short-term liquidity needs, but other than a few notable exceptions (Apple, for example), most firms do not hoard cash. Instead, any excess cash is often invested in Marketable Securities.

It is important to note that there are two kinds of cash: *restricted cash* and *excess cash*. Excess cash is what we typically think about when we talk about the cash account. Excess cash can be spent whenever we want to spend it; there are no restrictions on its use. This is like the cash in your checking account. Restricted cash is different. For example, the firm might have a deal with its bank that allows the firm to borrow money on a revolving line of credit at any time up to say a $100k limit. In return, the bank will require an interest payment on the outstanding balance and might also require the firm to keep a minimum of $30k in deposits at the bank at all times. In this case, that $30k is called restricted cash, and cannot be used for any other purpose than maintaining this minimum balance. Moving forward, when we talk about cash, we will be talking about excess cash, unless we specifically say otherwise.

## *Marketable securities/cash equivalents*

The second account we will most often see on a firm's balance sheet is called Cash Equivalents (also called Marketable Securities). These are highly-liquid, low-risk financial assets in which the firm invests short-term to earn some interest on funds for which it does not have an immediate need, but which it might need in the near future. Let us say, for example, that our firm had a million dollars in excess cash for which we did not have an immediate need, but that we will need in a month or so. What could we do with that extra million dollars? Well, we could let it sit safely in our firm's checking (cash) account or in our safe, but the problem is that our money would earn a very low, or in the case of keeping it in the safe, no interest rate (as of the date of the initial writing of this chapter, interest rates in Switzerland are actually negative!) Our asset wouldn't be earning any money for us. So, what does a smart Chief Financial Officer (CFO) do? They invest that million dollars of excess cash in the money market (short-term financial instruments) in order to earn a higher interest rate.

The key is that to be considered a cash equivalent or marketable security, the asset must, in general, meet two criteria: (1) it must be highly liquid, and (2) it must be very safe; that is, there is little risk to us for not getting back the full amount of our initial investment quickly. Typically, a firm will invest its excess cash in highly liquid and very safe market traded securities, such as US Treasury bills or bonds, certificates of deposit (CDs), and commercial paper. Things like bank cashier's checks, bank treasury checks, postal money orders, Western Union Money Orders, American Express Traveler's Checks, and even foreign currency deposits are all considered Cash Equivalents. An equity investment in a promising new start-up or an investment in a corporate bond or equity would not be considered marketable securities or cash equivalents, since there is a substantial risk that we could not quickly recover the full amount of our initial investment; consequently, these investments need to be listed somewhere else, farther down on the balance sheet.

### *Accounts receivable*

The next account we encounter is called Accounts Receivable (AR). AR represents sales of products or services that have already happened but for which our firm has not yet been paid, that is, our firm shipped goods to our customer, and invoiced our customer for the goods, but we are waiting to collect payment. AR thus accounts for a firm's uncollected sales invoices. It represents sales, and thus the future promise of cash, but not actual cash.

AR can also be thought of as an interest-free loan to your customers (or an "I Owe You," IOU); assuming you are not charging them any interest for paying within your payment terms. Standard payment terms for goods and services vary by industry and range from due-upon performance payment (COD — Cash on Delivery) for services such as a plumbing or electrical repair to 90 to 120+ days for much of the healthcare industry. Common shorthand terms used by firms to state their payment terms on invoices are things like 2/10 Net 30, which, if seen on an invoice we received, would mean the company is willing to offer us a 2% discount (take 2% off the invoice total) if we pay the invoice within 10 days, otherwise the invoice needs to be paid in full within 30 days of the date on the invoice. We might also see 1/10 Net 60 (which is increasingly becoming more common), which would mean the company is willing to offer us a 1% discount if you pay them within 10 days, otherwise full payment on the invoice is due within 60 days from the date on the invoice.

Accounts Receivable should be driven directly by Revenues since they are created directly as a result of the firm selling a product or providing a service. In fact, when forecasting AR, we often consider the historical ratio of AR to Sales, and if nothing material about the firm or its customer relationships has changed, then, for forecasting purposes, we typically use this historical ratio as our estimate of what will be the future relationship between AR and Sales.

We would like to note that the AR account only arises when a firm is using the Accrual Basis of accounting. Recall, with the cash basis, we don't book a sale until we get paid, thus there is no waiting, and hence no accounts receivable.

### *Doubtful receivables*

Doubtful receivables is a balance sheet account that is reported at management's discretion, specifically, when the management team believes that there is serious risk that a customer will not pay its outstanding invoices. Doubtful receivables means that the firm hasn't given up hope yet (if it had, then the receivables would be impaired and written down), but things aren't looking good with respect to getting paid. Doubtful receivables is considered a *contra asset*, in that it reduces the outstanding receivable balance. So, if the firm has $1MM in receivables, but $100k of those are doubtful receivables, then the net receivables (those that we actually expect will monetize) are $900k.

### *Inventory*

The next account we are likely to see on the Balance Sheet is called Inventory. Inventory represents the total value of goods a firm has available for sale. For example, the inventory of a retail firm would be the value of all the goods the firm has available for sale in its stores and in its warehouses. The inventory of a manufacturing firm is the sum of the value of three different categories of goods: finished goods, work-in-process (WIP), and raw materials. Take, for example, a car manufacturer such as Ford Motor Company. The inventory number that Ford reports on its Balance Sheet is the sum of the value of the completed cars it has waiting to be sold to dealers, plus the value of any vehicles it has in some stage of production, plus the value of raw materials (e.g., steel, glass, tires, etc.) that Ford owns that are waiting to be put into production.

The Inventory account, like all the other balance sheet accounts, is reported at historical cost: the lesser of its current book value or what it is actually worth today. That means that the value of a firm's Inventory can never exceed what the firm paid for it (its historical cost), however, the inventory can be reported at less than what was paid for it if the firm feels that value of the inventory has been *impaired*. Impairment is an accounting concept that occurs whenever the value of an asset has permanently and irreversibly decreased. Accountants call this decrease in value "Impairment."

The value of a firm's inventory can be impaired by obsolescence, perishability, and/or changes in the market for the firm's products. Impairment due to obsolescence has to do with a product no longer being relevant to the market, for example, if you happened to still own a warehouse full of Pentium 386 microprocessors from the late 1990s, the value of that inventory would be severely impaired today and would need to be reported at a very low value compared to what was originally paid for those processors 30 years ago. Similarly, if your firm's inventory was a container full of bananas that got held in customs for a few months (causing all the bananas to rot), then your firm would need to impair the value of that inventory due to perishability. In general, if the management of a firm has any reason to believe that the market value of its inventory has permanently fallen below the cost the firm paid for that inventory, then in order to comply with GAAP accounting standards, the firm would be required to impair, or decrease, the value of its inventory to the lesser of what the firm paid for it or what they feel that inventory is worth today. In this case, the firm's equity would be reduced by the amount of the impairment. In addition, the firm would report the loss of value as an increase in Costs of Goods Sold (see Chapter 3, on the Income Statement).

Another component of inventory accounting has to do with what assumption a firm chooses to make with respect to the flow of its inventory through the organization. There are three methods of inventory accounting permitted under GAAP: First-In-First-Out (FIFO), Last-In-First-Out (LIFO), and Average Cost. The difference among these inventory accounting methods pertains to the assumptions of each with respect to the flow of goods. We won't be going into details about the difference in these methods, but we wanted to bring them to your attention.

### *Pre-paid expenses*

Continuing to work our way down the Current Assets section of the Balance Sheet, the next account we encounter is called Pre-paid Expenses. The pre-paid expenses account represents something for which the company has paid for in advance, but whose associated benefit the company hasn't fully utilized yet. Most often this is for an expense like insurance (also a service contract or a subscription service) where instead of paying for the annual policy in monthly payments, the firm chooses to pay for the entire policy up-front at the beginning of the policy period. Doing this would create a pre-paid expense — Insurance or a Service Benefit, which would decrease by one-twelfth each month until the end of the 1-year policy term.

### *Long-term assets*

Next, we will look at the Non-Current or Long-Term Asset accounts. These are also called Long-Lived Assets, Tangible Assets, or Capital Assets. Recall that the Current Asset accounts represent those assets that are expected to be converted into cash within the next year; in contrast, the Long-Term Asset accounts represent everything else. For many firms, the largest Long-Term Asset account is usually an account called Property, Plant & Equipment (PP&E).

## *Capital/financial leases and right of use assets*

There are two types of leases: Operating Leases and Capital (now called Financial) Leases. Operating Leases are effectively long-term rental agreements (like renting an office), and thus their value has up until recently not been accounted for on the balance sheet, but this has changed. They are now reported as *Right of Use Assets* with a corresponding offsetting *Operating Lease Liability*. Capital (Financial) Leases, in contrast, are very similar to long-term loans, since the lessee leases the asset for most of its useful life; consequently, accountants report *Financial Leases* as the asset that has an identical offsetting, corresponding liability called *Financial Leases*. The value of all leases (Right of Use Assets and Financial Lease assets and their corresponding liabilities) is calculated as the present value of all the future lease payments (we will learn how to take present values later in the book). Note that creditors have historically treated Capital/Financial Leases as debt. The same is now true for operating leases. As payments are made on a Right to Use Asset or a Capital Lease, both the asset and the liability will be reduced symmetrically by the principal component (versus interest) amount of the payment, until the Lease has been paid off and its balance is zero.

## *Property, plant, and equipment*

The *PP&E* account comprises *Property*, which is land, *Plant*, which includes edifices built on the land, and *Equipment*, which includes any durable machines or fixtures the company owns that are used to manufacture products or provide services.

The PP&E account increases with Capital Expenditures (investments made in PP&E) and decreases with Depreciation. *Depreciation* is an accounting concept that takes an asset's value and allocates it over the asset's useful life. For example, let us say that a firm decided to purchase a new piece of manufacturing equipment for one million dollars and that the useful life of that equipment was 10 years. Under *straight-line* depreciation, the firm would depreciate \$1,000,000 divided by 10 = \$100,000 each year for the next 10 years. For simplicity, let us also assume that, for this example, this piece of equipment is the only PP&E asset the firm owns. In this case, at the end of the first year, the firm's PP&E account would look like this:

| End of Year 1 | |
|---|---|
| PP&E — Equipment | 1,000,000 |
| Less: Accumulated Depreciation — Equipment | 100,000 |
| PP&E — Net | 900,000 |

As we can see from this example, the PP&E account is sometimes reported as Gross PP&E minus any accumulated depreciation. This difference is typically referred to as Net PP&E. In this example, we would say that book value of the firm's gross PP&E was $1,000,000, but the net PP&E was $900,000. At the end of year 2, the PP&E account would look like this:

| End of Year 2 | |
|---|---|
| PP&E — Equipment | 1,000,000 |
| Less: Accumulated Depreciation — Equipment | 200,000 |
| PP&E — Net | 800,000 |

Here the net PP&E account now reflects 2 years of accumulated depreciation ($100,000 from year 1 plus $100,000 from year 2 for a total of $200,000). This reduction in value will continue each year until the asset is fully depreciated in year 10, when the PP&E account would be reported as follows:

| End of Year 10 | |
|---|---|
| PP&E — Equipment | 1,000,000 |
| Less: Accumulated Depreciation — Equipment | 1,000,000 |
| PP&E — Net | 0 |

At the end of an asset's useful life, the book value of the asset is zero. The useful life of an asset is determined by both GAAP and the Internal Revenue Service (IRS) for just about every type of asset imaginable. It is worth noting that the GAAP and IRS useful life numbers do not always align. This non-alignment in useful lives between GAAP and the IRS is one of the reasons why a firm's financial statements for tax reporting purposes may be different than the firm's financial statements for Securities and Exchange Commission[1] (SEC) reporting purposes.

In the above example, we assumed that the Equipment asset was depreciated using straight-line depreciation. Straight-line depreciation is the most conservative (i.e., the least aggressive) form of depreciation, in which the asset depreciates by the same amount for each year of the asset's useful life. The benefits of straight-line depreciation are that (1) it is very easy to calculate and to explain to others and (2) we minimize the impact of the depreciation on near-term profits, since we are evenly spreading out the depreciation over the asset's useful life; consequently, it is very common to find this method utilized for GAAP financial statements. The disadvantage of straight-line depreciation is that, for IRS tax purposes, we are minimizing the near-term benefits of the tax shield that is provided by the reduction of pre-tax earnings that comes from depreciation, so under straight-line depreciation, we pay the highest amount of tax.

Firms typically prefer a more aggressive form of depreciation for tax purposes. An example of one such type of depreciation is called MACRS (Modified Accelerated Cost Recovery System). Under MACRS, the asset is not depreciated by a uniform amount every year over its useful life; instead, more of the depreciation is applied during the early years of the asset's life versus the later years.

For example, the following is a summary straight line versus MACRS depreciation schedule:

| | **Percentage per Year** | |
|---|---|---|
| **Year** | **Straight Line** | **MACRS** |
| 1 | 10.00% | 13.28% |
| 2 | 10.00% | 18.00% |
| 3 | 10.00% | 14.40% |

*(Continued)*

[1]The United States Securities and Exchange Commission is the governing body for publicly traded companies in the United States. The SEC determines the reporting requirements for all the publicly traded companies, which the SEC appoints to the Financial Accounting Standards Board (FASB) to detail its Generally Accepted Accounting Principles (GAAP).

(*Continued*)

| | Percentage per Year | |
|---|---|---|
| **Year** | **Straight Line** | **MACRS** |
| 4 | 10.00% | 11.52% |
| 5 | 10.00% | 9.22% |
| 6 | 10.00% | 7.37% |
| 7 | 10.00% | 6.55% |
| 8 | 10.00% | 6.55% |
| 9 | 10.00% | 6.55% |
| 10 | 10.00% | 6.55% |
| | 100.00% | 100.00% |

As you can see, the MACRS schedule is more aggressive in the early years of the asset's useful life than is the straight-line method of depreciation. So why would a firm use MACRS? MACRS is used by firms, when permitted by the IRS, to decrease the firm's IRS tax liability, since it can claim more of the asset's cost as a pre-tax income and thereby reducing tax expense earlier in the asset's life.

We should also note that, like the Inventory account, the firm's PP&E account needs to be reported at the lesser of book value or what the asset is worth today. Stated another way, a firm's Long-Term Assets, such as land, buildings, and equipment, can never appreciate (get written up), they can only depreciate (get written down). To be completely accurate, Land (unlike Plant and Equipment) is not depreciable. We don't get a tax break from buying land. We get a tax break only from buying buildings and machines, which supposedly get worn down and consumed and will one day need to be replaced. This means that should the market value of land or a building or a machine that the firm owns double in value, the book value would never be adjusted to reflect the increase in market value. However, if management believes that the market value of a Long-Term Asset has been permanently reduced to an amount less than the current book value of that asset, then management should reduce or impair the value of that asset to reflect the current market value.

### *Other long-term assets*

Other assets listed under Long-Term Assets can include things like property held for sale, start-up costs in connection with a new business, cash surrender value of life insurance policies, long-term advance payments, long-term financial investments (like a 401k plan or an investment account), capitalized financing fees, and intangibles.

### *Intangible assets*

Intangible Long-Term Assets are separated into two types: Identifiable and Unidentifiable Intangible Assets. Identifiable Intangible Assets are those that GAAP allows to be reported on the balance sheet, and include things such as Goodwill and assets associated with a firm's intellectual property, such as patents, trademarks, and copyrights. These assets have a physical document that exists that grants some form of market protection (either a government-issued patent, a copyright, or a trademark), thus they are "tangible." Unidentifiable Intangible Assets don't have a physical document associated with them, but are still important and have real-world value, like brand, trade secrets (e.g., the formula for Coca-Cola), and expertise contained in human capital. Unfortunately, GAAP does not allow Unidentifiable Intangible Assets to be included on the balance sheet. That sounds silly, doesn't it? Things like brand can be incredibly valuable!

Why doesn't GAAP allow for these potentially extremely valuable things to be reported on the balance sheet? They certainly affect the value of equity, don't they? The answer is actually very simple. GAAP's standards revolve around the reporting of the value of assets at their historical cost; this is why inventory and PP&E have to be booked at the lesser of what they are worth today or what we paid for them. That means that for a brand or a patent, for example, the only historical expenses we can record on the balance sheet are the costs that the firm actually incurred in trademarking the brand or filing the patent application: that's it. In other words, if the firm internally created the Intangible Asset, such as a patent on one of the firm's new products or the firm's brand recognition resulting from years of expensive advertising campaigns, then the market value of the brand or the patent would not appear on the firm's balance sheet;

instead, only the historical cost basis would appear. However, if the firm were to instead acquire (purchase) the Intangible Asset (like a patent) from someone else, then the Intangible Asset would be recorded on the acquiring firm's balance sheet at the price that was paid to purchase it (i.e., the market value at the time of the purchase).

### *Amortization*

If the Intangible Asset's life is finite, such as a US patent that expires in 20 years, then the cost of the Intangible Asset is *amortized* over its useful life on the books of the acquiring firm. Amortization is very similar to depreciation: it allocates the cost of an Intangible Asset over its useful life and simultaneously reduces the balance sheet account by the same amount. If, however, the intangible asset has an indefinite life, such as a brand (which would be reported as goodwill — see what follows), then the asset must be assessed each year for impairment (that is, is the current market value of the asset greater than the historical basis, if so then nothing happens, if not, then the asset gets impaired).

Many people are shocked that accountants do not value assets at their fair market values when preparing balance sheets. However, FASB and other organizations that oversee accounting standards have the philosophy that financial statements should be reliable, consistent, and comparable across different firms and across different accountants; consequently, they prefer the use of objective and concrete historical costs, rather than less objective and potentially subjective estimates of current fair market values.

### *Goodwill*

GAAP's focus on historical cost means that an asset's value must be reported at the lesser of its historical cost or what it is worth today. With respect to goodwill, this means that if we purchase a company that has brand value (or human capital or trade secrets, etc.) or we purchase just the brand from another company, then we account for money that we paid for the brand (that is our historical cost of acquiring the brand) under the asset category called *Goodwill.*

Goodwill arises when the price paid for the equity of a target company is greater than the difference between the sum of the fair market value of its total identifiable balance sheet assets (e.g., Cash, AR, Prepaid, Inventory, PP&E, Identifiable Intangibles) and the fair market value of the liabilities. That is a mouthful. In a nutshell, the price we paid is greater than what the accountants can actually find "buckets" for when they allocate the value of the things that we bought. They allocate all that they can, but there is still some value left over. Remember, GAAP has no buckets for Unidentifiable Intangible Assets, so any money that we spent for these things must go somewhere. Where does it go? Goodwill.

Goodwill = Equity purchase price
— (Total MV of identifiable assets
— Total MV of liabilities)

Goodwill = Equity purchase price – Net asset value

For example, imagine that we plan to acquire a target for $100MM. At the time of acquisition, we assess the fair market value of all the assets that are reported on the target's balance sheet and determine them to be worth a total of $80MM. We then do the same for the market value of the firm's liabilities and arrive at a total of $40MM. We take the difference between these two values in order to arrive at the target's net asset value, $80MM – $40MM = $40MM. This means that we are effectively paying $100MM for a firm that has $40MM in net assets. So, if we borrowed all of the money to fund the acquisition, the right-hand side of our balance sheet would increase by $100MM, but the left-hand side of the balance sheet would only increase by $40MM. The balance sheet wouldn't balance, so we have to find a way to account for the $60MM difference. Note, we absolutely did NOT overpay for the target by $60MM. Instead, we paid for assets (perhaps brand, or trade secrets, for example) that did not appear on the target's balance sheet when we bought it. In order for our balance sheet to balance, the $60MM difference would be recorded on our balance sheet as Goodwill.

Goodwill is accounted for slightly differently for public firms versus private firms, but the general idea of Goodwill remains the same. It is an account that captures the excess of purchase price to net asset value of all the acquisitions the acquiring firm has made since its founding. The Goodwill account thus represents a running tally of all the goodwill that it accrued from each of its acquisitions over the life of the firm.

Publicly traded firms are not allowed to amortize Goodwill but are instead required to get a market estimate of their Goodwill accounts each year in order to determine if any impairment has occurred, and if so to reduce Goodwill by the amount of the impairment. This is called conducting an *annual impairment test* of the Goodwill. As mentioned above, amortization is a similar concept to depreciation, but whereas depreciation pertains to capitalizing the cost of a Tangible Asset (such as buildings and equipment), amortization pertains to capitalizing the cost of Intangible Assets (such as patents and goodwill). Note that much like other asset accounts on the balance sheet, the Goodwill account can never increase in value (unless there are more acquisitions). Goodwill can decrease, however, if impairment occurs. Privately held firms may elect to amortize Goodwill over a period of 10 years or less, but they should check with the firm's accountant in order to make sure.

## Liabilities

A firm's Liabilities represent an accounting of all the monies owed by the firm to others. The firm's Total Liabilities tell us how much of the firm's asset value is in fact owed to others. And just like there are two categories of Assets (Current and Long-Term), there are the same two categories of Liabilities — with the firm's Current Liability accounts representing any accounts that the firm expects to pay off within the next year, and the firm's Long-Term Liability accounts representing any accounts that the firm does not expect to pay off within the next year.

### *Accounts payable*

One of the first accounts found in the Current Liability section of the firm's Balance Sheet is the Accounts Payable (AP) account. AP represents the flipside of the firm's Accounts Receivable (AR) account; that is, while the AR account represents monies owed *to* the firm by its customers for goods or services the firm has provided, the AP account represents monies owed *by* the firm to its vendors for goods or services those vendors have provided to the firm. While AR can be thought of as a zero-interest rate loan from the firm to its customers, AP can be thought of as a zero-interest rate loan to the firm from its vendors. When the firm pays an invoice from one of its vendors, the firm's AP account is reduced by the amount of the invoice payment.

### *Deferred taxes*

Accrued (or Deferred) Taxes is another account we often find under the Current Liabilities section of the firm's Balance Sheet. Accrued Taxes represent taxes that the firm owes and expects to pay within the next year. These tax liabilities often result from temporary differences in a firm's recognition of revenues and expenses for tax (IRS) versus investor (SEC) reporting purposes.

### *Notes payable*

Notes Payable is often the next account we see under Current Liabilities. The Notes Payable account represents the outstanding balance on all the firm's revolving lines of bank credit plus the balance the firm owes on any notes payable to its suppliers. The firm's revolving lines of credit are similar to credit card accounts, in that the firm can draw on these lines of credit as needed until the credit line reaches its limit. The firm can then pay down the balance on these lines of credit whenever cash flow permits.

Similar to a credit card, the minimum payments due on the revolving lines of credit are typically interest-only payments due monthly or quarterly. These types of bank lines of credit typically get reviewed and renewed annually. Hence, they are listed under Current Liabilities, even though the firm could technically carry a balance on these lines for longer than a year. It should also be noted that any debts reported on the Balance Sheet represent the principal amounts due and do not include any interest, unless that interest is already payable. Hence, the amounts listed for any debts the firm owed reflect the amount required to pay off that debt in full as of the date on the Balance Sheet.

### *Current portion of long-term debt*

Another debt account we find listed under Current Liabilities is an account called Current Portion of Long-Term Debt. The balance in this account represents the next 12 months' worth of payments on all the term loans the firm has that mature in more than a year. For example, if the firm had a 25-year mortgage loan and a 5-year truck loan, then the balance shown in this account would represent the next 12 months' worth of payments due on both the mortgage loan and the truck loan (principal only).

You might be asking, why do accountants bother reporting the firm's Current Portion of Long-Term Debt? The answer lies in a commonly calculated ratio called the Current Ratio, which is calculated as the ratio of a firm's Current Assets to Current Liabilities. The Current Ratio is used as a measure of the firm's liquidity (or availability of cash). Remember that the firm's Current Assets represent all of the cash the firm expects to collect in the next year, and its Current Liabilities represent all of the cash the firm expects to pay out in the next year; hence, by looking at the ratio of the two, we can see how likely the firm is to experience a shortage of cash (liquidity) within the next year. Any ratio of Current Assets to Current Liabilities resulting in a number less than one means the firm is expecting to pay out more cash than it is expecting to collect in the next 12 months. The larger the Current Ratio, the better the firm's short-term liquidity. Since long-term loans often require monthly payments, the inclusion of the Current Portion of Long-Term Debt account under Current Liabilities makes the Current Ratio more accurate with respect to the amount of cash the firm will need to pay out within the next year.

## *Accrued liabilities*

Accrued Liabilities (AL) is another account found under Current Liabilities. The account or accounts listed here will include any other monies the firm owes that it expects to pay within the next 12 months. These are things that the firm has enjoyed but hasn't paid for yet. A great example of this would be the firm's utility bill. We get our utility bills at the end of the month after we have used the utility, not at the beginning of the month before we use it. Thus, our unpaid utility balance is an accrued liability. Another extremely important accrued liability is payroll, often recorded on the balance sheet as "Accrued Liabilities — Payroll." This account would represent any payroll monies the firm owes to its employees as of the date on the Balance Sheet. Such an account would be created if, say, the firm ran a bi-monthly payroll and the Balance Sheet reporting date fell 1 week into the firm's 2-week pay period. The firm would hence owe all of its employees 1 week's worth of pay. That amount would be reflected in the Accrued Liabilities — Payroll account under the Current

Liabilities section of the firm's Balance Sheet. Note… do not miss making a payroll payment!

## *What is working capital?*

Working Capital is the difference between non-interest-earning current assets minus non-interest-bearing current liabilities (we will learn more about these later in this chapter). Working Capital is all about waiting for money to be paid either to us or by us. If we have Accounts Receivable, then we are waiting for customers to pay us. If we have Accounts Payable, then we are waiting to pay our vendors. If we have Accrued Expenses,then we are waiting to pay our employees. And, if we have Inventory, then we are waiting to sell our products. You might encounter the phrase, "tied up in working capital." For each working capital item, there is a period of time before the asset turns into cash or the liability gets paid by us in cash. Until that point in time, the balance sheet item is "tied up in working capital." Thus, we can think of the working capital assets and liabilities as temporary storage bins for cash that will soon come into the firm or leave the firm.

## *Long-term liabilities*

Next, we will look at the Non-Current or Long-Term Liability accounts. In doing so, we recall that the Current Liability accounts represent any types of liabilities that are expected to be paid in cash within the next year, while the Long-Term Liability accounts represent any types of liabilities that are not expected to be paid in cash within the next year. For many firms, the largest Long-Term Liability account is usually an account called Long-Term Debt.

## *Operating and financial leases*

See the discussion under Long-Term Assets.

## *Long-term debt*

The Long-Term Debt account represents the outstanding principal balances (remember, interest would not be included unless already accrued) on all the debt obligations that the firm has that mature in more than 1 year. Examples of such debt obligations are mortgages, equipment loans, and bonds. Most of you are probably familiar with loans. Loans amortize, which means that each loan payment includes a portion that goes toward paying off the loan's principal and a portion that will cover the interest payment on the outstanding balance. Note that the amortization of a loan is very different than the amortization of an Intangible Asset. It is the same word but has a different definition in this case. Over time the outstanding balance of the loan will decrease steadily as the periodic payments are made. Now recall that the next 12 months' worth of payments on these long-term loans is accounted for in the Current Liability account called Current Portion of Long-Term Debt. Thus, the amount shown here does not include the next 12 months' worth of payments on these loans, as those amounts are already being accounted for in the Current Liabilities section.

*Bonds* are a little different than term loans. They are still debt obligations, but they act just like interest-only loans; that is, they do not amortize. That means that all of a bond's principal (the amount that we borrowed, it is typically called *par value*) is paid off in one massive lump-sum payment at the end of the bond's life. So, how does the lender get paid if they don't get any of their principal back until the bond matures? The lender gets periodic interest payments called *coupon payments*, which are usually made on a semi-annual (every 6-month) basis. A typical corporate bond will make interest payments every 6 months until it matures, at which point the lender will get all of their principal amount back. For example, if the bond's interest rate is 10% semi-annual, that means that the bond will pay 5% of the principal amount every 6 months, that is, 10% of the principal amount split into two equal payments of 5% each. So, if the bond has a $10MM par value, the lender should expect to receive $500k in interest (the coupon payment) every 6 months until the bond matures, at which point they will receive their last $500k interest payment and also get back their $10MM initial investment. That means that if the firm has a bond on its balance sheet, we should expect that the amount recorded for the bond will not change at all from year to year. In this case, the accountant would report $10MM for Long-Term Debt every year until the bond finally matures, at which point it will be paid off and the bond would completely disappear from the balance sheet.

### *Other long-term liabilities*

Other Long-Term Liabilities is another account you find under Long-Term Liabilities. This account represents a catch-all account for any other miscellaneous long-term liabilities the firm might have. What we know is that the balance in this account represents obligations the firm has that it does not expect to pay within the next year. It is best to read the notes in the firm's financial statements to understand what exactly the firm is including in this account. Commonly included items in the Other Long-Term Liabilities account include Tax Contingencies, Construction Liabilities, and Long-Term Deferred Tax Liabilities.

### *Commitments and contingencies*

Another account you might find listed under Long-Term Liabilities is an account called Commitments and Contingencies. You will never see a dollar amount listed next to this account. The presence of this account under the Long-Term Liabilities section of the firm's Balance Sheet is meant to alert the reader to the fact that the firm has some large, but as of yet, undetermined amount of pending liabilities.

When you see the Commitments and Contingencies account listed, you should VERY CAREFULLY read the notes on the account included with the firm's financial statements. A Commitment is a non-cancelable obligation for the firm to do something or pay something. An example of a commitment is a manufacturer that has signed a non-cancelable contract to buy 50,000 light bulbs during the following 8 years. This large commitment of future spending should be disclosed to investors. If the firm had contractual commitments with third parties, then it might provide a summary table as to the nature of their contractual commitments and their respective amounts.

In many respects, Contingencies can be even worse than Commitments. Contingencies represent potential future liabilities that are currently not reported on the balance sheet but that would be reported contingent on something bad happening. The classic example is a pending lawsuit. If a firm had litigation pending (a class action lawsuit, for example), then they would list the Commitments and Contingencies account under their Long-Term Liabilities. There would be no amount reported (since there is no actual liability… yet!), but there would likely be a footnote that contained a description of the nature of the class action lawsuit. Don't be surprised if you read something like, "We believe that the pending lawsuit will have no substantial impact on the firm." Yeah, right! When you see a line item for Commitments and Contingencies, be on high alert, since there is something potentially very nasty waiting for you in the footnotes. If so, then be sure to do your due diligence. Internet search engines can be your first line of defense.

### *Preferred stock*

Preferred Stock is a type of stock typically issued to large, institutional investors in exchange for a large investment in the firm. Preferred Stock typically carries special rights and privileges, which are negotiated directly between the large investor and the firm. Unlike Common Stock, Preferred Stock typically does not have voting rights; the holders of Preferred Shares will usually have negotiated more direct control, such as one or more seats on the firm's Board of Directors, as part of the terms of their Preferred Shares. Also, unlike Common Stock, Preferred Stock usually carries a fixed quarterly dividend payment, which is set at a fixed percentage of the Preferred Stock's par value (the amount invested). Like Common Stock, the quarterly dividends owed to preferred shareholders can be paid at the discretion of the firm. However, unlike Common Stock, the dividend payments due to preferred shareholders, if unpaid, accrue in arrears. The terms of most Preferred Shares state that no dividends can be paid to common shareholders until all preferred Shareholders' dividends are current. That is, the firm is prevented from distributing any of the firm's profits to its common shareholders until all dividends owed to its preferred shareholders are paid.

The amount shown in both the Common Stock and Preferred Stock accounts of a publicly traded firm relate to the number of shares of each type of stock the firm has outstanding and the par value of that stock. The par (the base) value of the stock is selected by the owners of the firm at its founding; however, because there is a tax liability generated by the par value assigned to the firm's stock in the year of its founding, the par values selected by the firm's owners tend to be very low, for example, $0.01 per share or lower.

### *Shareholders' equity*

The last section on a firm's Balance Sheet is the Owners' or Shareholders' Equity section. The firm's Shareholders' Equity section tells us how much of the firm's assets are in fact owned by the Shareholders (typically as Common Stock) of the firm. If we own shares of a publicly traded firm, odds are that we own Common Shares of stock in that firm. Common Stock usually has voting rights that are typically set at one vote per share. Common Stock may also pay a dividend at the firm's discretion. It also participates in capital gains, meaning that as the value of the firm increases, the market value of the Common Stock also increases. Note that even though the market value of the firm's Common Stock may go up or down over time, this change in market value will not be reflected in its book value.

Recall our original equation that governed the Balance Sheet: Assets = Liabilities + Shareholders' Equity. The equation states that the value of all the stuff the firm owns (its Assets) has to be equal to the value of all the money it owes others (its Liabilities) plus the value of the Shareholders' Equity.

It is easy to rearrange the Balance Sheet equation to see how Shareholders' Equity = Assets − Liabilities. While this relationship is mathematically true, that is, given a firm's Total Assets and its Total Liabilities, you can always subtract the firm's Liabilities from its Assets to arrive at the book value of the firm's Equity, it is not always the way the Shareholders' Equity section is accounted for on the Balance Sheet.

From an accounting perspective, the Owners' Equity section represents the sum of all the money the owners of the firm have invested in the firm, plus the sum of all the profits the firm has reinvested since it was formed; that is, the sum of its profits minus the sum of all dividends the firm has paid out since it was formed. This is represented as:

$$\begin{aligned}\text{Owners' equity} = {} & \text{Initial paid-in capital} \\ & + \sum_{t=1}^{\text{Today}} (\text{Profit}_t - \text{Losses}_t \\ & \qquad + \text{Additional paid-in capital}_t - \text{Dividends}_t)\end{aligned}$$

Thus, the Owners' Equity section can be divided into two parts: the contributed capital accounts and the retained earnings (Profit – Losses – Dividends) account.

In a privately held firm, the contributed capital account is usually called Contributed Capital or Owners' Capital, and the balance shown in the account represents all the monies the owner or owners of the firm have contributed to the firm since its founding. In a publicly traded firm, the contributed capital accounts comprise the Common Stock, Preferred Stock, and Additional Paid-In Capital accounts. When added together, the three contributed capital accounts in a publicly traded firm represent the total amount of money paid to the firm by its shareholders (owners) in exchange for shares of the firm's stock.

In the following example, we see that firm HJK has 1,000,000 shares of Common Stock outstanding and 200,000 shares of Preferred Stock outstanding, which were issued at par values of $0.01 and $0.001, respectively. If we multiply the number of Common shares outstanding, 1,000,000, by their par value, $0.01, we arrive at the balance shown in the Common Stock account of $10,000. Similarly, if we multiply the number of Preferred shares outstanding, 200,000, by their par value, $0.001, we arrive at the balance shown in the Preferred Stock account of $200.

| **Firm HJK's Equity Accounts** | |
|---|---|
| Common Stock Outstanding | 1,000,000 |
| Common Stock Par Value | $0.01 |
| Common Stock Account | $10,000 |
| Preferred Stock Outstanding | 200,000 |
| Preferred Stock Par Value | $0.001 |
| Preferred Stock Account | $200 |

Additional Paid-In Capital (APIC) is another account you will find under the Equity section on the Balance Sheet. The Additional Paid-In Capital account is closely related to the Common Stock and Preferred Stock accounts. While the balances shown in the firm's Common Stock and Preferred Stock accounts represent the par value of those shares, the APIC account shows the *excess* amount received for each share of stock, if that stock is sold for a price greater than its par value. For example, if firm HJK actually sold its stock at a price of $1.01 per share, then the APIC would be ($1.01 – $0.01) or $1.00 times the number of shares issued. Since the firm issued 1,000,000 shares, then the APIC would be $1,000,000 of APIC.

## *Treasury stock*

Treasury Stock is another account you will sometimes find in the Equity section on a publicly traded firm's Balance Sheet. Like any other investor, a firm can buy its own stock on the open market at any time. When it does, the value of those shares is recorded, either at cost or at par value, on the firm's Balance Sheet as Treasury Stock. Treasury Stock thus represents issued common shares of stock in the firm that the firm itself owns. The shares held in Treasury Stock are no longer considered outstanding and are not included in the distribution of dividends or the calculation of Earnings per Share (EPS) — the firm doesn't get to pay itself dividends! Treasury Stock also has no voting rights and the amount of Treasury Stock a firm can purchase is governed by the SEC. Treasury shares can either be held for resale by the firm or they can be retired. When retired, the shares are permanently canceled and cannot be reissued. Once retired, the shares are no longer listed as Treasury Stock on the firm Balance Sheet. You will notice that the Treasury Stock account always has a negative balance. That is because the Treasury Stock account is a *contra equity* account that decreases Shareholders' Equity. A *contra* account is one that reduces the balance of the account to which it references, so contra equity makes the equity account smaller. Doubtful Receivables is also an example of a contra asset account.

## *Retained earnings*

Last but not least, we find an account called Retained Earnings. The Retained Earnings account represents an important connection between the firm's Income Statement and its Balance Sheet. Every year at the end of the firm's fiscal year, all the revenue and expense accounts on the firm's Income Statement are reset to zero. But wait! What happened to the profit (Net Income or Net Loss) the firm generated during that period? Where does it go? At the end of every fiscal year, what is left over of the firm's Net Income (or Net Loss) after the firm pays dividends or buys back shares of stock is captured in the firm's Retained Earnings account. The balance in the firm's Retained Earnings account starts at zero when the company is formed. The Retained Earnings account then accumulates the firm's profits or losses for every year since the firm was founded. Net Income (profit) increases the balance in Retained Earnings, while a Net Loss decreases the balance in the firm's Retained Earnings account. Dividends to shareholders (Common and Preferred) are paid from the firm's Retained Earnings account. The firm's Ending Retained Earnings balance can be calculated as follows:

$$\begin{aligned}\text{Retained earnings}_t &\\ &= \text{Retained earnings}_{t-1} + \text{Net income}_t \\ &\quad - \text{Dividends}_t - \text{Share repurchases}_t\end{aligned}$$

From the equation, we can see that when the firm's operations generate a profit (Net Income), then that profit increases the balance in the firm's Retained Earnings account, thus increasing the firm's Shareholders' Equity. When the firm's operations generate a loss (negative Net Income or a Net Loss), or the firm decides to pay a dividend to its shareholders or buy back shares of stock, then the firm will decrease its Retained Earnings account, thus decreasing the firm's Shareholders' Equity. Think of the balance in the firm's Retained Earnings account as the total amount of profits the firm has chosen to retain inside itself for future use.

## Key Takeaways

- Assets = Liabilities + Shareholders' Equity. There is no free lunch: the Balance Sheet must always balance.
- The Balance Sheet provides a snapshot of a firm's financial condition at any given point in time.
- Balance Sheet items are reported at the lesser of historical cost or current value. That means that the value of a firm's assets cannot be increased but can only be decreased, most often by depreciation, amortization, or impairment.
- The Balance Sheet is organized by decreasing liquidity. The high liquidity assets such as Cash & Marketable Securities are first and Intangible Assets are last.

- Accrual Accounting → Revenues are recorded when ownership is transferred, or a service is provided, and not necessarily when the customer actually pays. Expenses are recorded simultaneously with revenues, again, not necessarily when the firm pays its vendors. Because of this there is often a misalignment between profit and cash flow.
- Cash Accounting → Revenues are recorded when cash is received and expenses are recorded when they are actually paid.
- Amortization of a loan's principal and interest ≠ Amortization of Intangible Assets.

# Chapter 3

# The Income Statement

## Understanding the Drivers of Profit

The Income Statement (also known as the statement of profit and loss or the P&L) provides an accounting of how a firm generates profits: revenues minus costs and taxes. Profit and cash flow are not always, or even usually, the same thing. For example, you will see non-cash charges, such as Depletion, Depreciation, and Amortization on the Income Statement. Accounting for these charges is important, because although they might have a negative impact on this period's profit, they have a positive impact on this period's cash flow, since they shield some of the firm's hard-earned revenue from taxes.

The general definition of Net Income is given by the following relationship:

**Revenues – Costs – Taxes = Net income**

As you will see, there are four ways to increase profit margins: (1) raise your prices if demand is inelastic, (2) cut your variable costs, (3) cut your fixed costs, and (4) cut your taxes. We will discuss each of these in turn. Understanding the income statement and the relationship among its component parts is essential to valuation, and you can expect heated discussions about the growth rate in revenues, since revenues are such an important driver of profit.

The following is Alpha Brewing's Income Statement, the components of which we will review in this chapter.

| **Year** | **2017** | **2018** | **2019** |
|---|---|---|---|
| Total Revenues | 1,209,600 | 1,663,200 | 1,829,520 |
| Total Excise and Sales Tax | 85,365 | 117,376 | 129,114 |
| Net Revenues | 1,124,235 | 1,545,824 | 1,700,406 |
| Cost of Goods Sold (COGS) | 166,320 | 199,584 | 172,553 |
| Gross Profit | 957,915 | 1,346,240 | 1,527,853 |
| Selling, General and Administrative Expenses | 771,494 | 893,223 | 916,380 |
| Depreciation & Amortization | 74,506 | 74,506 | 85,006 |
| Operating Income | 111,916 | 378,510 | 526,467 |
| Interest Expense | 38,336 | 35,300 | 32,070 |
| Earnings Before Taxes | 73,580 | 343,210 | 494,397 |
| Income Taxes | 15,452 | 72,074 | 103,823 |
| **Net Income** | **58,129** | **271,136** | **390,574** |

## Revenues

The income statement begins with Revenues. The assumptions that we make with respect to revenue growth are among the most important in any financial model and will likely be the ones that are most contested by our counterparty in a negotiation. In the world of accrual-based accounting, revenues are booked when a seller provides a service or transfers ownership of a product to a customer. That transaction is instantly booked as a sale and is recorded on the revenue line, irrespective of when the customer is expected to pay for the goods — provided that they actually are expected to pay for them (see Doubtful Receivables).

Revenue is a product of two things: Price and Quantity. So, when you want to forecast the revenue line, you need to consider the interaction between these two factors. What limits the firm's ability to raise prices? What factors lead to or limit the firm's ability to sell more products? If the firm raises its prices, will the demand suddenly dry up or will there be very little impact on demand? For example, think about our demand for gasoline for our cars. If gas prices increase by ten cents per gallon, will this have a meaningful impact on how much we drive? Will we drive less or consume less gas because of it? Most people that we know are not all that price sensitive to relatively small changes in gasoline prices.

The sensitivity of demand to a change in price is called price elasticity. It can be defined or explained as "For a given percentage change in price, what is the percentage change in demand?" Elasticity is given by the following relationship, where *Quantity* is the number of units (kgs, liters, things, etc.) sold at a given price, $\delta$ *Quantity* is the change in the number of these units sold after the price changes, Price is the price of units, and $\delta$ *Price* is the change in price of the units.

$$\text{Elasticity} = \frac{\dfrac{\delta\ \text{Quantity}}{\text{Quantity}}}{\dfrac{\delta\ \text{Price}}{\text{Price}}}$$

If the demand isn't really all that price sensitive — we call that inelastic demand — then perhaps the firm might want to think about raising its prices if it wants to squeeze out more profit. But what if the demand is hypersensitive — we call this elastic demand — to changes in price? In this case, the firm needs to be very careful when it thinks about raising prices, since its revenues might drop precipitously. Most people think about the elasticity of an increase in price, but it also makes sense to think about the elasticity of a decrease in price. The elasticity of demand at any given point doesn't have to be symmetrical for an increase and a decrease in price. What we mean by that is that a 1% increase in price might cause demand to crash, but a 1% decrease in price might have little effect at all or alternately might cause demand to skyrocket. Because demand elasticity impacts the firm's ability to raise price, and hence affects how it grows revenues, understanding the factors that drive demand elasticity are very important for valuation.

### *Factors that lead to price elastic demand and to subsequent volatility in revenues*

Competition is at the heart of price elasticity. If there is a lot of competition, then customers have many choices and there will be pressure on prices. There is a big difference between a firm that has a monopoly in its product market and one that is facing perfect competition. In a monopoly, the firm is the only supplier; that is, it has no competitors. This is great for the firm because it doesn't have to worry about someone offering a lower price and stealing its customers, so the firm can set whatever price maximizes its profit without having to concern itself with anything else. Monopoly is associated with maximum profit and relatively inelastic demand that is not as sensitive to price. Perfect competition is the polar opposite of a monopoly. There are many sellers, all of whom are selling the exact same item — there is no differentiation at all. Customers in this kind of market have many choices as to from whom they can buy their products. All the sellers are competing for the same business, and prices (and profits) get driven down to the lowest possible level. In a perfect competition, if a seller tries to raise prices, they will lose all of their demand — perfectly elastic demand — after all, it is all about price, since everyone is selling the exact same thing. The winner (if you want to use that term) is the firm that has the lowest manufacturing costs, because they are able to set the lowest price and still make a profit.

There are several factors to think about that can help you understand what drives competition in a product market and ultimately what affects the revenue line.

**Barriers to entry and exit** effectively keep potential competitors out of your markets. Barriers to entry include high start-up costs, legal barriers (such as government-granted licenses or permits), or economies of scale that are necessary to be able to manufacture a product at a reasonable price in order to be competitive. Patents, trademarks, copyrights, and other types of intellectual property (such as trade secrets) also create barriers to entry. The absence of entry or exit barriers leads to a market that is contestable; that is, a market where prices and profits tend to lean toward the perfect competition level, regardless of the number of firms within the industry. Whether or not a market is contestable depends on the existence of **sunk costs**.

Sunk costs are non-recoverable investments in industry-specific assets that are required for a firm to enter an industry. If no such non-recoverable investment is required — the nail salon business, for example — then the industry becomes vulnerable to "hit-and-run" entries by new competitors, who can easily close shop with impunity when things start going poorly. How many nail salons are there in your hometown? How long do they stay in business? What happens if one nail salon offers a $10 off coupon?

**Competition from substitute products** is another key driver of price elasticity. If there are easily identifiable and available substitutes for the firm's products or services, then customers have a choice and, as a result, there is competition. Think about what happens to the market price of a blockbuster drug when it comes off patent: it tanks! While the drug was on patent, the manufacturer had a monopoly on it. There was no competition, so the drug company could charge whatever price the market would bear. However, when the drug comes off patent, the monopoly disappears and market competition in the form of generic market clones drives down prices very rapidly. The bottom line is that if customers can easily substitute a firm's product or services with someone else's (like a branded drug versus a generic drug), then there is great risk that revenue growth will be unstable.

**Product differentiation** is important in warding off potential substitutes from stealing customers away and hurting the revenue line. How similar is the firm's product to that of its competitors? Is the product or service faster, better, or cheaper? And, importantly, how likely is it to remain faster, better, or cheaper? Because if the product or service is not faster, better, or cheaper in the future, then one would expect competitors to begin to chip away at the firm's market share, which should reduce expectations about future revenue growth.

The notions of "faster" or "cheaper" are fairly self-explanatory, but "better" is a little nebulous. Products can be better for a whole variety of reasons, some of which include being more reliable, more attractive, more prestigious, or a host of other reasons. The most important factor when thinking about the notion of "better" is to ensure you are better in a way that matters to your customers and not just to you. Be sure your product or service is better with respect to a criterion that materially affects your customer's purchasing decision, and not your own personal preferences.

**Brand recognition** and **customer loyalty** are two important factors that differentiate a firm's product or service as being "better" than that of its competitors in the perception of its customers. Customers that are loyal to a given brand are less likely to leave it and switch to the competition in the event that the firm increases its prices, or the competitor aggressively lowers its prices by offering deep discounts or other sales incentives.

These perceptions are likely to be much higher for personal hygiene products or fashion brands. When customers are loyal to a specific brand, new entrants into the market must spend a tremendous amount of money upfront on advertising and promotion just to get customers' attention, and then spend even more to ultimately gain their trust in order to win their business away from their trusted or preferred brand. This creates an effective and expensive barrier to entry and helps to keep the older firm's revenue line healthy and stable.

Another factor that impacts the extent of competition in a product market, and thus the volatility of revenues, is the extent to which one of the firms enjoys an **Absolute Cost Advantage**. This competitive advantage comes from the acquisition of very low-cost raw materials or labor. An excellent example of this is Saudi Aramco, an oil company which enjoys a three-times cost advantage over competitors Shell and Exxon Mobil. When one competitor can make something three times as cheaply, it is very difficult to compete on price.

Absolute cost advantages may also result from economies of learning. This advantage comes from specialized, time-consuming, or very expensive training and knowledge that yields profitable and differentiated goods and services. In order to enter a market that has learning economies, a new competitor would have to spend disproportionately on the acquisition of specialized knowledge; this too is an effective entry barrier that helps keep revenues from dropping precipitously because of new competition.

The last entry barrier that we will discuss is **limited access to channels of distribution**. If competitors cannot get their products into the hands of customers, then customers cannot buy them. If only one firm has access to the channels of distribution, then this firm effectively has a monopoly. The one worry is whether that proprietary access is likely to continue in the future.

Irrespective of the cause of the entry or exit barriers, the purpose that they serve is to keep competitors out of the firm's product market so that the firm can enjoy unhindered access to its customers. Entry and exit barriers help to create inelastic demand and stabilize the firm's revenue.

### *Other factors that can drive volatility in revenues*

The aforementioned is just a short list of things that might potentially cause volatility or instability in revenues. There are many more things about which we should be concerned. A sampling of these includes the possibility of natural disasters (such as hurricanes and earthquakes), regulatory intervention by the government, structural changes in the product market, geopolitical risk, global recessions, financial crises, or any other factors that might in some way compromise the firm's ability to sell products to its customers (and thus impact revenues). Therefore, it is very important to consider macroeconomic factors when predicting revenues. Our goal is to come up with revenue forecasts that are both reasonable and defensible (see Chapter 12), given our expectations about the firm's prospects for the future.

### *Net versus gross revenues*

Now that we have discussed the factors that can drive volatility in the revenue line, it is important that we understand the differences between net revenue and gross revenue: the difference between the two can have a huge impact on gross margins (which we'll be using later to better understand the power and value of a brand). When we sell something, either a product or a service, it gets recorded as "gross" revenues. "Net" revenues refer to the amount that we actually expect to get paid from what we sold. The difference between these two is potentially very important, because things like licensing fees, rebates, coupons, or other customer incentives all have to be deducted from gross revenues before we can actually determine how much money we will actually receive from the sale. These reductions can potentially have a huge impact on the revenue line.

### *Growth in revenues: A key assumption*

One of the most important assumptions that we make in financial modeling is the assumption of what will be the long-run rate of revenue growth, which is also known as the *terminal growth rate*. As you will see later, when we value a firm, long-run revenue growth will be one of the key drivers. Revenue growth is not only a direct driver of profits and operating cash flows, it also drives the need for working capital items, such as accounts receivable, inventory, pre-paid expenses, and accounts payable. Thus, because revenue growth is so important, it will be one of the most contentious and hotly challenged parts of any valuation. This chapter is going to prepare you to defend your assumptions.

Sometimes it is helpful to deconstruct revenue growth into price growth and quantity growth, and then think of the factors that may affect each of these differently. As we discussed above, if demand is relatively inelastic, then it might be possible to raise prices without affecting quantity demanded. However, if demand is highly elastic, then increasing prices can be disastrous for demand.

Understanding this trade-off between the price of a firm's product and the quantity of that product that the firm can sell at that price is essential to getting a good revenue forecast.

### *Be careful about deferred revenues*

Deferred revenues occur when a firm is prepaid in advance for the services that it will provide over a future period of time. For example, imagine a software service provider who gets paid a lump sum of $100,000 in January to provide service for the next 12 months. The cash is received in January, which is all fine and good, but how do we report the revenue? Do we report it all in one shot in January? If we do, then there will be a disconnect between the revenues and the future costs incurred generating those revenues.

Accrual basis accounting is based on the notion that revenues and costs need to be matched. Revenues should only be recognized when a product has been sold or service has been provided. The firm gets payment in January, but they have the obligation to provide service over the course of the year. Thus, they have a liability to provide service and this liability shows up as deferred revenues on the balance sheet. As the service is provided each month, the deferred liability account will go down, and the associated revenue will be recognized, as will the associated cost of goods sold.

Be very careful, when you see spikey jumps in revenue either at the beginning of the year or at various other times over the course of the year, to ascertain whether you're dealing with a potential deferred revenue situation. If so, the revenues may have been prematurely recorded and the firm's cash flows distorted. This is especially worrisome if we are lenders considering whether to make a loan to the firm with hidden deferred revenues. Note, that spikes in revenue can also come from acquisitions, but more on that later in the book.

## Costs and Expenses

### *Start with revenue then take out all the relevant costs*

There are two types of costs that you are likely to encounter: costs that are **capitalized** and costs that are **expensed**. If a cost of an asset is expensed, then we recognize that cost all at one time. If the cost of the asset is capitalized, then we recognize that cost over the useful life of the asset. The useful life of an asset is defined, usually in years, as the length of time that the asset is expected to last before wearing out (i.e., it stops generating revenues).

How can we tell whether a cost should be expensed or capitalized? A cost is expensed if the asset or service purchased does not provide any future benefits beyond the current period. For example, you buy a pencil. That pencil is expected to be fully consumed within a year; thus, it is expensed. In contrast, a cost is capitalized if the asset generates revenues or provides a benefit beyond the current period. When an asset is capitalized, you do not need to take the full hit to current profit all at once; you would only recognize either the depreciated or amortized amount for the period, which in many cases is only a small fraction of the full price. Consequently, your profit for that period would be higher if the cost were capitalized relative to being expensed. Note however that this year's tax burden will be higher when expenses are capitalized versus expensed.

### *Cost of goods sold/cost of sales*

The first cost that we're likely to encounter on an income statement is Cost of Goods Sold — for service companies that really don't use any inventory this is called Cost of Sales. Cost of Goods Sold (COGS) represents the direct labor and raw material costs associated with the product or service that we're selling. Cost of Sales refers to the labor involved in providing the service. There should be a one-to-one relationship between the quantity of units being sold and Cost of Goods Sold. A similar relationship should hold between the Cost of Sales and the amount of service being provided. When there isn't a one-to-one relationship, then we need to ask questions. That is, if sales go up by 10%, then we would expect the cost of goods sold to go up by 10%. It's unusual to see sudden changes in this relationship, not that the ratio cannot change naturally, but things like impairment of obsolete inventory can lead to sudden positive spikes in the relationship between the Cost of Goods Sold and Sales.

## *Gross profit and gross profit margin*

Gross profit is the difference between Sales and Cost of Goods Sold. It measures the extent to which the firm can markup the cost of its labor and raw materials. Firms with a strong competitive advantage will be better able to markup their direct costs than firms that don't have a competitive advantage.

$$\text{Gross profit} = \text{Sales} - \text{COGS}$$

The gross profit *margin* is calculated as gross profit divided by net sales.

$$\text{Gross profit margin} = \text{Gross profit/Sales}$$

Many people view the gross profit margin as an indicator of the power of a firm's brand or the extent to which the firm has a competitive advantage in its product market. As a market becomes more competitive, the gross margin starts to shrink.

Many people get confused with the difference between an item's ***markup*** and its gross profit margin. Markup is calculated by first taking the difference between the item's sales price and its manufacturing cost, and then dividing this difference by the manufacturing cost.

$$\text{Markup of an item} = (\text{Sales price} - \text{Cost})/\text{Cost}$$

And with some simple algebra,

$$\text{Selling price} = \text{Cost}(1 + \text{Markup})$$

For example, if a firm sells an item for \$100 and the cost is \$75, then the markup is (\$100 – \$75)/\$75 = .333 or 33.3%. The reciprocal is true: if the markup is 33.3% and the cost is \$75, then the final selling price would be \$75 (1 + .333) = \$100. By way of comparison, the gross profit margin is (\$100 – \$75)/\$100 = 0.25 or 25%.

The concept of markup can be useful at the firm level as well.

Average markup for the firm
 = (Net revenue – COGS)/COGS
 = Gross profit/COGS

So, markup is Gross Profit/COGS and Gross Margin is Gross Profit/ Net Revenues. The difference lies in the denominator.

### *Selling, general, and administrative expenses*

Selling, general, and administrative expenses (SG&A) are commonly referred to as *overhead*. These expenses are also often called *functional costs* or operating costs and are incurred in support of the firm's operations but are not directly linked to the manufacturing in the way that the costs of labor and raw materials would be. Think of these as the costs that we must incur in order to be able to generate our gross profit; that is, the firm would not be able to make their product and thus generate revenues without incurring these expenses, so they are essential. These expenses include facilities fees, administrative salaries, insurance, research and development, brand marketing expenditures, and other expenses. We discuss each of the component parts of SG&A expenses as follows.

### *Selling expenses*

Selling expenses are the first component of functional costs and are considered to be any expense that is associated with the actual "selling" of a good or a service or associated with actually making the sale. Selling expenses include commissions and salaries paid to salespeople and reimbursement of their out-of-pocket selling-associated expenses, logistical costs, shipping costs, and other selling-related direct expenses. **Brand marketing expenses** are included in selling expenses, and are essential to creating brand awareness, customer loyalty, and driving revenues.

You should be suspicious when there is a lot of volatility in selling or brand marketing expenses. Sometimes a firm may reduce these expenses in the short-term to bolster their current period's earnings. However, a big reduction in marketing expense today should lead to a reduction in revenues tomorrow, especially in a competitive market. We would expect a fairly stable relationship between brand marketing expenditures and revenues. Note that firms that are entering into a competitive market for the first time may have to spend disproportionately on brand marketing expenses in order to create brand awareness and lure customers away from existing market participants.

### *General and administrative expenses (G&A)*

General and Administrative expenses are often called "fixed" costs, in that they are fairly stable from quarter to quarter and do not really move one-for-one with sales or the quantity of units sold. Note, they really aren't fixed: many of the component parts of G&A expenses increase over time (medical insurance costs, for example) and G&A can increase abruptly if there is a large upswing in revenues that require an increase in capacity; for example, the firm might have to lease another office building or take out another expensive insurance policy. General and Administrative expenses include all operational expenses necessary to support the firm net of selling expenses. They include things like office supplies, printing supplies, rent, managerial salaries and expenses, insurance, salaries of support staff, legal expenses, etc.

### *Research and development*

Similar to brand marketing expenses, investment in research and development should lead to future revenue growth. The difference is that depending on the product market, research and development investments today may take a long time before they yield fruitful results in terms of revenues. The pharmaceutical industry is a great example of this, since it might take 15 years from an initial investment in research to yield a drug that is safe and useful to society (and hence can be sold).

Other industries, such as technology industries, have a much shorter time-to-market. Firms that are committed to innovation typically have a stable relationship between research and development and the revenue line. Large swings in R&D spending should be carefully analyzed to ascertain whether they will have an impact on the long-run revenue growth of the firm.

### *Operating leverage*

The relationship between fixed (SG&A) to variable costs (COGS) is called *Operating Leverage*. When you see the word "leverage" it means the use of fixed costs. Financial leverage means the use of debt, which involves fixed interest payments. Operating leverage has to do with the use of fixed costs. If Operating Leverage is high, that is, when most of the firm's costs are fixed costs rather than variable costs, then when revenue increases, costs will not change much, and the firm will generate a lot of profit. The opposite is true if revenues drop suddenly. High operating leverage (high fixed cost) makes profit very sensitive to changes in the revenue line: it makes the good times better and the bad times worse.

$$\text{Operating leverage} = \frac{\text{Fixed cost}}{\text{Total cost}}$$

For example:

| **Operating Leverage** | **2021** |
|---|---|
| Fixed Cost | $1,829,520 |
| Variable Cost | $526,467 |

$$\begin{aligned}\text{Operating leverage} &= \frac{1{,}829{,}520}{(1{,}829{,}520 + 526{,}467)}\\ &= \frac{1{,}829{,}520}{2{,}355{,}987}\\ &= 0.78\end{aligned}$$

A fixed cost is defined as any operating cost that *does not* vary with sales. These costs are typically found in G&A expenses such as rent and salary expenses. A variable cost is any operating cost that *does* vary with sales such as cost of goods sold and sales commissions.

In the above example, we see that Operating Leverage is 0.78, which is relatively high as Operating Leverage is bound between 0 (no operating leverage, 100% variable cost structure) and 1 (100% operating leverage, 100% fixed cost structure).

### *Depreciation, amortization, and depletion*

Depreciation, amortization, and depletion reflect the allocation of the cost of long-term assets in accordance with the revenues associated with the utilization of those assets. All three of these expenses are non-cash charges. They result from a cost being capitalized, rather than being expensed. Depreciation allocates the cost of PP&E during the useful life of the asset. Amortization allocates the cost of leasehold improvements, and identifiable intangibles such as patents, copyrights, trademarks, and franchises. Depletion allocates the cost of natural resources, such as oil fields and mines. For example, if the firm were to buy tools, machines, or other capital equipment, these costs would be capitalized rather than expensed. Intangible assets that can be capitalized include acquisition costs of obtaining a patent or copyright from another entity. R&D costs such as the salary of the scientists are typically expensed, but legal fees involved in acquiring R&D, as well as patents, can be capitalized.

## Profits and Remaining Expenses

### *Operating profit and earnings before interest and tax: EBIT*

Operating profit, also known as Earnings Before Interest and Tax or EBIT, is the difference between revenues and all the operational costs incurred to generate those revenues. Whereas revenues represent the "top line" on the income statement and net profit represents the "bottom line" on the income statement, EBIT is often referred to as the "line."

That is, EBIT draws a line between operating and non-operating pre-tax inflows and outflows. All the items included in operating profit should be tied directly to the firm's product market strategy, that is, its core business operations.

Often the firm may experience inflows or outflows that, although may influence net profit, have nothing to do with the normal business operations of the firm. For example, imagine if we were to sell off an unwanted asset at a price higher than book value. The proceeds would certainly be taxable, and they would definitely be included as part of our pre-tax income. However, they should not be included as part of our operating income because they have absolutely nothing to do with our product market strategy or normal business operations. Consequently, such inflows or outflows would appear below the EBIT "line" rather than above it.

## *EBITDA — Earnings before interest, taxes, depreciation, and amortization*

Although EBITDA is not an "official" line item on GAAP financial statements, it has evolved to become a very important measure of pre-tax profitability. It is literally net revenues minus cash cost of goods sold minus the cash cost of selling and general and administrative expenses, which is why EBITDA is also called "cash operating profit." Another way of calculating EBITDA is to take EBIT and add back in the non-cash expenses of depreciation and amortization.[1]

$$\text{EBITDA} = \text{EBIT} + \text{Depreciation} + \text{Amortization}$$

EBITDA first came into use in association with leveraged buyouts in the early 1980s. Although EBITDA is a measure of cash operating profit, it ignores important things like CAPEX and changes in working capital, so it really isn't a perfect measure of the amount of pre-tax cash flow that is actually generated by the firm's operations — to get that, you would have to take out CAPEX and changes in working capital. This being said, the use of EBITDA as a measure of operating profitability is quite appropriate for service companies and dot coms, which typically have neither of these expenses. Originally, in the late 1970s and early 1980s, the use of EBITDA was limited to these kinds of companies, but EBITDA is now used ubiquitously, even in sectors such as heavy manufacturing where its use is not really warranted, because they have a lot of CAPEX and increases in working capital as they grow.

EBITDA is a key performance indicator for many firms and is a critical metric in comparable value analysis through its use in the enterprise value to EBITDA multiple (more on this later in the book). EBITDA is also used extensively by lenders when doing credit analysis. Specifically,

[1] If the firm has amortizable depletion or exploration expenses, such as a mining or oil company, then it is common to use Earnings Before Interest, Taxes, Depreciation, Depletion, Amortization, and Exploration Expenses (EBITDAX).

lenders use coverage ratios like the ratio of EBITDA to interest expense or EBITDA–CAPEX to interest expense to set the ceiling on the amount of funds a firm can borrow and as a measure to assess the firm's ability to service debt.

Be careful, since oftentimes, in the interest of parsimony, accountants will bundle depreciation in with cost of goods sold and amortization with selling, general and administrative expenses. Thus, you will sometimes see the line items "cash cost of goods sold" and "cash selling and general administrative expenses." When in doubt as to whether there is any depreciation or amortization buried in COGS and SGAE, always defer to the statement of cash flows (a financial statement that we will be examining more fully in the next chapter). The information about depreciation and amortization that appears on the statement of cash flows will dominate the information found on the income statement for the purposes of calculating EBITDA.

### *Non-operating inflows and outflows*

Non-operating income is the pre-tax profit that comes from non-core business operations. Non-operating gains and losses are usually non-recurring in nature and are consequently reported below EBIT. They include things like gains and losses from investments, dividends, foreign exchange transactions, and asset and property sales (among other things). If a firm were to sell its art collection for a profit, this is where the income would show up.

### *Interest expense*

Interest expense is the firm's cost of borrowing money for a given period of time. To be precise, interest expense reflects the interest *accrued* over a given time period, rather than the interest that is actually *paid* during that period. Luckily for firms, interest payments are tax deductible, that is, they can be deducted from EBIT prior to calculating the firm's pre-tax income. Thus, interest expense reduces the amount of tax the firm would otherwise pay. The easiest method to compute interest expense is to multiply the average interest rate by the firm's total debt at the end of the period. However, a more precise method would be to use the average level of debt over the period; that is, the beginning debt balance plus the ending debt balance divided by two.

### *Taxes*

Firms and individuals are required by law to pay their fair share of tax. The corporate tax on income is calculated over a given period of time. The calculation is very simple: multiply the taxable level of income by the tax rate (note, the corporate tax rate in the US is 21% in 2022). Note that the reported taxable income on a firm's income statement will often differ somewhat from the taxable income that is used to determine the tax that is actually paid to the government.

For example, a firm might employ a straight-line method to calculate depreciation on its accounting statements (to show higher earnings), but then employ some kind of accelerated depreciation — the tax code allows for this — for actual tax purposes (to pay less actual cash tax). The result is that their taxable income for Federal income tax purposes is actually lower than their reported taxable income according to GAAP.

### *Net income*

Net Income (also known as Net Profit or Net Earnings) represents the amount left over after starting with Net Revenues and subtracting out all expenses, that is, cost of goods sold, operating expenses, non-operating expenses, interest expense, taxes, and any dividends that might be paid to the preferred stockholders. Net profit is the bottom line on the income statement and is often referred to as "the bottom line."

Net profit is an important indicator of a firm's financial profitability and is closely watched by market participants. It is very important to understand that net profit is not a direct measure of cash flow. It is not the amount of cash that a company created or used in any given period; for example, if you have \$100 in profit, it does not necessarily mean that your cash account balance went up by \$100 this year. The reason why is that the net profit includes non-cash expenses (such as depreciation and amortization), and it also ignores changes in working capital or additional CAPEX spending that might have happened during the period. For example, we might have \$100 in reported profit, but have not yet received payment from any of our customers; thus, the revenues that would have generated that profit are sitting in Accounts Receivable rather than in our checking account.

Net profit can vary tremendously across firms and industries, so sometimes it doesn't make sense to directly compare the net profit of two firms: the comparison isn't often all that informative. Firms with greater revenues will, all other things held equal, have higher net profits. It is usually better to think about net profit as a percentage of net revenues. This is called the "net profit margin," and is calculated as the ratio of net profit to net revenues.

$$\text{Net profit margin} = \text{Net profit}/\text{Net revenues}$$

A higher net profit margin is better irrespective of the size or scale of the firm. What percentage of the revenues did the firm actually manage to turn into profit? The higher the percentage, the better.

### *Earnings per share*

Another popular measure of profitability is called earnings per share (EPS). It is calculated as net profit divided by the number of shares outstanding.

$$\text{Earnings per share} = \frac{\text{Net profit}}{\text{Number of shares outstanding}}$$

EPS is a performance measure that is closely followed by Wall Street, with investors hanging on the edge of their seats waiting for firms to make their earnings announcements. Firms that fail to meet earnings expectations usually have their stock prices punished by the financial markets. If managers continue to miss earnings targets, they run the risk of being replaced.

## Key Takeaways

- **Revenues – Costs – Taxes = Net income.** Net Income (also known as net profit) is what remains of the revenues after all costs, interests, and taxes have been paid.

- Four ways to increase profit margin: (1) raise your prices if demand is inelastic, (2) cut your variable costs, (3) cut your fixed costs, and (4) cut your taxes.
- $\text{Elasticity} = \frac{\frac{\delta\,\text{Quantity}}{\text{Quantity}}}{\frac{\delta\,\text{Price}}{\text{Price}}}$, it is a measure of the sensitivity in the revenue line to changes in price and is driven by the nature of competition in the product market.
- Cost is Capitalized or Expensed? If the asset creates value for more than 1 year (e.g., a machine), then it is capitalized, else (a pencil) it is expensed.
- Gross profit = Sales – COGS.
- Gross profit margin = Gross profit/Sales is a measure of the power of brand and our ability to markup our variable costs.
- Markup = (Sales price – Cost)/Cost.
- Operating leverage = $\frac{\text{Fixed cost}}{\text{Total cost}}$ is a measure of the sensitivity of the profit to changes in revenues.
- EBITDA = EBIT + Depreciation + Amortization is a popular proxy for operating cash flows. Note, EBITDA is typically NOT a cash flow since it ignores CAPEX and changes in working capital.
- Net profit margin = Net profit/Net revenues.
- $\text{Earnings per share} = \frac{\text{Net profit}}{\text{Number of shares outstanding}}$.

# Chapter 4

# The Statement of Cash Flows/The Statement of Sources and Uses

**The Statement of Cash Flows**, also known as the Statement of Sources and Uses, documents a firm's sources and uses of funds. The sources and uses are separated into three categories: (1) operating cash flows, (2) investing cash flows, and (3) financing cash flows. Each of these three categories can either be a source or a use of funds. A source of funds means that the particular activity is generating funds, and a use of funds means that the activity is consuming funds.

The Statement of Cash Flows helps us to understand from where the firm is getting its funds and how the firm is using its funds. It provides a summary of the amount of cash that enters and leaves the firm. It is important that the sources and uses of funds make sense given what the firm says it is supposed to be doing with the money. For example, if a firm was expecting revenue growth this period, then we would expect that the firm would generate more Accounts Receivable (since these should grow proportionately with increases in sales) and probably need more inventory; these would be considered uses of funds. However, if the firm had to borrow money from a bank to fund the increase in Accounts Receivable and Inventory, then the bank borrowing would be considered a source of funds.

A simple rule of thumb is that if an asset increases, then we consider that to be a use of funds, since the funds are put into that asset "bin" and they stay there until they are released. We literally "used" the funds to support that asset. If an asset decreases, then the funds are liberated from the bin to be used elsewhere, and we can consider that to be a source of funds. The exact opposite is true for liabilities and equity relative to assets. If a liability increases, then that is a source of funds (but, we will have the liability to eventually pay those funds back). Similarly, if equity increases, then that is also a source of funds (but we don't have the liability to pay those funds back). And if a liability or equity decreases, either because we paid back a loan, for example, or bought back shares of stock or paid a dividend, then that would be a use of funds. When we net out all of the firm's sources and uses of funds, you get the firm's net change in their cash balance from one period to the next (which is shown on the firm's Balance Sheet).

Imagine if last year the firm had \$100,000 in inventory on its balance sheet, but this year the firm has \$120,000 in inventory. That means that, over the last year, the firm had to spend an additional \$20,000 for inventory relative to what it spent the year before. In order for the funds to be used to buy inventory, those funds had to come from somewhere (they certainly didn't grow on trees). Alternatively, imagine if last year the firm had \$100,000 in accounts receivable, but this year it only has \$75,000 in accounts receivable. That means that \$25,000 worth of receivables have been collected and are now available to be used for other purposes. As mentioned above, when receivables (or any other asset for that matter) go down, then we consider that to be a source of funds. In contrast, when receivables (or any other asset) increase over the reporting period, we consider that to be a use of funds.

In total, the Statement of Cash Flows reconciles the firm's cash balance from the beginning of the period to the end of the period. It answers the question, "How did my cash balance get from $x$ dollars at the beginning of the period to $y$ dollars at the end of the period?" The Cash Flow Statement shows us what activities generated cash for the firm (a source) and what activities consumed cash from the firm (a use). It is worth noting that the Statement of Cash Flows is created by looking at all of the activity from the firm's Income Statement and Balance Sheet from a cash flow perspective. From a financial perspective, all of the firm's activity is captured on either the firm's Income Statement or Balance Sheet. The Cash Flow Statement groups all of that activity into one of three categories: (1) Operating activity, (2) Investing activity, and (3) Financing activity. It shows us whether each activity was overall either a source of funds to the firm or a use of funds for the firm. Given two periods of a firm's Income Statement and Balance Sheet, you can always create a Cash Flow Statement for the time period covered.

## Operating Cash Flows

Operating cash flows are funds either created or consumed as a result of the firm implementing its business strategy. If operating cash flow is positive, then (after paying all its bills associated with running its operations) the firm has some funds left over to make capital investments, acquisitions, pay dividends, pay down debt, buyback shares of stock, or even to put the money in a savings account if it chooses to do so. Thus, positive operating cash flows are a source of funds for the firm. However, if operating cash flows are negative, then the firm is consuming more funds in its operations than it generates. This means that in order to fully fund its operations, the firm must obtain funds from other sources; in this case, either from selling off assets, borrowing money, selling new equity, or dipping into its savings.

### *How to calculate operating cash flows?*

Operating Cash Flow reconciles Net Income, which is an accounting measure of profit (or loss), to Cash Flow from Operations, which is a financial measure of cash generation (or consumption). The calculation of operating cash flow begins with net income. However, we already know that net income is not the same thing as cash flow, so we will have to make some adjustments. Why? Because things like depreciation and amortization are included in the net income calculation, and these are non-cash charges. These will need to be added back into net profit in order to determine how much operating cash flow we actually generated. Moreover, we have to worry about increases in working capital over the reporting period that can also eat up our funds and create differences between profit and cash flow.

For example, were the invoices that were created by our revenues (and hence the associated accounts receivable) paid by customers? Because, if not, then those potential revenues are sitting in accounts receivable, and are not available for the firm to spend elsewhere. Sales that have not been paid for yet might result in profit (because of the accrual basis of accounting), but not in cash flow; specifically, those sales are still sitting in accounts receivable, and are hence a use of funds. Thus, we would have to subtract out any increase in accounts receivable from net profit in order to get a truer representation of how much actual cash was generated by the operations.

**Operating cash flow = Net income + Non-cash expenses – Changes in working capital**

where Non-Cash Expenses include Depreciation, Amortization, and Depletion.

## Investing Cash Flows

Cash flows from investing activities tell us how much cash has been created or consumed from investment-related activities over a given period of time. Similar to operating activities, investing activities can either be sources or uses of cash. Investment activities that are uses of cash include capital expenditures (the purchase of property, plant, and equipment), investments in financial securities, or the purchase of a subsidiary (among other things). Those that are sources of cash include the sale of capital assets (property, plant, and equipment), the sale of a subsidiary, or the sale of securities.

## Financing Cash Flows

The cash flows from financing activities section of the Cash Flow Statement give us information about the net flow of funds into and out of the company; that is, how did cash flow between the firm and its various claimholders: owners, creditors, and investors. Financing activities include borrowing and paying back debt, selling and buying back equity, and paying dividends.

Financing cash flows are determined as follows:

**Financing cash flows = Net cash inflows from issuing new equity and new debt – Cash paid out as dividends – Cash used to repurchase shares of equity or repayment of the principal on debt**

You may be thinking to yourself "what about interest expense?" Principal repayments on debt are included, but why not interest expense? We don't include interest expense here because it was already accounted for in the cash flows from operating activities section. Specifically, it was included when we calculated Net Income, the line item that starts off the Operating Cash Flow section. By including interest expense in the cash flows from financing activities section, we would be counting it twice and end up with an incorrect ending cash balance.

## *Net change in cash*

If we sum up the firm's cash flow from its Operating, Investing, and Financing activities, we get the firm's Net Change in Cash for the time period. The firm's Net Change in Cash tells us over the course of any period of time, given all the firm's sources and uses of funds, whether the firm's cash balance went up or whether it went down. When we add this Net Change in Cash to the firm's Beginning Cash Balance, we get the firm's Ending Cash Balance.

In this way, the Statement of Cash Flows reconciles the firm's cash balance at the beginning of the period to the firm's cash balance at the end of the period. It shows us how the firm went from having *x* dollars in its account at the beginning of the period to having *y* dollars in its account at the end of the period.

The following is Alpha Brewing Co.'s Cash Flow Statement:

| **Year** | **2017** | **2018** | **2019** |
|---|---|---|---|
| CASH AND CASH EQUIVALENTS, BEGINNING OF PERIOD | — | 93,466 | 213,709 |
| OPERATING ACTIVITIES: | | | |
| Net income | 58,129 | 271,136 | 390,574 |
| Adjustments to reconcile net income to net cash from operating activities: | | | |
| Depreciation | 74,506 | 74,506 | 85,006 |
| Changes in working capital: | | | |
| Accounts receivable | (21,602) | (76,883) | (64,568) |
| Inventories | (15,632) | (2,211) | (2,330) |
| Security Deposit | (20,000) | — | — |
| Accounts Payable | 3,829 | 3,920 | 5,070 |
| Net cash provided by (used in) operating activities | 79,229 | 270,468 | 413,752 |
| INVESTING ACTIVITIES: | | | |
| Capital Expenditures | (996,500) | — | (52,500) |
| Net cash provided by (used in) investing activities | (996,500) | — | (52,500) |
| Cash Available for Debt Repayment | (917,271) | 363,933 | 574,961 |
| FINANCING ACTIVITIES: | | | |
| Equity Investment from Founders | 423,170 | — | — |
| Long-Term Debt — proceeds | 634,755 | — | — |
| Long-Term Debt — principle repayment | (47,189) | (50,224) | (53,455) |
| Dividends | — | (100,000) | (255,000) |
| Net cash provided by (used in) financing activities | 1,010,736 | (150,224) | (308,455) |

| Year | 2017 | 2018 | 2019 |
|---|---|---|---|
| Net increase/(decrease) in cash and cash equivalents | 93,466 | 120,244 | 52,797 |
| **CASH AND CASH EQUIVALENTS, END OF PERIOD** | **93,466** | **213,709** | **266,507** |

## Key Takeaways

- There are three Sources and/or Uses of Cash for a firm: Operating, Investing, and Financing cash flows.
- The Statement of Cash Flows details the firm's net change in the Balance Sheet's Cash account from the beginning of the period to the end of the period. It does this by correcting for non-cash charges (e.g., Depreciation, Amortization, etc.), investing cash flows such as CAPEX, and financing cash flows such as the borrowing or repayment of debt or the sale or repurchase of shares.

# Chapter 5
# Financial Statement Analysis

Now that we know the basics of the three financial statements, let us turn our attention to interpreting them so that we can form insights with respect to the firm's performance and financial condition. Specifically, we are interested in assessing four characteristics: (1) Profitability, (2) Efficiency, (3) Leverage, and (4) Liquidity.

We will examine each of the four characteristics in great detail in what follows, but, in short, Profitability and Efficiency are measures of the firm's performance. Leverage relates to how much debt the firm is employing and Liquidity tells us how well the firm is positioned to satisfy its upcoming liabilities (will it be able to pay its upcoming bills or not?). As we will see later in this book, our insights with respect to these four critical dimensions will help us confirm the validity of the assumptions that will ultimately drive our financial forecasts.

## Profitability

Let us start with Profitability. To measure Alpha Brewing's profitability, we will first calculate its Return on Equity (ROE), which is the percentage return that we get as owners of the company for investing a dollar in it. We will then break down the firm's ROE using a DuPont Analysis. The DuPont Analysis will allow us to deconstruct the firm's ROE by analyzing the product of three ratios: (1) Profit Margin (profitability), (2) Asset Turnover (efficiency), and (3) The Equity Multiplier (debt ratio).

Our DuPont Analysis will reveal which areas of our firm are driving the returns to our shareholders. It will also allow us to see which areas of the business might be performing well and which areas might need improvement. We will also look at our firm's Price to Earnings (P/E) ratio to get additional insights into firm profitability.

## *Return on equity (ROE)*

Alpha Brewing's ROE can be calculated by taking the firm's Net Income (from its Income Statement) and dividing it by the firm's Shareholders' Equity (from its Balance Sheet).

$$\text{Return on equity} = \frac{\text{Net income}}{\text{Shareholders' equity}}$$

In doing so, let us look at 3 years of Alpha Brewing's (AB) historical financials, where 2017, 2018, and 2019 are Year 1, Year 2, and Year 3, respectively. Here we see that last year (Year 3), Alpha Brewing's Net Income was $390,574, and our Owners' Equity was $788,008. In this case, our ROE would equal 390,574/788,088 = 0.496 = 49.6%.

The following is AB's ROE for the last 3 years, with Year 3 (2019) representing the last year:

| | Year 1 | Year 2 | Year 3 |
|---|---|---|---|
| ROE | 12.1% | 41.6% | 49.6% |

You can think of a firm's ROE as the earnings the firm generates per dollar of equity capital. In this case, last year AB generated $0.50 for every $1.00 of equity capital invested in the business. Thus, the Owners earned a 49.6% return for every dollar of equity capital they have in the business. Think of ROE as a sort of an owners' "bang for the buck" measure, with higher returns being better than lower returns. Please note that 49.6% is a very high ROE capital. Once microbreweries are up and running, they can be incredibly profitable; that is one of the reasons why there are so many of them! In your analyses of other companies, please don't be surprised if you encounter ROEs that are less than 10% or even negative.

## ***DuPont analysis***

Next, let us deconstruct AB's ROE by performing a DuPont Analysis. A DuPont Analysis decomposes a firm's ROE into three components — (1) Profitability, (2) Efficiency, and (3) Leverage. Therefore, a firm's ROE can mathematically be shown to be the product of three inputs; specifically, ROE equals Profitability × Efficiency × Leverage.

This ROE decomposition is as follows:

$$ROE = Profitability \ x \ Efficiency \ x \ Leverage$$

$$ROE = \underset{Margin}{Profit} \ x \ \underset{Turnover}{Asset} \ x \ \underset{Multiplier}{Equity}$$

$$ROE = \frac{Net\ Income}{Sales} \ x \ \frac{Sales}{Assets} \ x \ \frac{Assets}{Shareholders'\ Equity}$$

$$ROE = \frac{Net\ Income}{\cancel{Sales}} \ x \ \frac{\cancel{Sales}}{\cancel{Assets}} \ x \ \frac{\cancel{Assets}}{Shareholders'\ Equity}$$

$$ROE = Net\ Income/Shareholders'\ Equity$$

So, what is it that drives AB's return? Let's use the DuPont equation to find out.

## ***Profit margin***

Let's first examine AB's Profit Margins over the last 3 years. A firm's Profit Margin tells us how much profit the firm is able to squeeze out from every dollar of its sales. It tells us how efficient the firm is at turning top-line sales into bottom-line profit for the firm's owners. The higher a firm's Profit Margin, the better its profitability.

Imagine a firm that has zero expenses, so every dollar of sales would go straight into the owners' bank account as profit. In this theoretical example of a firm with no expenses, the firm's Profit Margin would be 100% (the highest theoretically possible profit margin) minus whatever is paid out in taxes. Of course, all firms have expenses, many quite significant, so Profit Margins can be in the single digits for many firms or even negative if the expenses are greater than the revenues.

For calculating ROE, we use the firm's bottom-line measure of profitability: Net Income. The firm's Net Income is the profit the firm earns after paying all its expenses, including taxes. Now, we know that Net Income is not the same thing as the firm's free cash flow; instead, the firm's Net Income equals the book value of all the profits the owners (shareholders) of the firm have earned from the firm's operations.

While Net Income includes all expenses, it is also interesting to look at the firm's profitability at two other points on the firm's Income Statement. In addition to calculating a firm's Net Income-based Profit Margin, senior management and investors often keep a close eye on the firm's Gross Profit Margin and its Operating or EBIT (Earnings Before Interest and Taxes) Profit Margin.

A firm's Gross Profit Margin, which is calculated as Gross Profit/Sales, is a measure of the firm's pricing power and its ability to control its manufacturing costs. If Gross Profit margins are declining, that means one, or both, of two things is happening — either its selling price is declining and/or its Costs of Goods Sold (or Cost of Sales) is increasing. If its selling price is declining, then the firm is losing its pricing power, meaning it is no longer able to demand the prices it once did. As we mentioned in our discussion of the firm's Income Statement, this may mean that the firm's competitive advantages are eroding, allowing its competitors to exert pricing pressure. If the firm's Cost of Goods Sold (or Cost of Sales) is increasing, that means that the firm needs to do a better job controlling its manufacturing costs.

A firm's Operating (EBIT) Profit Margin measures the firm's profitability after subtracting all the firm's operating expenses from the firm's Gross Profit. Thus, the firm's Operating Profit Margin lets managers and investors see how good, or bad, of a job the firm is doing controlling its operating expenses (overhead). Holding the firm's Gross Profit Margins steady, if the firm's Operating Profit Margin is declining, this would mean the firm needs to do a better job controlling its operating expenses.

The following are AB's Profit Margins:

| | **Year 1** | **Year 2** | **Year 3** |
|---|---|---|---|
| Profit Margin (Gross) | 79.2% | 80.9% | 83.5% |
| Profit Margin (EBIT) | 9.3% | 22.8% | 28.8% |
| Profit Margin (Net) | 4.8% | 16.3% | 21.3% |

### *Asset turnover*

The next component in our DuPont Analysis after Profit Margin is Asset Turnover. Asset Turnover is a measure of a firm's efficiency and is calculated as Sales/Total Assets. This ratio tells us how efficient the firm is at utilizing its Assets to generate Sales. It tells us for every dollar of Assets the firm owns, how many dollars in Sales is it able to generate. The higher this ratio, the more efficiently the firm's Assets are being utilized to generate revenues.

Since the firm's Assets represent capital that is tied up in the business, we want this capital to be used as efficiently as possible, simply meaning that we want that our hard-earned capital generates as much revenue (and hopefully profit) as possible. A firm capable of generating billions of dollars in sales with little to no assets would be very capital efficient (think of most software companies) and, all other things equal, more valuable than a firm that requires huge amounts of assets (i.e., capital) to generate the same level of sales. For example, think of asset-intensive businesses like chemical manufacturing, and to a slightly lesser degree, breweries, which require a fair amount of equipment (and therefore capital) to operate.

The following is AB's historical Asset Turnover:

| | Year 1 | Year 2 | Year 3 |
|---|---|---|---|
| Asset Turnover | 1.13 | 1.39 | 1.42 |

### *Financial leverage — The equity multiplier*

To complete our DuPont Analysis, we next need to look at a measure of AB's financial leverage. To do this, we use the Equity Multiplier, which is the ratio of AB's Total Assets to its Shareholders' Equity. This ratio tells us how many dollars of equity are being used to finance each dollar of the firm's Assets. Another way of expressing the Equity Multiplier is 1 + D/E, where D is the firm's total debt and the E is the Shareholders' Equity, thus the more debt a firm has, the higher will be its Equity Multiplier. At any ratio above 1, we know the firm is using some amount of debt to finance its assets, in which case we might start to look at some debt coverage or liquidity ratios to better understand whether or not the firm's financial condition is at risk. We will explore this concept more when we later analyze liquidity ratios.

The following are AB's historical Equity Multiplier ratios:

| | Year 1 | Year 2 | Year 3 |
|---|---|---|---|
| Financial Leverage | 2.23 | 1.84 | 1.63 |

### *Breakdown of DuPont analysis results*

The following is a Summary of our DuPont Analysis on AB:

| | Year 1 | Year 2 | Year 3 |
|---|---|---|---|
| Profit Margin (Net) | 4.8% | 16.3% | 21.3% |
| Asset Turnover | 1.13 | 1.39 | 1.42 |
| Financial Leverage | 2.23 | 1.84 | 1.63 |
| ROE | 12.1% | 41.6% | 49.6% |

In the above DuPont Analysis, we can think of the firm's Net Profit Margin as summarizing the firm's Income Statement. The Asset Turnover ratio summarizes the left-hand side (Asset) of the firm's Balance Sheet, while the firm's Equity Multiplier ratio summarizes the right-hand side (Liabilities and Owners' Equity) of the firm's Balance Sheet. Thus, in ROE, we see all of the firm's financial performance being captured in one succinct number.

As we can see, AB's ROE has been steadily increasing over the last 3 years; that is great news for the owners. But what is driving that increase? As the DuPont Analysis demonstrates, this increase has been driven by two things: a large improvement in the company's profitability and a moderate improvement in the firm's efficiency. AB has done a good job over the last 3 years by increasing its Net Profit Margin every year, so management should be commended for its efforts there. By looking at the other Profit Margins we discussed earlier (gross margin and EBIT margin), management should be able to see exactly where this increase is coming from and commend the people in those areas.

Asset Turnover has also been increasing every year. AB's increase in Asset Turnover is mainly caused by the firm's steadily increasing sales, the PP&E slowly depreciating (yet the firm is still operating comfortably and has the excess capacity to continue increasing sales), and management's dividend payouts keeping the cash balance lean (cash is an asset, so keeping this from unnecessarily inflating actually increases the efficiency of the operations). The firm's balance sheet overall has been shrinking over the 5-year period, but its sales and profitability have been increasing, thereby generating more net income using less assets over time, which fits the very definition of efficiency that the asset turnover calculation looks to measure.

Lastly, we see that the firm's financial leverage is decreasing steadily. The decrease in leverage puts downward pressure on ROE, but the upward pressure on ROE contributed by the massive increase in profitability and solid increase in efficiency dominates the downward pressure that comes from decreasing leverage. The declining amount of financial leverage comes from the natural amortization of the firm's debt. As the firm's loans are paid off over time, the firm's leverage decreases. We spoke to the owners, and they have no intention of taking on more debt when the current loan is retired, so eventually the debt balance will go to zero. The decrease in leverage reduces the expected return the firm's owners receive on their equity (ROE), but also decreases the firm's risk, as less debt means lower interest and principal payments and thus less of a chance that the firm will default on those interest payments; overall, it means less financial risk for the firm. AB is doing very well. If the firm can continue this excellent performance, then the owners are going to be very happy indeed!

### *Price to earnings*

Another ratio that is used to measure the value, or shall we say investor optimism, of publicly traded companies is a firm's price to earnings ratio, or P/E ratio. A firm's P/E ratio is calculated as the firm's Stock Price divided by its Earnings per Share[1] (EPS). The resulting ratio tells us how much the market is willing to pay for every dollar of the firm's earnings.

[1] Earnings per Share (EPS) = Net Income/Average Outstanding Common Shares. Note that if the firm had Preferred Shares that were paid a dividend during the period, that dividend amount would be subtracted from the firm's Net Income before calculating the firm's EPS.

For example, let's say that a firm's common stock price is \$120, and its trailing (last reported) EPS was \$10 per share. This firm's P/E ratio (or multiple, as it is sometimes called) would hence be calculated as \$120/\$10 = 12 x. In this example, the market is saying it is currently willing to pay \$12 for every dollar of this firm's earnings. That is, the price investors are currently willing to pay for the earning power of this firm.

A firm's P/E ratio is dependent on two variables: (1) the amount of earnings the firm generates and (2) the multiple investors are willing to pay for that firm's earning power. The higher a firm's P/E ratio, all things equal, the more optimistic investors are about the future prospects of the firm, that is, the higher investor's expectations are about future profits. This is typically why young firms with a lot of growth potential have relatively high P/E ratios (above 20 x) when compared to older, more mature, and more slowly growing firms.

### *Market to book*

Another popular valuation ratio is the *market-to-book* (M/B) ratio; specifically, the market value of equity divided by the book value of equity. Sometimes this ratio is specified as the *book-to-market* (B/M) ratio, which is just the reciprocal of the M/B. The market-to-book multiple gives an indication of how optimistic the market is about the future prospects of the firm. Glamour stocks, the darlings of Wall Street, tend to have high market-to-book ratios. Their market value of equity is much higher than their corresponding book value of equity; this is often the case, because their stock prices are extremely high (perhaps even inflated). In contrast, value stocks tend to have relatively low M/B ratios.

The M/B ratio can also be high for firms that have a substantial amount of off-balance-sheet assets such as unidentifiable intangibles (trade secrets, brands, or a substantial amount of knowledge tied up in human capital). These off-balance-sheet assets are not included in the book value of equity, but they are absolutely included in the market value of equity. The M/B can also be high for firms that have a lot of property, plant, and equipment, whose cost basis is very low (because it was purchased many years ago); remember, PP&E cannot get written up in value — it is reported at the lessor of what we paid for it or what it is worth today. So, if the market value of the firm's PP&E has substantially appreciated in value over time, this will cause the M/B ratio to increase as well.

## Efficiency

In completing our DuPont Analysis, we discussed one measure of a firm's efficiency, which is a ratio called Asset Turnover. Most measures of a firm's efficiency relate to the firm's ability to manage its Working Capital accounts, that is, its Current Asset and Current Liability accounts. A firm's Working Capital accounts are accounts we would expect to see fluctuate in direct proportion to the firm's sales, specifically, the quantity being sold. That is, any increase or decrease in the quantity sold should translate directly to a similar increase or decrease in the firm's Inventory, Accounts Receivable, and Accounts Payable accounts. The firm's Fixed or Long-term Asset and Liability accounts, such as Plant, Property, and Equipment (PP&E) and Long-Term Debt, do not demonstrate this same direct correlation to sales. The firm's Fixed Asset accounts tend to move more in discrete and discontinuous increments, as equipment is purchased, and loans are secured.

A firm's ability to properly manage its Working Capital accounts can have a large effect on the firm's financial performance and hence its value. Efficiency measures such as Inventory Turnover, Days Receivables (also called Days Sales Outstanding), and Days Payables (also called Days Payables Outstanding) help us see how well a firm is managing three of the firm's critical Working Capital accounts: Inventory, Accounts Receivable, and Accounts Payable. As we shall see, these measures of efficiency can also be very helpful in correctly forecasting a firm's future financial statements.

### *Inventory turnover*

Inventory Turnover is calculated as the firm's Cost of Goods Sold (COGS) divided by Inventory. The ratio tells us how often the firm turns over or sells every item in its inventory. If you take the number of days in a calendar year (365) and divide it by the firm's Inventory Turnover, the resulting number is called Days Inventory Outstanding or DIO.[2] DIO tells

---

[2] Sometimes bankers will use a 360-day commercial year instead of the 365-day calendar year when calculating Inventory Turnover.

us how long, on average, every item sits in the firm's inventory. It provides a unit of time for how long inventory has been held on hand. This measure is useful on a relative basis for comparing with other firms' inventory practices or for comparing to the firm itself over a period of time.

AB's historical Inventory Turnover and Days Inventory are calculated as follows:

| | **Year 1** | **Year 2** | **Year 3** |
|---|---|---|---|
| Inventory Turnover | 10.6 | 11.2 | 8.6 |
| Days Inventory | 34.3 | 32.6 | 42.7 |

Forecasting inventory can be a challenge, since it can be a combination of finished goods, work in process, and raw materials. Since the value of finished goods and work in process inventory both are driven by labor and raw materials, and the value of raw materials is driven by its purchase costs, people tend to forecast inventory as a percentage of Costs of Good Sold. Specifically, unless the firm made substantial changes to its manufacturing process, qualified new vendors, or required a substantial amount of overtime hours in order to create the inventory, a reasonable assumption is to assume that the historical ratio of Inventory to COGS will remain stable over time. So, if the historical ratio of Inventory to COGS was 11%, and COGS costs were forecasted to be \$100MM, then a reasonable estimate for the value of inventory would be (.11)(\$100MM) = \$11MM.

Inventory Turnover can also be used to forecast your Inventory. For example, let's say your lead time for the goods you sell is 3 months. That means you are planning to always have 3-months' worth of inventory on hand. 3-months' worth of inventory means you turn your inventory 4x per year (12 months per year/3 months of inventory = 4x). To calculate your firm's Inventory level, divide your annual COGS by 12 and then multiply that number by your Inventory Turnover (in this case 4x).

### *Days sales outstanding*

A firm's Days Sales Outstanding, abbreviated as DSO (also called Days Receivable) tells us how many days' worth of sales is waiting to be collected. Days Sales Outstanding represents the average number of days between the date of sale and the date payment is received. It is calculated as (Accounts Receivable (AR) divided by Sales) times 365.

Closely monitoring DSO or similarly the ratio of Accounts Receivable to Sales can provide us with a warning sign if the firm is secretly selling to uncreditworthy customers. The warning lights should go on whenever we see DSO (or the ratio of AR/Sales) start to increase over time. Why might this mean trouble? Because AR is an account that we would expect to see fluctuate in direct proportion to sales, for example, if sales were to increase 10% during a given period of time, then AR should also increase 10% during that same time period. Likewise, if sales were to decrease 10%, we would expect to see AR decrease by 10%. The warning sign should appear whenever AR is increasing at a greater rate than sales, for example, sales increased 10% last quarter, but AR increased 40%. What would that mean?

If revenues increase 10% but AR increased 40%, that means that the company is booking sales but not collecting payment for those sales. If something like this happens, then it is time for us to start asking the management team some tough questions. Why is the firm having trouble collecting its receivables? One reason may be totally benign: the firm intentionally extended its payment terms in order to lure more customers. For example, instead of giving customers 30 days to pay their invoices, they increased their payment terms to 45 or 60 days. In this case, it is understandable why customers are taking longer to pay and why receivables are increasing relative to sales. If this intentional change in payment terms were in-line with what the rest of the industry is doing with respect to payment terms, then there would be no cause for concern. If, however, this change were not in line with that of its competitors, then it might potentially be foreshadowing a decline in the competitiveness of the firm's products or services.

In a worst-case scenario, a disproportionate increase in AR to Sales could be an early indicator of outright fraud, as was the case with "Chainsaw Al" Dunlap and Sunbeam back in 1998. Chainsaw Al, as they called him, was a swashbuckling Chief Executive Officer (CEO) who built a name for himself turning around companies.[3] Wall Street liked him, and Al was hired by Sunbeam (circa 1998) to help turn around the

[3] Why did they call him "Chainsaw"? Because usually the first thing he would do when he took over a company was to cut, or chainsaw, headcount, that is, lay off lots of people.

struggling consumer products manufacturer. So, what happened after Chainsaw Al became CEO?

Well, 6 months to a year went by, and things were looking good at Sunbeam — sales were up, expenses were down, and Wall Street was happy, as it appeared that Chainsaw Al was doing his thing and his thing was working. But one Wall Street analyst noticed something worrisome: the firm's accounts receivable account was exploding relative to sales. It looked like Sunbeam was not collecting any of the money from its new sales. Well, this seemed odd, so the analyst dug a little deeper.

It turns out Chainsaw Al, in an attempt to appear successful in his turnaround efforts, had set up a wholly owned subsidiary of Sunbeam and was booking bogus sales from Sunbeam to this subsidiary. In other words, Sunbeam was booking sales to itself. Well, this ended up resulting in investor fraud, Wall Street was not so happy anymore, and Chainsaw Al went to spend some time in prison. The moral of the story: pay close attention to AR as a percentage of sales.

AB's historical Days Receivables are as follows:

| | **Year 1** | **Year 2** | **Year 3** |
|---|---|---|---|
| Days Receivables | 6.5 | 21.6 | 32.5 |

## *Days payables outstanding*

A firm's Days Payables Outstanding (DPO, also called Days Payable) shows us, on average, how many days it takes for the firm to pay its vendors. It is calculated as Accounts Payable (AP) divided by annual Purchases multiplied by 365. Note that sometimes data on Purchases is not available, in this case we would use Cost of Goods Sold instead.

AP is one of those accounts, like AR, that is worth keeping a close eye on. Just like the AR account, AP can flash a warning sign. The AP is another account that we would expect to see fluctuate in direct proportion to a change in the quantity of the goods that a firm sells. More precisely, AP should grow in proportion with purchases, which are driven by the quantity of what is being sold. If the firm's purchases increased 10%, then, if everything is stable, the firm's AP should increase 10%. We would hence expect to see a firm's AP remain relatively constant as a percentage of the firm's purchases over time. Remember that a firm's AP balance represents all the bills the firm has received from its vendors but has not yet paid, so if a firm were to slow down its payments to its vendors, then that would result in an increase in the firm's AP-to-Purchases ratio, which would trigger a red flag.

In a best-case scenario, this increase in the firm's AP-to-Purchases ratio could simply be a result of the firm renegotiating better (longer) payment terms with its vendors. Longer payment terms effectively allow the firm to use its vendor's money for a longer period of time. Longer payment terms are a good thing, since (when the interest rate associated with monies is zero, as is the case with AR and AP) firms generally want to collect monies owed to them as quickly as possible and pay monies owed to others as slowly as possible. Who doesn't like free money?

A less pleasant cause for the increase in the firm's AP-to-Purchases ratio involves the firm *dragging its payables*, which could be a leading indicator of a potential liquidity problem and impending financial distress. When a business (or an individual for that matter) is experiencing liquidity problems, they often cannot pay all their bills on time. For example, rather than paying their vendors in 30 days, they might pay in 35 days; this is called "*dragging their payables*." Some bills may get paid late, while other bills may not get paid at all, resulting in an unhealthy build-up of AP. So, when the AP/Purchases ratio is increasing over time, it pays to ask the management team, "Why aren't you paying your bills on time?"

The following is AB's historical Days Payables Outstanding (DPO):

| | **Year 1** | **Year 2** | **Year 3** |
|---|---|---|---|
| Days Payables | 8.4 | 14.2 | 27.1 |

### *Cash conversion cycle*

The three previous metrics can then be used in conjunction to further analyze the firm's efficiency in generating cash from their working capital management. This can be accomplished by calculating the firm's Cash Conversion Cycle. By combining all the measures together into one equation, you can measure how many days an initial cash investment in the inventory and operations is tied up before being converted into cash profits via sales.

A firm's Cash Conversion Cycle is calculated by adding Days Inventory and Days Receivables together, followed by subtracting out Days Payables (DI + DR – DP).

AB's historical Cash Conversion Cycles (CCC) are as follows:

| | Year 1 | Year 2 | Year 3 |
|---|---|---|---|
| Days Inventory | 34.3 | 32.6 | 42.7 |
| Days Receivables | 6.5 | 21.6 | 32.5 |
| Days Payables | 8.4 | 14.2 | 27.1 |
| Cash Conv. Cycle | 32.4 | 40.1 | 48.1 |

## Leverage

Next, we can look at some measures of how much debt (also referred to as leverage in the US or gearing in many of the UK Commonwealth countries) a firm has used to finance its assets. The amount of debt a firm has is a decision made by the management of the firm. As management chooses to finance more and more of the firm's assets with debt, the firm's financial leverage ratios will increase. As a firm's financial leverage increases, so does the firm's risk, since more debt means more future financial obligations (principal and interest payments) that need to be met. The more future obligations a firm has, the more likely it becomes that the firm will encounter business conditions (e.g., an economic recession or a supply chain bottleneck) that will cause the firm to be unable to meet its obligations. Should this happen, the debt holders of the firm could potentially gain control of the firm through bankruptcy and wipe out the firm's shareholders. In general, a firm's leverage ratios are more easily understood in relation to the leverage ratios of other firms in the industry and to industry averages.

Be aware that the use of debt increases the volatility of a firm's cash flows. The use of debt makes the good times better, since the bank is getting a fixed rate of return (its interest payment) and anything the firm earns from using the borrowed funds that is above and beyond the interest payment, it gets to keep. The flip side is that the use of debt makes the bad times worse, because the firm has to make interest payments irrespective of whether it has a good year or a bad year. Even if the firm has no revenues, it still has to make interest payments. Think about the situation with COVID-19. So many firms buckled underneath the crushing pressure of required interest payments when there were very little revenues to be had. Debt makes the bad times worse.

### *Debt-to-assets and debt-to-equity*

In our DuPont Analysis, we used the ratio of Assets to Shareholders' Equity as our measure of financial leverage. Other common measures of financial leverage include Debt-to-Assets and Debt-to-Equity ratios. Debt-to-Assets is calculated as Total Liabilities divided by Total Assets and Debt-to-Equity is calculated as Total Liabilities to Shareholders' Equity.

AB's historical Debt-to-Assets and Debt-to-Equity ratios are calculated as follows:

| | **Year 1** | **Year 2** | **Year 3** |
|---|---|---|---|
| Debt-to-Assets | 55.1% | 45.5% | 38.7% |
| Debt-to-Equity | 1.23 | 0.84 | 0.63 |

In Year 1, we see that AB was financing 55.1% of its Assets with debt. The Debt-to-Equity ratio for Year 1 tells us that for every dollar of equity the firm had, it had $1.23 of debt. As you see, both ratios decline as AB pays down its loans over time. This decline in AB's use of financial leverage decreases the firm's ROE but also decreases the risk of the firm.

## Liquidity

A firm's ability to service its short-term liabilities is captured by various liquidity ratios. These include the Interest Coverage Ratio (some books include this under leverage ratios), the Current Ratio, and the Quick Ratio. These ratios are often reviewed by a firm's lenders in order to assess a firm's ability to pay its debts, both current and future. The ratios are also useful in financial forecasting, a discussion we shall defer until Chapter 12.

### *Interest coverage ratio*

The Interest Coverage Ratio, also called the Times Interest Earned (or TIE) ratio, is calculated by dividing the firm's EBIT (or Earnings Before

Interest and Taxes) for a given time period by its Interest Expense for the same time period. The resulting ratio tells us how many dollars of operating profit or EBIT the firm has for each dollar of interest it owes — a margin of safety measure for the firm's ability to service its debt. The higher a firm's interest coverage ratio, the greater its ability to service its debt. If two firms, Firm A and Firm B, both have high amounts of debt, but Firm A is much more profitable than Firm B, that is, Firm A has more EBIT than Firm B, then Firm A will have a higher Interest Coverage Ratio than Firm B. This tells us that Firm A has a better ability to service its debt than Firm B.

AB's historical Interest Coverage Ratios are calculated as follows:

| | **Year 1** | **Year 2** | **Year 3** |
|---|---|---|---|
| Interest Coverage Ratio | 2.9 | 10.7 | 16.4 |

We can see that the brewery's TIE ratio has been steadily increasing. This is not surprising, since its leverage has been decreasing.

### *Current ratio and quick ratio*

Two commonly used liquidity measures are the Current Ratio and the Quick Ratio (also called the Acid Test). A firm's Current Ratio is calculated by dividing its Current Assets by its Current Liabilities. The Current Ratio compares all of the cash the firm expects to collect in the next year (its Current Assets) to all of the cash the firm expects to pay out in the next year (its Current Liabilities). The resulting ratio tells us how many dollars expected to be collected in cash within the next year are available to be paid out for each dollar of liabilities due within the next year. The higher the current ratio is, the better, supposedly, is the firm positioned to service its short-term (less than 1 year) obligations. We would like this ratio to be well greater than one, as the resulting ratio compares how many dollars we expect to collect in cash within the next year (our Current Assets) versus how many dollars we expect to pay out in cash within the next year (our Current Liabilities). If a firm's Current Ratio were less than one, we might be concerned that the firm would be facing a pending liquidity crisis sometime within the next 12 months, which is why a Current Ratio under one is usually a major concern for management.

A closely related ratio to the Current Ratio is called the Quick Ratio. The Quick Ratio simply subtracts any less liquid Current Asset accounts, most often the Inventory account, from the firm's Current Assets before dividing by its Current Liabilities. The Quick Ratio should be used in place of the Current Ratio whenever you feel the liquidity of one or more of the firm's Current Asset account(s) is questionable. By removing the value of any illiquid Current Asset account(s) from the ratio, we get a more accurate picture of the firm's ability to service its current obligations. Again, just like the Current Ratio, the higher the Quick Ratio, the better. The expectation would be for this ratio to always be greater than one to avoid a potential liquidity crisis, should those potentially questionable account(s) prove to be either overvalued or illiquid.

AB's historical Current Ratios and Quick Ratios (without Inventory) are calculated as follows:

| | **Year 1** | **Year 2** | **Year 3** |
|---|---|---|---|
| Current Ratio | 2.4 | 5.4 | 6.5 |
| Quick Ratio | 2.1 | 5.1 | 6.2 |

While Profitability, Efficiency, and Leverage ratios help us measure firm performance and risk, Liquidity ratios help us understand a firm's prospects for survival. Cash is king, and if a firm is facing a shortage of cash (i.e., a liquidity crisis), then that needs to be addressed before any other matters. The Liquidity ratios we looked at are often calculated using a firm's annual or quarterly financial statements, but there is no reason why they cannot be calculated using 1-week, 2-week, or 1-month financial forecasts should we have grave concerns about the firm's future liquidity.

Generally, businesses with more stable cash flows are able to comfortably operate with lower Interest Coverage Ratios and Current or Quick Ratios than businesses with greater variability in their cash flows. As we mentioned, debt is a source of risk. The greater is a firm's debt, the greater is its financial risk. The total risk of the firm can be thought of as a combination of the firm's financial risk (debt) and its business risk (earnings variability and operating leverage).

## *Risk analysis*

In thinking about the overall risk of a firm, one must consider both its business risk and its financial risk. Business risk has to do with the precision with which we can forecast the firm's operating cash flows. If we can forecast them with a high degree of accuracy, then there is relatively little business risk. One way to think about a firm's historical business risk is to evaluate the firm's variability in earnings over time, as well as its operating leverage (the proportion of its costs that are fixed costs).

Further, one way to evaluate a firm's historical variability in earnings is look at the firm's EBIT or EBITDA over the last 5 to 10 years. Do the firm's operating earnings (EBIT) exhibit slow, steady growth, like one might expect from a utility company? Or do they exhibit large variations over time, like one would expect from a movie production company that sometimes releases blockbuster movies (e.g., the movie *Titanic*) and other times total flops (e.g., the movie *Cats*)? To the extent that one firm's earnings are more stable over time relative to that of another firm, we can say the firm with more stable earnings has less business risk than the firm with the higher variability in earnings.

### *Operating leverage*

Another source of business risk is the amount of operating leverage employed by the firm. Operating leverage is defined as the proportion of the firm's fixed expenses to total expenses. The higher that proportion, that is, the more fixed costs the firm has, the higher the firm's operating leverage. Now, much like financial leverage (debt), operating leverage acts as a lever to the firm's performance, once again making the good times better and the bad times worse.

Imagine two firms, Firm A and Firm B. On the one hand, Firm A has a 100% fixed cost overhead structure, where none of the firm's expenses vary at all in direct relation to sales (there is zero correlation between the firm's sales and expenses); so, irrespective if sales are up 50% or down 30%, the firm's total costs are the same. On the other hand, Firm B has a 100% variable cost overhead structure, where all of the firm's expenses vary in direct relation to sales, that is, if sales increase 50%, then the firm's total expenses also increase 50%, but if sales decrease 30%, then the firm's total expenses decrease 30%.

Now, imagine that Firm A and Firm B both experienced a 100% increase in sales, meaning that sales doubled at both firms from one year to the next. Assuming both firms were profitable before the increase in sales, every dollar of that increase in sales would go straight to the EBIT of Firm A. Why? Because Firm A would not experience an increase in expenses in relation to its doubling of revenues. Firm A's EBIT would skyrocket by the amount of the sales increase ("good times better");

however, not so with Firm B. Firm B's expenses would also double along with its sales, resulting in more EBIT than the year prior, but not nearly as much as in Firm A.

| Base Case | | | Sales Increase 100% | | |
|---|---|---|---|---|---|
| | **Firm A** | **Firm B** | | **Firm A** | **Firm B** |
| Sales | 100,000 | 100,000 | Sales | 200,000 | 200,000 |
| Expenses | | | Expenses | | |
| Fixed | 65,000 | 0 | Fixed | 65,000 | 0 |
| Variable | 0 | 65,000 | Variable | 0 | 130,000 |
| Total Expenses | 65,000 | 65,000 | Total Expenses | 65,000 | 130,000 |
| EBIT | 35,000 | 35,000 | EBIT | 135,000 | 70,000 |
| Difference | 0 | | Difference | 65,000 | |

Now, let us imagine the opposite scenario. Let us assume that sales decreased by 50% for both Firm A and Firm B. Firm B would show a much smaller decrease in EBIT than Firm A, because as Firm B's sales declined, so would its expenses, resulting in a lower drop in profit relative to Firm A. Firm A's expenses, in contrast, would remain exactly the same as they were prior to the 50% sales decline, thus greatly reducing (or eliminating, as in our example) Firm B's profitability ("making the bad times worse").

| Base Case | | | Sales Decrease 50% | | |
|---|---|---|---|---|---|
| | **Firm A** | **Firm B** | | **Firm A** | **Firm B** |
| Sales | 100,000 | 100,000 | Sales | 50,000 | 50,000 |
| Expenses | | | Expenses | | |
| Fixed | 65,000 | 0 | Fixed | 65,000 | 0 |
| Variable | 0 | 65,000 | Variable | 0 | 32,500 |
| Total Expenses | 65,000 | 65,000 | Total Expenses | 65,000 | 32,500 |
| EBIT | 35,000 | 35,000 | EBIT | (15,000) | 17,500 |
| Difference | 0 | | Difference | (32,500) | |

As shown above, operating leverage, defined as the degree to which a firm has a fixed cost structure as opposed to a variable cost structure, has a huge effect on the performance and on the business risk of the firm. Firms with more operating leverage are deemed to be riskier than firms with less operating leverage, because just like financial leverage, operating leverage increases a firm's break-even point of sales. By increasing a firm's break-even point, we increase the probability that the firm will encounter a state in its market where the firm is unable to generate enough revenues to meet its obligations.

So, if a firm has a lot of variability in earnings and a lot of operating leverage, then that firm will have a lot of business risk. It is very dangerous to finance a firm that has a lot of business risk with a lot of debt (financial risk). High business risk combined with lots of financial risk can create a very problematic situation when things go poorly; again, think of all the COVID-19-related bankruptcies of highly levered firms. The Lesson: Do not overleverage firms with a lot of business risk, it is likely to not end well.

## Key Takeaways

- Financial Statement analysis involves the assessment of four things: Profitability, Efficiency, Leverage, and Liquidity.
- We access a firm's performance relative to itself historically and to its competitors.
- Performing financial statement analysis helps to identify problem areas before they become too severe and allows us to access areas for strengths and weaknesses both within the firm and among competitors.
- ROE can be deconstructed into three components: profitability, efficiency, and leverage. This relationship is delineated by the DuPont equation.
- Profitability has to do with the amount of profit that the firm generates given its Revenues.
- Efficiency allows us to determine how efficiently the firm is utilizing its Assets to generate Revenues. Is it lean and mean or is it bogged down with unproductive Assets? Remember A = L + E so someone has to pay for all of the firm's non-productive Assets.

- Leverage has to do with the firm's use of Debt in its Capital Structure. Higher leverage means that the firm has more Debt. Too much debt can lead to financial distress and perhaps even bankruptcy. Not enough debt can put the firm at a competitive disadvantage.
- Liquidity has to do with the firm's access to cash. The traditional accounting measures do not do a good job of measuring liquidity. If the firm has access to cash when needed it is said to be relatively liquid.

# Chapter 6

# The Time Value of Money

Valuation is the practice of determining what something should be worth today, given the costs, benefits, and risks associated with owning it. There are two things that drive the intrinsic value of an asset: (1) cash flows (whether they're inflows or outflows) and (2) the risk of those cash flows. The intrinsic value is what *we* think it should be worth based on our own research and our forecasts of the assets' cash flows and the risk of those cash flows. Our intrinsic value is often different from the market value, which is based on supply and demand conditions in the market. If our intrinsic value is much higher than the market value, then we might consider purchasing the asset.

So, one of the core requirements of valuation is understanding what the asset's fair value should be, given its expected cash flows and the riskiness of those cash flows. The higher the risk of any given stream of future cash flows, the lower the price that someone would pay today in return for those cash flows. As you will learn later in this book, there is a relationship between risk and required return: the higher the riskiness of an asset's cash flows, the greater is the rate of return that you will require for investing in the asset.

## Present Value and Future Value

A key concept in the determination of what future cash flows are worth today is the concept of the time value of money. Money has a time value to it. A dollar today is worth more than a dollar a year from now. The reason for this is that a dollar today can be invested and will thus earn a rate of return, so a year from now it will be worth more than the dollar that you initially invested. Specifically, it will be worth one dollar multiplied by one plus whatever the rate of return on that dollar investment is. Thus, the future value one year from now of a dollar today can be calculated as follows:

$$\text{Future value} = \$1.00 * (1 + \text{Rate of return})$$

For example, if the interest rate that we can earn on our money is 2% per year, then \$1.00 today is worth \$1.00 × 1.02 = \$1.02 a year from now. In other words, \$1.02 is the "future value" of a present value of \$1.00 today. More generally, the future value of any present value 1 year from now is just the Present Value $x$ (1 + Rate of return). So, for example, the future value 1 year from now of \$100 invested at 5% per year would be \$100 * (1.05) or \$105.

By extension, the future value (FV) of any present value (PV) 2 years from today can be calculated as follows:

$$\begin{aligned} \text{FV} &= \text{PV} * (1 + \text{Rate of return}) * (1 + \text{Rate of return}) \\ &= \text{PV} * (1 + \text{Rate of return})^2 \end{aligned}$$

Here is an illustration that will help give us some intuition for the above relationship. Using the previous example, instead of asking what the future value of \$100 invested at 5% 1 year from now is, what if we wanted to know what it would be worth 2 years from now? We know from the last example that, after 1 year, our investment should be worth \$100 * (1.05) = \$1.05. Then, we would take that \$1.05 and invest it at 5% for 1 year, which would yield \$1.05 * (1.05) = \$1.1025.

In general, the future value of any present value some "$N$" years from today can be calculated as follows:

$$\text{FV} = \text{PV} * (1 + \text{Rate of return})^N$$

This is called the *future value formula*, where PV is the dollar amount of the investment today, and $N$ is the number of years in the future that you will be investing the cash flow.

For example, the future value of \$100 invested at a 2% per year return, 5 years from now, can be calculated as follows:

$$\begin{aligned} &\$100 * (1.02) * (1.02) * (1.02) * (1.02) * (1.02) \\ &= \$100 * (1.02)^5 = \$110.408 \end{aligned}$$

Taking the future value of a cash flow is called *compounding*. Its counterpart, taking the present value of a future cash flow, is called *discounting*. The rate of return that we use to compound and discount the cash flows is called the *discount rate* (synonyms include the *hurdle rate* or the *required rate of return*). For example, if \$1.00 today invested at 2% per year interest is worth \$1.02 a year from now, then \$1.02 received a year from now, discounted back at a discount rate of 2%, must be worth \$1.00 today — there must always be parity between PV and FV calculations. Thus, if the future value is computed as

$$\text{FV} = \text{PV} * (1 + \text{Discount rate})^N$$

Then the present value of a future cash flow must be

$$\text{PV} = \frac{\text{FV}}{(1 + \text{Discount rate})^N}$$

This is called the *present value formula*.

For example, using the previous illustration, the present value of \$110.408 received 5 years from now, discounted back to today at a discount rate of 2%, is $\$110.408/(1.02)^5 = \$100.00$. It *has* to equal \$100.00 or else there will be an arbitrage opportunity — arbitrage means that we can make a return without taking on any risk. If the price is less than \$100.00, then everyone will want to buy it because it is underpriced. In contrast, if the price is more than \$100.00, then no one will want to buy it because it is too expensive. Instead, everyone will try to sell it.

### *How to get the PV of a finite sequence of cash flows*

Now that we are familiar with the way the time value of money works for an individual cash flow, we can apply this methodology to a stream of cash flows. Lucky for us, the present value of a sequence of cash flows is just the sum of the present values of each of the individual cash flows in the sequence.

$$\text{PV}\sum_{1}^{N}\text{CF}_t = \sum_{1}^{N}\text{PV}(\text{CF}_t)$$

For example, imagine that we had an asset that paid $100 at the end of the first year and $200 at the end of the second year. If the discount rate was 10%, then what is a fair price for the asset?

| | CF0 | CF1 | CF2 |
|---|---|---|---|
| Payout | 0 | $100 | $200 |

Since the present value of a sequence of cash flows is just the present value of the individual cash flows, then we can solve the example as follows:

$$PV = \frac{\$100}{(1.1)} + \frac{\$200}{(1.1)^2} = \$256.20$$

The fair price for the asset, if the discount rate were 10%, would be $256.20. Why is this said to be the fair price of the asset? Because at this price, the owner of the cash flows will earn a 10% rate of return: no more, no less. In fact, if someone gave us $256.20 today, then we could invest that amount at 10% return, and pay out $100 at the end of year 1 and $200 at the end of year 2.

| | CF0 | CF1 | CF2 |
|---|---|---|---|
| Rate of Return | 0.0 | 1.1 | 1.1 |
| Asset CF | ($256.20) | $281.82 | $200.00 |
| Payout | 0 | ($100.00) | ($200.00) |
| Remainder | $256.20 | $181.82 | $0.00 |

### *Using Excel functions to determine present values*

The calculation of Present Values is made very easy through the use of Microsoft Excel's NPV function.[1]

[1] For an excellent primer on the use of Excel in financial modeling, please see Ivan E. Brick, *Lecture Notes in Introduction to Corporate Finance*, Vol. 1 (World Scientific, 2017).

The function is used as follows:

= NPV(*rate*, *value1*, *value2*,..., *value N*)[2]

where *rate* is the discount rate and *value1*, *value2*,..., *valueN* are the cash flows from year 1 through the final year. So, for the example above, the formula for the NPV calculation would be

= NPV(.1, 100, 200)

which yields an answer of \$256.20.

*Example to tie it all together*

What would be the value today, if the discount rate were 10%, of the following cash flows: \$80 received a year from now, \$100, 2 years from now, \$150, 3 years from now, and \$200, 4 years from now?

**Solution**

$$PV = \frac{\$80}{(1.1)} + \frac{\$100}{(1.1)^2} + \frac{\$150}{(1.1)^3} + \frac{\$200}{(1.1)^4} = \$404.67$$

or using Excel

= NPV(.1, 80, 100, 150, 200) = \$404.67

### *Valuation of an infinite stream of cash flows*

Using the present value formula is computationally feasible when there are a finite number of cash flows (that is, a reasonable number of finite cash flows... it would likely require a supercomputer to compute the present value of billions of individual cash flows). However, you may encounter instances (e.g., pricing a stock) where the cash flows go on forever. The existence of an infinite number of cash flows makes the calculation of present value infeasible, since you could never get enough computational power to do an infinite number of calculations.

[2]Be sure to put an equal sign in front of the formula.

$$\text{Present value} = \frac{CF_1}{(1+\text{Discount rate})^1} + \frac{CF_2}{(1+\text{Discount rate})^2} + \frac{CF_3}{(1+\text{Discount rate})^3} + \frac{CF_4}{(1+\text{Discount rate})^4} + \cdots + \frac{CF_\infty}{(1+\text{Discount rate})^\infty}$$

Fortunately, there are a few situations where the cash flows are infinite, yet they can still be valued. The first situation is when the cash flow is a *perpetuity*. A perpetuity is a cash flow that is paid at fixed time intervals (perhaps the end of every year), never changes in value (thus is constant), and goes on forever. A good example of this is the Consol Bond: a perpetual bond which has a fixed payment and an infinite maturity. Consol Bonds were first issued by the British government back in 1917 to fund their World War II efforts. Those initial Consol Bonds paid 5% interest, and many are still in existence today.

The second situation is when the cash flows are growing at a constant growth rate other than zero. An example of this might be a utility stock, whose dividends are growing at a slow but constant rate. In each of these cases, the infinite stream of cash flows can be valued by employing an easy-to-use formula.

## *Valuation of an infinite stream of cash flows when the cash flow is growing at a constant rate — the Gordon Growth Formula*

Let's begin with the valuation of an infinite stream of cash flows that are growing at a constant rate, *g*. As we will see, a perpetuity is just a special case of this more general case, where the growth rate is zero.

Here is an example of a cash flow growing at a constant rate, *g*:

| Year 1 | Year 2 | Year 3 | Year 4 | Year 5 | Year ∞ |
|---|---|---|---|---|---|
| CF | CF(1+g) | $CF(1+g)^2$ | $CF(1+g)^3$ | $CF(1+g)^4$ | $CF(1+g)^\infty$ |

Using the present value formula, the above cash flow stream has the following present value:

$$\text{Present value}_{t=0} = \frac{\text{CF}}{(1+\ \text{Discount rate})^1} + \frac{\text{CF}(1+g)}{(1+\text{Discount rate})^2} + \frac{\text{CF}(1+g)^2}{(1+\text{Discount rate})^3} + \frac{\text{CF}(1+g)^3}{(1+\text{Discount rate})^4} + \cdots + \frac{\text{CF}(1+g)^{\infty-1}}{(1+\text{Discount rate})^\infty}$$

Since this calculation of this series involves an infinite number of calculations, it is computationally impossible. Fortunately for us, since the cash flow is growing at a constant rate forever, Myron Gordon and Eli Shapiro were able to prove that the infinite sequence above converges to a very simple and easy-to-use equation.[3]

$$\text{Present value} = \frac{\text{CF}}{\text{Discount rate} - g}$$

This famous equation is called the *Gordon Growth Formula.* So, if the cash flows' growth rate is expected to be constant (as it often is, for say, the dividends paid by utility companies), the only three things we need in order to value equity directly using the discounted cash flow method are: (1) next year's expected cash flow, (2) the discount rate, and (3) the growth rate.

For example, imagine that we were trying to value an asset that is expected to pay $100 in the first year, and whose cash flow is to grow at the rate of 2% every year forever.

The cash flows would look as follows:

| **Year 1** | **Year 2** | **Year 3** | **Year 4** | **Year 5** | **Year ∞** |
|---|---|---|---|---|---|
| 100 | 102 | 104.04 | 106.12 | 108.24 | ??? |

If the discount rate is 10%, then the value of this infinite cash flow stream would be as follows:

[3]M. J. Gordon and Eli Shapiro, "Capital Equipment Analysis: The Required Rate of Profit," *Management Science* 3, no. 1 (1956): 102–110.

$$\text{Present value} = \frac{\$100}{.1-.02} = \$1,250$$

Piece of cake!

### *A special case: Valuing a perpetuity — constant cash flows/a growth rate of zero*

As mentioned above, a perpetuity is a constant, non-changing cash flow received at fixed intervals of time, forever. Another way of saying this is that a perpetuity is a steady, periodic cash flow with a growth rate of zero. Growing a cash flow at a rate of 0% means that the cash flow will remain constant; that means that we can grow the cash flow at 0% infinitely many times and the cash flow will never change.

The following is an example of a perpetuity:

| Year 1 | Year 2 | Year 3 | Year 4 | Year 5 | Year ∞ |
|---|---|---|---|---|---|
| 100 | 100 | 100 | 100 | 100 | 100 |

If we were to value a perpetuity that has a cash flow equal to CF, we would have to solve the following calculation:

Using the $100 cash flow as an example…

$$\text{Present value} = \frac{100}{(1+\text{Discount rate})^1} + \frac{100}{(1+\text{Discount rate})^2} + \frac{100}{(1+\text{Discount rate})^3} + \frac{100}{(1+\text{Discount rate})^4} + \cdots + \frac{100}{(1+\text{Discount rate})^\infty}$$

But, lucky for us, we can use the Gordon Growth Formula and just put a zero in for the growth rate,

$$\text{Present value of a perpetuity} = \frac{\text{CF}}{\text{Discount rate} - 0}$$

or

$$\text{Present value of a perpetuity} = \frac{\text{CF}}{\text{Discount rate}}$$

So, if the cash flow is a perpetuity, then the only two things that we need to know in order to value it are: (1) the cash flow and (2) the discount rate.

For example, if the discount rate was 10%, and the cash flow was $100 per year, the value of this perpetuity would be as follows:

$$\text{Value of perpetuity} = \frac{\$100}{.1} = \$1,000$$

Again, why must $1,000 be the value of the perpetuity? Because, if we are given $1,000 and can invest this at a 10% rate of return, then we can replicate the $100 cash flow forever, since $1,000 invested at 10% will pay us $100 in interest per year, forever. We take out the $100 and reinvest the $1,000, so every year this investment will pay off $100 with no deterioration of the $1,000 principal.

## Key Takeaways

- Money has a time value. A dollar today is worth more than a dollar tomorrow (assuming interest rates are positive) because of the opportunity cost of capital.
- Taking the Present Value of a future cash flow is called discounting.
- Taking the Future Value of a present cash flow is called compounding.
- This chapter details how we calculate the Present and Future values of individual cash flows, Annuities and Perpetuities, and other cash flows.

# Chapter 7

# Valuation Tools for Financial Decision Making

Valuation is an essential skill for making profitable investment decisions. If we were to make an investment at the current price, would we be financially better or worse off? How do we know if we are overpaying? Is the current asking price reasonable? What "should" be the fair price given the cash flows and the risk? There are two dimensions involved in determining whether an investment is financially viable: (1) profitability and (2) liquidity. We will examine the financial tools that are used to assess these two important dimensions in the current chapter.

## Profitability

### *The net present value*

The first dimension, profitability, has to do with whether or not the investment is fairly priced. That is, whether the present value of the inflows that you receive from making the investment is greater than the present value of the outflows (the price) that you pay in order to make the investment. If the present value of the inflows is greater than the present value of the outflows, then we are better off if we make this investment since it provides more value than it costs. The difference between the present value of the inflows and the present value of the outflows is called the *net present value (NPV)*. The net present value is one of the key valuation tools that we will be using in order to make capital budgeting decisions. Let us look at an example.

Imagine our discount rate is 10% and we are offered the following investment:

| CF0 | Price ($100,000) |
|---|---|
| CF1 | $0 |
| CF2 | $0 |
| CF3 | $0 |
| CF4 | $0 |
| CF5 | $200,000 |

We are asked to invest $100,000 in an asset today, which is referred to on a timeline as CF0 or time zero, but then have to wait 5 years until we see any kind of cash return on that investment. How can we tell if this is a good deal? We can use the Net Present Value to help us decide. We will compare the present value of the inflows (what it is worth) to the present value of the outflows (what it costs). If it is worth more than it costs, then the asset is underpriced, and we should buy it. If it is worth less than it costs, then the asset's price is too high, in which case it is overpriced, and we should avoid it. In the example here, there is only one outflow: the price. $100,000 spent today is worth $100,000 today, so the present value of the outflows is easy to determine. All we need to do now is determine the present value of $200,000 received 5 years from now using a discount rate of 10%, which is, $200,000/(1.1)^5 = $124,186. The fair price of the investment is $124,168.

Luckily, we can make this investment for only $100,000, so it turns out that if the discount rate is 10%, then the above investment in the asset is a very good deal. The net present value of making this investment is $24,168. In other words, the asset is underpriced by $24,168. The fair price is $24,168 higher, so the asset is a bargain, and we should definitely buy it for the offered price.

If the NPV is greater than 0, then the Present Value of the inflows (what it is worth) is greater than the Present Value of the outflows (what it costs); consequently, positive NPV investments are underpriced and represent a good deal. In contrast, negative NPV investments are overpriced and should be avoided. If the NPV = 0, then the asset is fairly priced, since what it is worth is equal to what it costs.

The NPV decision rule is as follows:

NPV > 0, accept, asset is underpriced
NPV < 0, reject, asset is overpriced
NPV = 0, accept, asset is fairly priced

## *Internal rate of return*

Another tool for assessing the profitability of an investment is called the *internal rate of return (IRR)*. Unlike net present value, which will tell us by how many dollars an asset is under or overpriced, the internal rate of return is expressed as a percentage. What is the percentage rate of return that we would earn every year if we were to invest a given amount of money today, and in return receive a stream of cash flows in the future? We compare this percentage return (the IRR) to our discount rate to decide whether the investment is worth pursuing. Many people prefer IRR to NPV because it is sometimes easier to think in relative terms (percentages), rather than absolute terms (dollars). I need to earn 10% on my investment. Does it yield more than 10% or not? The decision is very intuitive and easy to explain to people that are not well trained in valuation.

The IRR decision rule is as follows:

IRR > discount rate, accept, asset is underpriced
IRR < discount rate, reject, asset is overpriced
IRR = discount rate, accept, asset is correctly priced

Although the use of the internal rate of return for decision-making is very easy and intuitive, its calculation is not so easy. We will start by providing some intuition behind how IRR is calculated. If you look at the above decision rule, you will see that when the *IRR = the discount rate*, then the asset is correctly priced. Correctly priced assets have an NPV = 0, so we can think of IRR as the discount rate that sets NPV equal to zero; that is, the discount rate that exactly sets the present value of the inflows associated with an investment equal to the present value of the costs incurred in order to make the investment.

$$\text{PV} = \frac{\text{CF}_1}{(1+\text{IRR})} + \frac{\text{CF}_2}{(1+\text{IRR})^2} + \frac{\text{CF}_3}{(1+\text{IRR})^3} + \cdots + \frac{\text{CF}_N}{(1+\text{IRR})^N}$$

or

$$0 = \text{NPV} = -\text{PV} + \frac{\text{CF}_1}{(1+\text{IRR})} + \frac{\text{CF}_2}{(1+\text{IRR})^2} + \frac{\text{CF}_3}{(1+\text{IRR})^3} + \cdots + \frac{\text{CF}_N}{(1+\text{IRR})^N}$$

The solution to this polynomial is a little complicated, but most financial calculators can easily compute it. The computation is extremely easy using Excel.

The Excel function is called *IRR*, and is used as follows:

$$= \text{IRR}(value0,\ value1,\ value2, \ldots,\ valueN)$$

For example, if our discount rate is 10%, and we are offered the following investment, then according to IRR should we make the investment?

| | |
|---|---|
| **CF0** | Price ($100,000) |
| **CF1** | $0 |
| **CF2** | $0 |
| **CF3** | $0 |
| **CF4** | $0 |
| **CF5** | $200,000 |

= IRR(-100000,0,0,0,0,200000) = 14.87%. Since 14.87% is greater than the required discount rate of 10%, we should definitely make this investment. Recall from the NPV example that the NPV of this investment is $24,168.

$$= -100000 + \text{NPV}(.10,0,0,0,0,200000) = \$24,168$$

But now, watch what happens if, instead of using 10% as our discount rate to determine the NPV of this cash flow stream, we use the IRR (14.87%) as a discount rate instead.

$$= -100000 + \text{NPV}(.1487,0,0,0,0,200000) = 0$$

Not surprisingly, the NPV is equal to zero. Remember that IRR is the discount rate that sets the NPV = 0. It is exactly the annual rate of return that you would earn if you invested the present value amount at time zero and received the future cash flow stream.

There are a few caveats to mention regarding the use of IRR as a decision-making tool. Because IRR is the solution to a polynomial, things can get a bit messy when the polynomial has multiple roots. What that means for us is that the IRR calculation works just fine when there is only one outflow over the life of the investment. For example, we make an investment at time zero (it is an outflow, so would be negative) but then make no further outflows over the life of the asset, and instead receive only positive future cash flows. This type of cash flow stream that doesn't change sign is called a "normal" cash flow. However, some assets require more than one outflow over the course of their life; that is, the cash flows switch signs from negative to positive more than once (an example of this would be the need for a large capital investment or a cost that might be incurred to shut down the project at the end of its life). Note that a firm (e.g., a start-up company) can have negative cash flows for the first several years and then positive cash flows thereafter, in which case there will still be only one solution to the polynomial, and, hence, only one solution for the IRR. Remember, the rule is that the sign of the cash flows can change only once. If they change more than once, then there can be multiple roots, and thus multiple IRRs. Here is such an example:

Suppose an investment will cost $90,000 initially and will generate the following cash flows:

| | |
|---|---|
| **Year 1** | $132,000 |
| **Year 2** | $100,000 |
| **Year 3** | ($150,000) |

If the discount rate is 15%, then should we accept or reject this investment?

So, we are solving the following equation:

$$0 = \text{NPV} = -90,000 + \frac{132,000}{(1+\text{IRR})} + \frac{100,000}{(1+\text{IRR})^2} - \frac{150,000}{(1+\text{IRR})^3}$$

Notice that the cash flows switch from negative to positive more than once. This equation has two roots; that is, there are two IRRs that will yield an NPV equal to zero: 10.11% and 42.65%. Let me show you using Excel.

$$NPV = -90000 + NPV(.1011, 132000, 100000, -150000) = 0$$
$$NPV = -90000 + NPV(.4265, 132000, 100000, -150000) = 0$$

Note the actual NPV of this calculation is slightly different from zero, but that is because we rounded the IRR to two significant digits. If we used Excel's full machine precision, then the NPV would be zero.

So, there are two IRRs? What do we do? If the IRR was 10.11%, then we would definitely reject the investment since that is less than our 15% required discount rate. But if the IRR was 42.65%, then we would accept the investment since that is greater than our discount rate. We are stuck. When the cash flows are non-normal (they switch sign more than once over the life of the asset) then we cannot use IRR as a decision tool; we should use NPV instead. So, if our discount rate is 15%, then is this a good deal or a bad deal? Should we accept or reject the investment? Let's find out using Excel.

$$NPV = -90000 + NPV(.15, 132000, 100000, -150000) = \$1,769.$$

Since the NPV > 0, we should definitely accept this project. This investment is a good deal.

**A rule of thumb: As long as the cash flows are normal (meaning they only switch signs once) NPV and IRR will always yield the same decision when you are analyzing only one investment.**

The reason for this is that since the IRR is the discount rate that sets NPV equal to zero, when IRR is greater than the discount rate, the asset will be underpriced. If the asset is underpriced, then the NPV > 0. In contrast, if the IRR is less than the discount rate, then the asset is overpriced, in which case the NPV < 0. And, if the IRR = the discount rate, then the asset is correctly priced, and the NPV = 0.

## *What if we are deciding among multiple investments?*

Whereas the investment decision is relatively easy when we are deciding to purchase an individual asset, things get a little more complicated when we have to decide among several *mutually exclusive* assets. Mutually exclusive means that if we select investment A, then we necessarily forego making an investment in B or C: there can be only one investment. For example, if we were deciding to either build a bridge, a tunnel, or a ferry terminal to cross a river, we would choose the solution that was the most financially viable. If that ends up being a tunnel, then we will not need a bridge or a ferry.

**When deciding among mutually exclusive projects, you should always use NPV as the decision tool**, because NPV will always tell you — in dollars — by how much you are actually better or worse off if you make the investment. Sometimes the rankings will differ if you use IRR. **When IRR and NPV disagree, always use NPV.**

**Deciding among multiple projects is easy: choose the investment that has the highest NPV.**

For example, imagine that our discount rate is 10%, and we are comparing the following two mutually exclusive investments, A and B, which have these cash flows:

| CF | Investment A | Investment B |
|---|---|---|
| 0 | ($100,000) | ($150,000) |
| 1 | $150,000 | $200,000 |
| 2 | $200,000 | $250,000 |

First, let's calculate the NPV of the two investments:

$$\text{NPV(A)} = -100000 + \text{NPV}(.1, 150000, 200000) = \$201{,}652$$
$$\text{NPV(B)} = -150000 + \text{NPV}(.1, 200000, 250000) = \$238{,}429$$

According to NPV, investment B is more profitable. But, what if we were to rank the investments by their IRRs? What would be our ranking then?

$$\text{IRR(A)} = \text{IRR}(-100000, 150000, 200000) = 135\%$$
$$\text{IRR(B)} = \text{IRR}(-150000, 200000, 250000) = 112\%$$

If we were to use IRR to rank these investments, then we would erroneously choose investment A, since A has a higher IRR than B. Why would the choice of A, rather than B, be a poor choice? The reason why is that investment B has an NPV of \$238,429, while A's NPV is only \$201,652: a difference of \$36,777. That is a lot of money! They are both underpriced and good deals, so we wish that we could invest in both, but we cannot. We can choose only one. Since we are \$36,777 better off if we choose B over A, then B should be our one and only choice. Remember that **NPV dominates IRR for mutually exclusive investments**. Please be warned that IRR by construction assumes that all the cash flows are reinvested at the IRR rate, which in this case would be 135%, which would be highly unlikely. NPV on the other hand assumes the cash flows are reinvested at the firm's cost of capital (WACC), which represents the firm's opportunity costs and is the appropriate hurdle rate for investments.

### *What if the investments are not mutually exclusive?*

Things are much easier if the investments are not mutually exclusive. When deciding among investments that are not mutually exclusive, we can use either NPV or IRR; either is fine, as long as the cash flows are normal. If the cash flows are non-normal, then always use NPV.

The decision rule is very simple: choose all the investments where the NPV > 0 and the IRR > discount rate. This will work perfectly as long as we don't run out of funds, but what happens if we are capital constrained? In other words, what if we just don't have enough funds to invest in all the profitable, positive NPV projects? How do we choose among them?

### *How to choose among good investments when we have limited funds?*

When funds are limited, we should choose the investments that give us the most profitable use of our limited funds. A very useful tool for determining the relative profitability of an investment is the *profitability index*.

$$\text{Profitability index} = \frac{\text{Present value of cash flows}}{\text{Initial investment}}$$

The profitability index scales the benefit received from making the investment by the cost of making the investment. The higher the profitability index, the more value we are getting out of our limited investment dollars.

Here is an example:

Assume that we have a total of $200,000 available to invest, and we have four choices, all of which have different investment requirements. Our discount rate is 10%. Which, if any, of the following investments should we choose?

| CF | Investment A | Investment B | Investment C | Investment D |
|---|---|---|---|---|
| 0 | ($125,000) | ($100,000) | ($74,000) | ($25,000) |
| 1 | $40,000 | $55,000 | $41,000 | $10,000 |
| 2 | $120,000 | $75,000 | $55,000 | $23,000 |

Let's first rank these projects by NPV. Remember, the projects are not mutually exclusive, so we can invest in as many as we can afford to fund.

| | Investment A | Investment B | Investment C | Investment D |
|---|---|---|---|---|
| NPV | $10,537 | $11,983 | $8,727 | $3,099 |

If we were to use NPV to rank the projects, then investment B has the highest NPV, and investment A has the second highest NPV. We would be delighted to buy them both, but unfortunately that choice would cost a total of $225,000, and that would put us over budget. We can't afford both A and B. We definitely want investment B, but we want to invest as much of the money as possible, so how do we decide what is the combination that will create the most value for us? The profitability index is a very useful tool for making this decision. The following are the profitability indexes for each of the investments:

| | Investment A | Investment B | Investment C | Investment D |
|---|---|---|---|---|
| PI | 1.084 | 1.120 | 1.118 | 1.124 |

**The rule for using profitability index is very simple: choose the highest profitability index, then the next highest, and so on until you have invested all of your money.**

According to the profitability index, it is actually investment D that gives us the most value for our investment dollar. Even though D has the smallest NPV, it is actually the one that offers us the most bang for our buck. In contrast, investment A is the loser of the bunch — it generates a lot of NPV, but it uses up a large chunk of our investment amount. Investment A just doesn't give us enough of a return to justify that large of an investment; there are better ways to spend our money.

So, according to the profitability index, we definitely want to invest in D and add that to our portfolio. That gives us $175,000 still left to invest. The investment with the next highest profitability index is B, which will cost us $100,000. So, we buy B and now have $75,000 left over. Investment C has the next highest profitability index, and it costs $74,000. If we buy C, then we have invested all but $1,000 of our budget. We are done: our investments are D, B, and C, for a total of $199,000. Note, there is no other combination of affordable investments that will yield a higher combined NPV for us than D, B, and C, which yields a total of $23,810.

| | |
|---|---|
| **DBC** | $23,810 |
| **AC** | $19,264 |
| **AD** | $13,636 |

For example, if we were to combine A and C, the NPV would be $19,264, and we would also only have $1,000 left over. If we were to combine A and D, then our NPV would be $13,636 and we would have $50,000 left over. The best combination, by far, is D, B, and C.

## Liquidity

Each of the three decision metrics discussed above (NPV, IRR, and PI) examine the first dimension of an investment's desirability: its profitability. The second dimension of an investment's desirability, liquidity, has to do with how long it takes us to recover our initial investment amount. Investments where the initial invested amount is recovered quickly are considered to be *liquid* investments and present less risk to us ceteris paribus than less liquid investments, because we get our money back sooner.

### *Payback period*

Perhaps the most widely used tool for measuring a project's relative liquidity is its *payback period*. The payback period tells us how many years it takes the project before we can recover the amount that we invested. Determining the payback period is a relatively straightforward endeavor. Keep a running total of the difference between the original invested amount and how much of that amount has been recovered every year.

Here is an example that will help to illustrate the concept. The project requires an initial investment of $100. It pays $30 in year 1, $40 in year 2, $50 in year 3, and $40 in year 4. If we require our projects to pay back their initial investment in 3 years or less, should we reject this project?

| Year | Cash Flow | Balance |
|---|---|---|
| 0 | ($100) | ($100) |
| 1 | $30 | ($70) |
| 2 | $40 | ($30) |
| 3 | $50 | $20 |
| 4 | $40 | $60 |

We will keep a running balance of how much of the initial investment has been recovered. The payback period occurs when the balance goes to zero. After the first year, $30 is received. We invested $100, so remaining balance is –$70. The payback period is definitely not less than 1 year. In the second year, we get $40. Our outstanding balance was $70, we've recovered $40, so there's still $30 remaining on our balance. Our payback is not less than 2 years either. Finally, in year 3 we receive $50, which will take us to the point where our balance crosses the zero threshold. Our payback period is somewhere between years 2 and 3.

Exactly when between years 2 and 3 depends on the timing of the cash flows over the course of the year. If the assumption is that the cash flows come in smoothly over the course of the year, then most people use a simple linear extrapolation to estimate the payback period. Using the previous example, we have $30 left in our balance at the end of year 2, and we receive $50 sometime between years 2 and 3. Using linear extrapolation, we can obtain an estimate of the payback period as 2 years plus $30/$50 = 0.6 years or 2.6 years.

Alternatively, if the $50 cash flow was received only at the end of the year, rather than smoothly over the course of the year, then the payback period would be 3 years, since the cash flows would not be received until the end of the year. Either way, since in the above example the required payback period was less than or equal to 3 years, we would not reject this project.

The payback period is popular because it is easy to calculate and even easier to understand. **The decision rule is to reject the project if the payback period is greater than what is acceptable, and do not reject it otherwise.**

There are a couple of problems with the payback period. The first is that it completely ignores the time value of money, which is especially problematical when discount rates are very high, such as in countries with hyperinflation, for example. The second problem is that the payback method completely ignores cash flows that occur after the payback period. For example, imagine that we have a required payback period of 3 years, and we have the chance to invest in the following asset that costs $100. It pays $20 in year 1, $30 in year 2, $40 in year 3, and $1,000,000,000 in year 4.

| Year | Cash Flow | Balance |
|---|---|---|
| 0 | ($100) | ($100) |
| 1 | $20 | ($80) |
| 2 | $30 | ($50) |
| 3 | $40 | ($10) |
| 4 | $1,000,000,000 | $999,999,990 |

The payback is not less than 3 years, so we would reject the investment. But, look at massive cash flow in year 4! How can we ignore it? Some people would think we were crazy to not make this investment: the asset is a massive bargain. Well, if all we use is the payback method, we would pass on it — which is exactly the weakness that we are talking about. Which leads us to the next important point...

**We should consider both an investment's profitability and its liquidity when making an investment decision.** The investment has to make sense in both dimensions.

### *Sunk costs*

Another factor worth mentioning in capital budgeting is the presence of *sunk costs*. A sunk cost is defined as any money that has been spent prior to the present that cannot be recovered. The financial rule for dealing with sunk costs is to ignore them. The reason is simple; the money has already been spent and cannot be recovered. Thus, from a financial perspective, the presence of sunk costs should in no way be used to determine the optimal financial decisions going forward.

As an example, the fact that the company has already invested a large sum of money into a given investment should have no effect on the current value of the investment. Stated another way, it is only the cash flows from time zero and forward that matter. The rest is history.

Of course, ignoring sunk costs in practice is easier said than done. The human psyche tends to cling to sunk costs, making them difficult to ignore, especially when great sums of time and money have already been invested. Remain disciplined; the presence of sunk costs should in no way affect your financial decisions going forward.

## Key Takeaways

- Net Present Value (NPV) is the difference between the present value of the firm's cash inflows and the present value of its cash outflows.
  The NPV decision rule is as follows:
  NPV > 0, accept, asset is underpriced
  NPV < 0, reject, asset is overpriced
  NPV = 0, accept, asset is fairly priced
- The Internal Rate of Return (IRR) is the percentage rate of return that we would earn every year if we were to invest a given amount of money today, and in return receive a given stream of cash flows in the future.
  The IRR decision rule is as follows:
  IRR > discount rate, accept, asset is underpriced
  IRR < discount rate, reject, asset is overpriced
  IRR = discount rate, accept, asset is correctly priced
  *Note*: the IRR is only valid with (normal) cash flows (maximum of one sign change).
- When choosing between Mutually Exclusive investments, use NPV, not IRR.
- The Profitability Index measures the investments' "bang for the buck"; specifically, how much NPV the investment generates per dollar invested.
- Payback Period is a straightforward measure of how long it takes us to recover our initial investment (ignoring the time value of money) and as such provides us with a measure of the investment's liquidity.

# Chapter 8

# Risk and Return

In the previous chapters, we discussed the concept of a discount rate for use in time value of money calculations. In this chapter, we will explore exactly how that discount rate is determined. An important rule to bear in mind is that the discount rate has to match (i.e., be consistent) with the nature of the cash flows that are being discounted. If dividends are being discounted, for example, then the cost of equity capital should be used, since dividends are cash flows that are received directly and only by shareholders. But, if we are trying to value the entire firm (and not just the equity) or if we want to value a project that is financed with a combination of debt and equity capital, then all of the capital providers (debt and equity holders) need to be compensated. In this case, we need a different risk measure; this measure is called the Weighted Average Cost of Capital (WACC). The WACC is the discount rate that we use to take the time value of money of cash flows that are available to all investors. We discuss in Chapter 9 how we use the cost of equity and the WACC to determine the fair price of the equity and firm's assets, respectively.

## Weighted Average Cost of Capital

Here is an example that will give you a glimpse of the essence of what the WACC is trying to capture. This example *assumes no taxes*, so it isn't the most realistic, but keeping things simple (for now) helps to get the idea across better. Imagine if we had to raise two dollars in order to fund our business. The first dollar we would obtain from a bank. The bank would charge a 10% interest rate in order to loan to us, based upon the risk that it perceives us to have. The second dollar would come from selling equity in the company.

Debt has a senior claim to equity; that means that in the event of financial distress the debtholders will get paid first before the equity holders see a dime of their investment. Also, the firm has to make mandatory interest payments before it can arrive at net income. So, either way the debt holders get paid first. This means that equity is riskier than debt. Since equity is riskier than debt, the equity holders will require a higher rate of return; in this case, it is 20% per year.

So, at the end of the year, we'd have to earn 10% on the first dollar that we raised from the bank and 20% on the dollar that we raised from equity. That means we have to earn 10 cents to satisfy the debtholder plus 20 cents to satisfy the equity holder, or a total of 30 cents, in order to make everyone happy. Well, if we take the 30 cents that we earned and divide it by the two dollars that we invested, \$0.30/\$2.00 = 15%, we find that we need to earn an average return of 15% on our invested capital in order to satisfy all of our investors. That 15% is our WACC.

What if we earn less than 15%? For example, what if we earn only 10%? Ten percent of \$2 is 20 cents. The bank gets paid first. We promised the bank 10 cents, and we pay them their 10 cents, so the bank is happy. But now there is only 10 cents left over for the equity holders. We promised them 20 cents, but can deliver only 10 cents. They are going to be very disappointed in us and will give us a very hard time. We might even get fired.

The opposite happens if we earn more than 15%; for example, what if we earn 20%? Twenty percent of \$2 is 40 cents. We pay the bank its 10 cents first, leaving us with 30 cents for our shareholders. We promised the shareholders 20 cents in return for their \$1 investment, but we have delivered 30 cents. We gave them more than what we promised, and they are delighted with us. They might even pay us a bonus for all our hard work.

Thus, the WACC is the discount rate of return that we need to earn in order to satisfy all of our investors. Recall that we accept projects if the IRR is greater than the discount rate. Well, the discount rate for corporations is the WACC. It should make a lot of sense now as to why when the IRR > WACC, we accept projects: all of your investors will be happy.

## *Formula for WACC*

Now that we understand the concept of the WACC, let's go into more detail on exactly how it is calculated. It is called a WACC because it is calculated by taking a weighted average of all the costs associated with the different kinds of capital that are used by the firm.

$$\text{WACC} = w_d K_d (1 - t) + w_p K_p + w_e K_e$$

In the above equation, $w_d$, $w_p$, and $w_e$ are the percentages of financing that comes from debt, preferred stock, and equity, respectively. Also, $K_d$, $K_p$, and $K_e$ are the costs of debt, preferred stock, and equity, and $t$ is the marginal tax rate. We will explore how to determine each of these components in this section.

The weights are very easy to calculate:

$$w_d = \frac{\text{Total debt}}{\text{Total capital}}$$

$$w_p = \frac{\text{Total preferred stock}}{\text{Total capital}}$$

$$w_e = \frac{\text{Total equity}}{\text{Total capital}}$$

where total capital equals total debt plus total preferred stock plus total equity. An interesting question arises as to what exactly should we use for these numbers. Should we use the current book values that are reported on the balance sheet? Should we use current market values using the prices at which the securities trade in the market? The right answer is neither.

Since the WACC will be used for valuation purposes to discount future cash flows, it should represent the rate of return that is required over the life of the investment; that is, the rate of return that will compensate investors for bearing risk over the life of the investment. So, *what matters is not the current weights of debt, preferred stock, and equity, but their expected future weights*. Will the firm's target capital structure (mix of debt, preferred stock, and equity) change significantly in the future? If so, then we need to capture that in our discount rate measure. Often times, the firm's capital structure remains constant over the life of an investment; in which case, it is perfectly acceptable to use the current relative weights of equity, preferred stock, and debt. But when we believe that the weights will change substantially, and in a permanent way, over the life of the investment, then using current weights is inappropriate.

For the purposes of the rest of this chapter, we will assume that the firm's target capital structure will not change substantially over the life of the investment — which is likely the assumption that you will encounter — in which case, using the firm's current capital structure to determine the weights is appropriate.[1]

## The Components of WACC

It would be great if we could obtain the actual market values of debt, preferred stock, and equity and use these values in our calculations. However, this is not usually feasible. Not all firms have equity that is publicly traded, and even though some firms have debt that is publicly traded, the debt usually isn't all that liquid (i.e., it doesn't trade all that often, so the prices really aren't as informative as they should be). Even worse, preferred stock is usually not publicly traded at all. So, what do we do? The following discussion on the components of WACC will answer this question.

### *The weight of debt — $W_d$*

Since debt isn't usually publicly traded, or when it is traded it is thinly traded, it is commonplace to use the book value of debt as a proxy for the market value. This proxy choice is a reasonable one for firms that are in good financial condition, since for those firms there is little concern that the firm will default on its debt, and the debtholders are likely to get not only all of their interest payments, but also all of their principal back.

When firms are in good financial condition, the book value (which should be equal to the present value of the future interest and principal payments when the debt was *issued*) and market value of debt (which reflects the present value of the future interest and principal payments as of today) should be relatively close to one another. Note, if the firm is in financial distress, then the standard discounted cash flow approach may not be appropriate — more on this later in the book — since the book value and market value of the debt can diverge substantially.

Ok, so for a financially solid firm we can use the book value of debt as a proxy for the market value. Now, what should be included as debt?

---

[1] Ivan E. Brick and Daniel G. Weaver. "A Comparison of Capital Budgeting Techniques in Identifying Profitable Investments," *Financial Management* 13, no. 3 (1984): 29–39.

Should we include short-term debt? What about things like financial and operating leases, which are very similar to debt in that they involve long-run payments with interest associated with them?

Let's begin with a discussion of long-term debt. Pretty much, if there is a liability that has an associated interest payment and has maturity of greater than a year (this includes things like term loans, mortgages, bonds, debentures, subordinated debt, and other forms of long-term debt), then we should probably include such a liability as debt for the purposes of the calculation of $w_d$.

Regarding the inclusion of short-term debt, it should only be included in $w_d$ if it is a permanent, long-run part of the firm's capital structure. For example, seasonal lines of credit are usually not included because they are temporary in nature; one might borrow heavily on the line of credit at the beginning of the selling season to buy inventory, and then pay off the line of credit as the inventory purchased with the funds obtained from the line of credit that gets sold. In this case, one would not expect the seasonal line of credit to be permanently on the books, hence it would be excluded from the calculation of $w_d$.

An easy way to check whether short-term debt is a permanent component of the capital structure is to look at the quarterly financial statements. Is the short-term debt balance relatively stable from quarter to quarter? If it is, then we would expect that the short-term debt is indeed a permanent component of the capital structure, and we would include it in the determination of $w_d$. Oftentimes, we have to look at the firm's 10Q statements to understand what exactly is included in short-term debt. Once we learn what is included in short-term debt, then we can make an informed decision as to whether or not it is a permanent component of the capital structure and thus should be included in the $w_d$ calculation.

| | Q1 | Q2 | Q3 | Q4 | Q5 | Q6 | Q7 | Q8 |
|---|---|---|---|---|---|---|---|---|
| **Firm A** | | | | | | | | |
| Notes payable | 200 | 198 | 201 | 203 | 200 | 200 | 200 | 202 |
| Accrued liabilities | 142 | 142 | 145 | 138 | 139 | 141 | 140 | 140 |
| **Firm B** | | | | | | | | |
| Notes payable | 200 | 400 | 523 | 0 | 0 | 0 | 180 | 172 |
| Accrued liabilities | 142 | 201 | 189 | 0 | 0 | 0 | 140 | 140 |

The above panel presents 2 years' worth of quarterly balance sheet information for Firm A and Firm B. we focus on notes payable and include accrued liabilities so that the reader knows where this would appear on the balance sheet. Notice that Firm A notes payable hovered steadily around 200, while Firm B notes payable are volatile. In this case, when calculating the total debt for Firm A, we would include the average of 200 for the contribution of short-term debt. Firm B is different. Since there is no permanency in the notes payable, their contribution to total debt is zero for the purpose of determining $w_d$.

Financial and operating leases are nowadays treated as long-term debt for the purposes of determining the WACC, since they involve a lease payment that comprises depreciation and interest.[2] Since leases share many of the features of long-term debt, it is common to include them in the calculation of $w_d$.

Once we have identified all of the sources of debt, then we add them up to obtain total debt. It is total debt that will be the numerator in the calculation of $w_d$.

## *The weight of preferred stock — $W_p$*

Preferred stock does not usually trade in the open market; thus, it is not often possible to obtain its market value. Consequently, the weight of preferred stock is most often calculated by using its book value as a percentage of total capital. This assumption of using book value as a proxy for market value makes sense for financially viable firms, since the market value of preferred stock and the book value of preferred stock are usually reasonably close to one another for financially secure firms. The same caveat applies here as with debt: if the firm is in financial distress, then the book value and market value of the preferred stock can diverge substantially and thus the book value would no longer be a good proxy.

## *The weight of equity — $W_e$*

If the firm is publicly traded, then obtaining the weight of equity is relatively easy. All we have to do is take the number of shares outstanding (that means trading in the market, also called *open interest*) and multiply

[2] See Chapter 2 for an in-depth discussion of leases.

them by the current price per share. For example, if there were 100,000,000 shares outstanding at a price of $5 a share, then the market value of equity would be $500,000,000. If there are both A shares and B shares, or any other category of shares (C, D, etc.), then we would get the market values of each of these individually and then add them up to obtain the total market value of equity.

### *What do we do if the firm is not publicly traded?*

If the firm is not publicly traded, then things become a little more complicated. What is often done is to assume that the firm will have a capital structure that is similar to comparable publicly traded firms in its industry. That is, we could use the weights $w_d$, $w_p$, and $w_e$ of comparable firms as estimates for what will likely be the future mix of debt, preferred stock, and equity for the firm we are trying to value. Another approach is to use trading comparables, such as the P/E multiple (or Price/Sales or EV/EBITDA — see Chapter 5) to back out an estimate of what the market value of equity might be if the firm were publicly traded — note this approach probably overstates the value of the equity because it ignores the fact that the private firm is illiquid, and thus would require an illiquidity reduction in multiple.

### *How to estimate $K_d(1-t)$, the after-tax cost of debt?*

Interest payments are tax deductible, which means that our effective cost of borrowing money is reduced. We get a tax break from paying interest. So, if the tax rate is 40% and the interest rate is 10%, then the after-tax cost of debt is 10% * (1 – .4) = 6%. Another way of thinking about that is if we have $100,000 in debt that carries a 10% interest rate, then we would expect to spend $10,000 a year in interest. That $10,000 in interest would reduce our taxable income by $10,000, and if the tax rate was 40%, we would end up saving $4,000 in tax. Consequently, the after-tax impact of interest expense on our profit is only $6,000. It is for this reason that we need to take the tax deductibility of interest into consideration when we calculate the cost of debt for the purposes of obtaining the WACC.

Getting the after-tax cost of debt requires us to estimate two things: $k_d$ (the cost of debt) and the tax rate. We will begin with a discussion of how to estimate the cost of debt, $k_d$.

## *Estimating $K_d$, the cost of debt*

Very rarely do we get lucky and find a firm that has only one source of debt financing. It is not unusual for larger firms to have dozens of loans and bond offerings, plus they usually have a revolving line of credit (or several lines of credit) as well. This makes for a bit of a challenge when we are trying to estimate an expected cost of debt. In theory, what we are trying to measure is on average overall what is the interest rate that the firm would expect to pay on borrowed funds over the life of the assets that we are trying to value.

One way to estimate this expected future interest rate is to use the average of the interest rates that the firm is currently paying. An easy way to calculate this is to sum up all of the interest payments that the firm made in the last year (note that this will appear on the income statement as interest expense) and divide that by total debt, which appears on the balance sheet. This ratio of interest paid divided by total debt gives a reasonable proxy for the average interest rate that the firm paid over the past year. The big assumption that is made when using this proxy is that this average interest rate will remain fairly stable over the life of the asset being valued. If you have reason to believe that this assumption is valid (and it very often is valid), then great. But if not, then this method of estimation should probably be avoided.

There are other methods commonly encountered for determining the cost of debt. One such method, if the firm has publicly traded debt, is to calculate the yield to maturity of a recent bond issue. We will not go into this calculation in deep detail here, but the yield to maturity of a bond is simply its internal rate of return (see IRR) and it can easily be found on Bloomberg. The price of the bond will move up as interest rates go down and vice versa. So, if we know the bond's price and we know its coupon (interest) payments, then we can solve for the internal rate of return (i.e., its yield to maturity) and then use this as our measure of $k_d$.

If the firm doesn't have any publicly traded debt but has been rated by say Moody's or Standard and Poor's, then another approach is to use the default risk spread published by these companies that is appropriate for the firm's debt rating, and then add this spread to the risk-free rate of return. If the firm's debt hasn't been rated, then it might be possible to compute an approximate bond rating for the firm using credit statistics — this method is beyond the scope of this handbook.

## *Estimating the tax rate*

We often get questions about whether one should use the firm's marginal tax rate or its effective tax rate (both to be defined in what follows) when calculating the WACC. The answer is: it depends.

The WACC is the discount rate that is employed when discounting *future* cash flows, which means that the tax rate that we should use is the one that we expect would most likely apply when we calculate those future cash flows. On the one hand, it is possible that the future effective tax rate might be similar to the current effective tax rate. But on the other hand, it is possible that the future effective tax rate can vary substantially from its current value.

Let's start by defining the two different tax rates:

$$\text{Tax}_{\text{eff}} = \frac{\text{Tax}}{\text{Earnings before taxes}}$$

where both taxes paid and earnings before tax (EBT) can be found on the most recent income statement. The other tax rate is known as the marginal tax rate given as follows:

$$\text{Tax}_{\text{marginal}} = 21\% + \text{State and local taxes}$$

The marginal tax rate is often called the *statutory* tax rate and represents the tax that would be paid on the next dollar of pretax income. Note, 21% is currently the US government-imposed tax rate on corporations.

So how do we decide between the two? Well, it all depends on what you think is going to happen in the future. The firm's effective tax rate and marginal tax rate will normally differ from one another because of various tax breaks that might be available to the firm. The effective tax rate is normally lower, and sometimes much lower, than the marginal tax rate. Also, if the firm operates internationally, it might be able to take advantage of additional tax savings opportunities that will further exacerbate the difference.

If you believe that the current effective tax rate is fairly representative of what the firm will pay in the future, then using it as an estimate of what the tax rate will be in the future is reasonable. But, if you believe that the effective tax rate is much lower now than what it will be in the future, because the tax breaks that it is currently enjoying will evaporate in the future, then you might consider slowly increasing the tax rate until it reaches the marginal tax rate — note that in this case, the tax rate will usually be increased to the marginal tax rate by the year in which we estimate the terminal cash flow (see DCF valuation as explained in Chapter 9).

### *Estimating $K_p$, the cost of preferred stock*

The next component of the WACC is the cost of preferred stock, $k_p$. It is calculated by dividing the annual dividend that is paid by the preferred stock by the preferred stock's price. If the preferred stock is publicly traded, then getting an estimate of $k_p$ is easy.

$$k_p = \frac{\text{Annual preferred dividend}}{\text{Market price}}$$

Since preferred stock is not usually publicly traded, the market price is not often available. So, instead of using the current market price, people typically assume that the price of preferred stock will remain stable over time. This assumption allows them to use the historical issuance cost of preferred stock as a proxy for the market price.

$$k_p = \frac{\text{Annual preferred dividend}}{\text{Issuance price}}$$

Note that preferred stock often pays a quarterly dividend, so be sure to add up all the dividends and use a full year's worth, rather than using a quarterly figure.

## The Cost of Equity Capital — $K_e$

Cost of equity, $k_e$, is more difficult to estimate than either $k_d$ or $k_p$. There are several approaches and there is substantial debate in the field about which approach available is the most appropriate. In addition, there is a big difference in the way this cost is calculated for a buyer that holds a well-diversified portfolio, where much of the idiosyncratic risk of any individual investment is diversified away and thus the risk can be ignored, or that holds the investment as a standalone, where the investor will bear the full brunt of the asset's individual idiosyncratic risk. We will begin with a discussion of how the cost of equity capital is calculated for the valuation of a firm that is publicly traded, and thus purchased by investors that most likely hold well-diversified portfolios.

## *The cost of equity for a public company or for an initial public offering*

There are several competing models for the estimation of the cost of equity, $k_e$. These include the Dividend Growth model, Capital Asset Pricing Model (CAPM), the Fama–French multifactor model, and the Arbitrary Pricing Theory (APT). Of these, the CAPM, with all of the criticisms leveled against it, is still used most often, so it will be the focus of this next section.

### *The dividend growth model*

The Dividend Growth model was initially developed by Myron Gordon and Eli Shapiro in 1956.[3] It explicitly values a firm's equity as the present value of the firm's dividends discounted back using the cost of equity capital. The next chapter will do a deep dive into the use of the model and its limitations (which are numerous). For our purposes here, it should be enough to be familiar with the model's components and how it is used. One critical (and limiting) assumption of the model is that the firm's dividends must grow at a constant rate. Yes, everyone knows that this assumption isn't reasonable for many (perhaps even most) firms, but the model does give us a nice starting point.

$$\text{Price} = \frac{(\text{Dividend})(1+g)}{K_e - g}$$

*Dividend* is the most recently paid dividend, $g$ is the expected constant growth rate, and $K_e$ is the firm's cost of equity capital. Some simple algebra allows for the following transformation of the Dividend Growth model to yield a formula for the cost of equity.

---

[3]M. J. Gordon and Eli Shapiro, "Capital Equipment Analysis: The Required Rate of Profit," *Management Science* 3, no. 1 (October 1956): 102–10. Reprinted in *Management of Corporate Capital* (Glencoe, Ill.: Free Press, 1959).

$$K_e = \frac{(\text{Dividend})(1+g)}{\text{Price}} + g$$

where the first part is the firm's expected dividend yield, and the $g$ represents the future capital gains yield. Notice that both the first and second term depend critically on the *expected* growth rate, $g$; thus, this is a formula that actually calculates the "expected" ROE. In order for this formula to yield an estimate of the required ROE, the formula requires the firm's stock price to be in equilibrium. The equilibrium price is the price at which the firm's expected and required returns are equal (i.e., all the information in the market has been fully incorporated into the current price), thus we can use the dividend growth formula to infer the required return.

Although this model is popular in introductory finance textbooks, it really doesn't get all that much use in practice. You will learn all the reasons why in the next chapter. The bottom line is that there are just too many assumptions that aren't realistic for most firms. That being said, the Dividend Growth model is taught in every introductory finance course, and you should be familiar with it. A more widely used approach is based on the CAPM.

## *The capital asset pricing model*

The CAPM was developed independently by Jack Treynor, William Sharpe, John Lintner, and Jan Mossin in the mid-1960s.[4] It provides a very intuitive way of representing the relationship between risk and return. We won't go into the details as to how the model is theoretically derived, but instead will share some intuition about it.

---

[4]Jack L. Treynor, "Market Value, Time, and Risk," 8 August 1961, Vol. no. 95–209; William F. Sharpe, "Capital Asset Prices: A Theory of Market Equilibrium under Conditions of Risk," *Journal of Finance* 19, no. 3 (1964): 425–42; John Lintner, "The Valuation of Risk Assets and the Selection of Risky Investments in Stock Portfolios and Capital Budgets," *Review of Economics and Statistics* 47, no. 1 (1965): 13–37; Jan Mossin, "Equilibrium in a Capital Asset Market," *Econometrica* 34, no. 4 (1966): 768–83.

The CAPM determines the required return to equity as a combination of the risk-free rate of return plus a premium for bearing risk.

$$k_e = k_{rf} + \text{Premium for bearing risk}$$

Any investment has to pay at least the risk-free rate of return; otherwise, we would prefer to just put our money into the risk-free asset. The risk-free rate of return, $k_{rf}$, is what we demand in order to invest in something that has zero risk of default and that is highly liquid, such as a US government treasury bond (T-bonds). As long as the market believes that the US government will not default on its financial obligations and that treasury bonds can easily be bought and sold in the market, then US T-bonds are a very good choice for a risk-free rate of return for US-based investments.

T-bonds come with many different maturities, so which is the most appropriate for use in the calculation of $K_e$? The answer depends on what exactly is the asset that we are trying to value. Recall that we are trying to get a good estimate of the required rate of return that will be used to discount a future stream of cash flows. If the cash flows are from a project that has a 10-year maturity, then we would like a discount rate that represents the required return over that 10-year period.

It is desirable to match the maturity of the project to the maturity of the T-bond that will be used in the calculation of the cost of equity; so, if you are valuing an 8-year project, use the rate on a T-bond that has 8 years left to maturity. But what do we do if we are trying to price a stock? Firms theoretically have potentially infinitely long lives, and there is no infinite maturity T-bond. In this case, valuation professionals usually use the 30-year T-bond as a measure of $k_{rf}$.

Now that we have our measure of the risk-free rate, we need an estimate of the premium for bearing risk that we will add to the risk-free rate in order to get the cost of equity capital. The higher the risk, the greater will be the return that we require for bearing that risk. The beauty of the CAPM lies in its simplicity of its risk measure: if investors hold a diversified portfolio of every asset in the universe, then the only risk that matters is the risk that cannot be diversified away; this risk is called *systematic risk*. The intuition is that if a portfolio is diversified, then all of the idiosyncratic, firm-specific risk associated with the individual stocks in the portfolio will be diversified away (some stocks will do extremely well, while others might do extremely badly) and the only thing that will remain is the systematic risk of the entire market portfolio that cannot be diversified away.

**Portfolio Diversification Ex.**

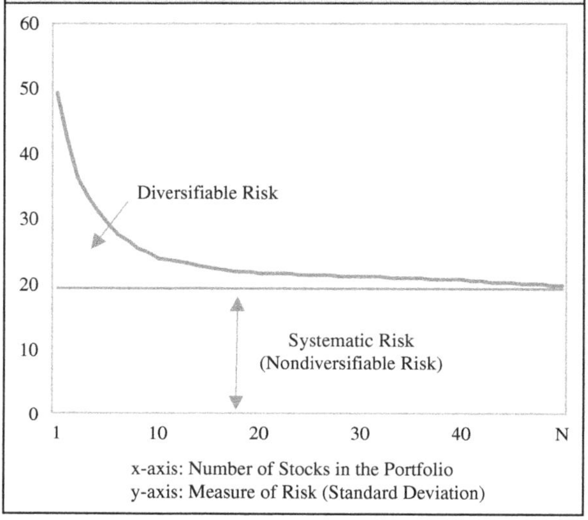


The measure of systematic risk is called beta, $\beta$. Beta measures the sensitivity of an asset's rate of return to changes in the market's rate of return.[5] If $\beta = 1$, then the firm has the same level of systematic risk as the overall market portfolio, so we would expect its stock to have a similar rate of return as the market.

If that is the case, then if the market goes up by 1% in any given year, then the firm's return would also be expected to go up by 1%. If $\beta = 0.5$, then if the market goes up by 1%, the firm's return is expected to go up by half as much as the market, or 0.5%. The beta of the risk-free asset is zero, which means that its future rate of return should be entirely independent from what happens in the market. Please note that the betas that are available are "historical" betas, that is, they reflect the historical sensitivity of the firm to systematic risk.

What we really would like for valuation purposes is the forward beta, which represents what we think will be the sensitivity to systematic risk over the life of the investment. The historical beta is a good estimate of

[5]Beta estimates for public companies can be obtained on Bloomberg, Barra, and S&P (for a fee), or at Yahoo! Finance (for free).

the forward beta if we believe that the sensitivity to systematic risk will not change in the future. If we do believe that it will change, then we have to make whatever adjustments we deem to be appropriate.

So, if beta is the measure of systematic risk, then what is the premium that we would require for bearing one unit of beta? That premium is called the "market risk premium," which is the difference between what investors believe will be the expected return on the market portfolio and the expected return on the appropriate maturity T-bond over the life of the investment. The market risk premium (usually people will use the equity risk premium because it is easier to calculate[6]) represents the extra return, above that of the risk-free rate, that investors demand in order to invest in the market portfolio instead of the risk-free asset.

$$\text{Market risk premium} = E[k_m - k_{rf}]$$

The market risk premium is not constant over time. As of the time of writing this book, the market risk premium is 5.5%. However, it was 5.3%, 5.7%, 5.4%, 5.6%, 5.6, and 5.5% for 2016, 2017, 2018, 2019, 2020, and 2021, respectively.[7]

We can also estimate the risk premium by subtracting the risk-free rate from the expected equity market return.

$$\text{Market risk premium} = \text{Expected rate of return} - \text{Risk free rate of return}$$

So, if the expected return on the market over the next 10 years is 8.0% and the rate of return on a 10-year T-bond is 3.0%, then we would expect the equity risk premium to be 5.0% over the life of our 10-year asset.

Putting all these pieces together, the CAPM says that:

$$k_e = k_{rf} + \beta * E[k_m - k_{rf}]$$

That is, the required ROE, $k_e$, equals the risk-free rate of interest, $k_{rf}$, plus the premium for bearing systematic risk, $E[k_m - k_{rf}]$, times the amount of systematic risk, $\beta$.

---

[6]The difference between the market risk premium and the equity risk premium is that the market risk premium should include every single possible asset in the investment universe, while the equity risk premium includes just stocks.

[7]https://www.statista.com/statistics/664840/average-market-risk-premium-usa/. Aswath Damodaran provides ERPs for free on his website: http://pages.stern.nyu.edu/~adamodar/. Both Morningstar/Ibbotson and Duff & Phelps provide ERPs for a fee.

For example, assume we want to solve for the cost of equity that will be used for a public stock valuation. The 30-year T-bond rate is 2.2%, beta is 1.2, and the market risk premium is 5.6%. Then the cost of equity capital would be: $k_e = 2.2\% + 1.2(5.6\%) = 8.92\%$.

## Innovations to CAPM — Fama–French 3-Factor CAPM

Fama–French (1992) innovated upon the original CAPM to add factors for size risk and value risk.[8] We won't go into very much detail here about the three-factor CAPM in this handbook, but so that the reader is at least familiar with it, the Fama–French, three-factor CAPM is represented as follows:

$$k_e = k_{rf} + \beta_1[k_m - k_{rf}] + \beta_2[\text{SMB}] + \beta_3[\text{HML}]$$

where:

- $[k_m - k_{rf}]$ is the market risk premium
- SMB is a premium for size. Fama–French show that, holding beta constant, small stocks tend to, on average, perform better than large stocks, thus, they include a premium for small minus big stocks in their cost of equity equation. The factor is calculated as the historical difference in excess returns of small-cap firms relative to large-cap firms.
- HML (high minus low) is a premium for value stocks. Fama–French find that, again holding beta constant, relatively inexpensive value stocks (those with a high B/M ratio) tend to on average outperform relatively expensive glamour stocks (those with a low book-to-market ratio), thus, they include a premium for high minus low book-to-market ratio stocks. The HML factor is calculated as the historical difference in returns of value stocks relative to growth stocks.

$\beta_1$, $\beta_2$, and $\beta_3$ are the coefficients on each of the three Fama–French factors. The following are some historical values for the three factors:

---

[8] E. F. Fama and K. R. French, "The Cross-Section of Expected Stock Returns," *The Journal of Finance* 47, no. 2 (1992): 427–465. Also see E. F. Fama and K. R. French, "Common Risk Factors in the Returns on Stocks and Bonds," *Journal of Financial Economics* 33 (1993): 3–56.

| | Dec 2021 | Dec 2020 | Dec 2019 |
|---|---|---|---|
| $K_m - K_{rf}$ | 3.10 | 8.26 | 23.57 |
| SMB | –1.58 | –5.26 | –3.81 |
| HML | 3.22 | 2.08 | 25.3 |

Professor French keeps an updated list of these factors on his publicly available website.[9]

## Innovations to CAPM — size and country risk

Another innovation of CAPM that is popular is to include premia for both size and country risk.

$$k_e = k_{rf} + b_1\ [k_m - k_{rf}] + \text{Size premium} + \text{Country premium}$$

Typical size and country risk premia are as follows:

| Country Risk Premia | |
|---|---|
| United States | 0.0% |
| United Kingdom | 0.5% |
| Germany | 0.0% |
| Australia | 0.0% |
| France | 0.5% |
| China | 1.1% |
| India | 3.4% |
| Middle East | 1.4% |
| Eastern Europe | 3.1% |
| Brazil | 3.0% |
| Africa | 5.9% |

*Source*: Damodaran

[9]https://mba.tuck.dartmouth.edu/pages/faculty/ken.french/data_library.html.

## *The cost of equity for a private company*

If the company is private (i.e., its stock is not publicly traded), then its stock is illiquid, in which case anyone purchasing that stock would want to be compensated for illiquidity risk. Illiquidity risk is the risk that they won't be able to sell their stock at a fair price when they want to sell it. Not only that, but it is likely that the stock would not be part of a fully diversified portfolio, so firm-specific risk would be important to the buyer as well. Remember that the CAPM was originally created to determine the cost of equity of a well-diversified portfolio of perfectly liquid investments. So, when we solve for the cost of equity for these firms, investors will demand a higher rate of return than that which would be predicted by the CAPM.

Specifically:

$$k_e = k_{rf} + \beta * E[k_m - k_{rf}] + \text{Illiquidity risk premium} \\ + \text{Idiosyncratic risk premium}$$

Ibbotson Associates[10] recommends that, for illiquid stocks, an *illiquidity* premium of 3–4% be added to the cost of equity capital, but one must be careful using this range because even the tiniest stocks that are listed in their publication are much larger and more liquid than that of the typical privately held firm.

Another approach for estimating the illiquidity risk premium comes from Venture Economics, which documents that the rate of return earned on stock investments made by venture capital investors is on average 4% higher than those earned on similar stocks that are traded in the market.

Lastly, another approach for valuing private companies is to apply an illiquidity discount of between 20 and 30% of the value of a publicly traded company in order to obtain an estimate of the value of a similar private company. This is often much easier than trying to incorporate an illiquidity premium into the cost of capital.

The *idiosyncratic risk premium* (also known as the company-specific risk premium) is far more difficult to nail down since each firm is different and thus has its own firm-specific risks. What the idiosyncratic risk premium is trying to capture is the additional risk, beyond market systematic risk and illiquidity risk, that the investor will bear if they

---

[10] R. G. Ibbotson *et al.*, "Liquidity as an Investment Style," *Financial Analysts Journal* 69, no. 3 (2013): 30–44.

purchase the stock. The greater this company-specific risk, the higher will be the idiosyncratic risk premium.

Since the idiosyncratic risk premium is based on firm-specific risk, which will vary from company to company, there isn't really an established model or formula or even data set that we can rely on to reliably obtain this premium. The bottom line is that we will have to rely upon our own experience and judgment to attain a defensible estimate. Note that if you are doing forensic valuation (in support of litigation), the use of company-specific risk premium is not universally accepted by judges. It can vary substantially by jurisdiction, so be mindful.

Here are some of the factors that we consider in determining an appropriate idiosyncratic risk premium.

- Is the firm at risk due to regulatory changes that could hurt its cash flow?
- Does most of the company's revenue come from one primary customer?
- Does the firm have patents, copyrights, or trademarks that are expiring soon?
- Is the firm currently involved in litigation?
- Is there "key person" risk? That is, is there an individual (a salesperson or artisan, for example) upon which the firm's revenues are critically reliant?
- Is the firm dependent on a specific supplier?

One purchasable source of information on company-specific risk is the *Risk Premium Report* that is published annually by Duff & Phelps.[11] The report uses information found in historical financial statements to show the correlation between stock returns and firm-specific risk. Again, please note that if you are doing a valuation in support of litigation, courts are often skeptical about the use of discount rates that are subjective. They like to see substantial quantitative evidence that the firm is sufficiently "different" to merit an explicit premium for its differentness.

## *Calculating Alpha Brewing Co.'s WACC*

Next, we would like to calculate the WACC for Alpha Brewing. Recall that the formula for the WACC is

$$\text{WACC} = w_d K_d(1 - t) + w_p K_p + w_e K_e$$

[11] Please note that "Duff & Phelps" changed their name to "Kroll" in 2021.

We will begin with a discussion on how to obtain the weights on equity and debt. The firm has no preferred stock so the weight on preferred stock will be zero. According to Alpha Brewing's balance sheet, in 2020 (the time of the valuation) the firm has $426,995 of debt on its books and $991,711 in assets. In order to get the weights of debt and equity, if the firm were publicly traded, we would normally calculate the market capitalization (market value of equity) and add that to the book value of debt to get the total value of the firm's capital. Once we had that, then we would take the ratios of debt to total capital and equity to total capital. Voila, we have our weights.

Unfortunately, since Alpha Brewing is not publicly traded, we don't have access to its market stock price so we cannot easily get the market value of its equity. Instead, we will attempt to estimate it by using a comparable market-to-book ratio. We do this by locating a comparable small publicly traded craft brewery and use its Market/Book ratio to get an estimate for AB's market value of equity: take the comparable M/B ratio and multiply it by Alpha's book value of equity. Note, we could also do this by using comparable P/E multiples; the same caveat that we discuss next applies. The challenge here is that Alpha Brewing is not publicly traded, so it would have a lower M/B ratio (and potentially MUCH lower M/B ratio) than a publicly traded firm due to illiquidity.

After looking at public craft breweries, we believe that a reasonable market/book ratio for Alpha Brewing, at this early stage in the firm's life cycle, should be very close to one. Remember, Alpha Brewing isn't ever going to be a growth stock; that isn't the management's intention. They want the firm to be a dividend-paying machine that will generate steady and reliable income for the rest of their lives. So, if we assume that the M/B ratio is one, then that implies that our total capital will be $991,711, which means that $w_d$ will be 43.1% and $w_e$ will be 56.9%. We have our weights!

Next, we will obtain the cost of debt capital, $k_d$. The firm has one outstanding loan, and it carries an interest rate of 6.25%. So, getting the cost of debt capital is very simple: $k_d$ is 6.25%.

Now that we have the cost of debt, we need to determine an appropriate tax rate for the firm. The firm is incorporated in a state that has no state income tax; that means that the only tax we need to worry about is the federal tax rate which is 21%. So, $t$ is 21%.

The only remaining piece of the puzzle is to attain Alpha Brewing's cost of equity. Alpha Brewing is a private company, so its stock doesn't trade in the market; consequently, we need to worry about things like illiquidity risk, and thus make sure that that risk is priced into our cost of equity capital. Recall, that the cost of equity for a stock that is held in a well-diversified portfolio can be obtained by using the CAPM.

$$k_e = k_{rf} + \beta * E[k_m - k_{rf}]$$

The CAPM has three component parts: the risk-free rate, beta, and the market risk premium. We will discuss how to obtain each of these factors in turn. We begin with the risk-free rate, $k_{rf}$. Remember, as mentioned earlier in this chapter, that when selecting the risk-free rate, we should try to match the maturity of the risk-free rate to the maturity of the asset that we are pricing. The reason for this is that we want to capture the opportunity cost of our capital over the life of the investment. Since we are valuing equity, which is infinitely lived, and there is no infinite maturity treasury bond, we will use the longest possible maturity treasury bond available to us: the 30-year treasury bond. For 2020, the average yield for the 30-year treasury was 1.56% per year.[12] This will be our value for $k_{rf}$.

The next component in the CAPM is beta. As we can see in the following table, as of the writing of this chapter, publicly traded breweries have betas that vary substantially from one another; from Kirin, which is not all that sensitive to the market with a beta of 0.68, to Constellation brands (which also sells wine and spirits) that has a beta of 1.07.[13]

| **Brewery** | **Beta** |
|---|---|
| Constellation Brands | 1.07 |
| Boston Beer Company | 0.81 |
| Kirin | 0.68 |
| Molson Coors | 0.86 |

Our challenge is that Alpha Brewery is tiny compared to these multi-billion-dollar behemoths that have product portfolios that contain numerous brands at different price points. They really aren't great comps for Alpha. Even taking an industry average doesn't make much sense, because Alpha is focused on making premium craft beer for discerning

[12] https://www.macrotrends.net/2521/30-year-treasury-bond-rate-yield-chart

[13] All betas are from finance.yahoo.com

buyers: it is a luxury product meant to be consumed fresh, not bought off the shelf at the local liquor store. As a firm selling a luxury product, its revenue is likely to be more susceptible to changes in the macroeconomy than that of the massive breweries listed above. Because of this, we believe that Alpha Brewing's beta would be slightly higher than even the highest beta on this list. From our experience, we believe that a reasonable estimate for Alpha Brewing's beta would be around 1.1.

The last piece to the puzzle is the market risk premium. Getting this is relatively easy: just Google "current market risk premium." As of the writing of this chapter, the current market risk premium is 5.6%.

Now that we have all the component parts of the CAPM, we can solve for the cost of equity capital.

$$k_e = 1.56\% + 1.1 * 5.60\% = 7.72\%$$

If the brewery were publicly traded, then 7.72% would be our estimate for the cost of equity capital. Unfortunately for us, the brewery is private; that means that investors would likely demand a premium for bearing liquidity risk. As discussed earlier in this chapter, liquidity risk premia typically range between 1% and 3%. We pick the midpoint (2%), since the last three deals of firms of this size that we have done transacted with a 2% liquidity risk premium with little push back from the counterparty. Note, we can always change this when we do our sensitivity analysis, to see if changing the liquidity premium has a substantive impact on our valuation. So, all in all our cost of equity capital is 9.72%.

We finally have all of the component parts of the WACC. All that remains is to input our values and solve for the WACC.

$$\begin{aligned} \text{WACC} &= w_d K_d (1 - t) + w_p K_p + w_e K_e \\ \text{WACC} &= .431(6.25\%)(1 - .21) + 0(K_p) + .569(9.72\%) \\ &= 7.66\% \end{aligned}$$

Our estimate for the WACC for Alpha Brewing Company is 7.66%.

## Key Takeaways

- The discount rate must match (i.e., be consistent) with the nature of the cash flows that are being discounted.

- Debt has a senior claim to equity; that means that in the event of financial distress the debtholders will get paid first before the equity holders.
- The WACC is the discount rate of return that we need to earn to satisfy all of our investors. Hence, when the IRR > WACC, we accept projects.
- WACC = $w_d K_d(1 - t) + w_p K_p + w_e K_e$.
- The effective tax rate is normally lower, and sometimes much lower, than the marginal tax rate. Because of various tax breaks that might be available to the firm.
- The higher the risk, the greater the required return for bearing that risk.
- The historical beta is a good estimate of the forward beta if the sensitivity to systematic risk will not change in the future.

# Chapter 9

# The Income Approach to Valuing a Firm

The goal of this chapter is to explain how to value a firm's equity using the *Income Approach*, which is also known as the *Discounted Cash Flow (DCF) Approach*. The discounted cash flow valuation of equity can be done in one of two ways: either directly valuating the equity or directly valuating enterprise value (which we will discuss in great detail in a little bit) and from there indirectly calculating the value of equity. Either of these two approaches will yield an "intrinsic" value that is based upon our own individual assumptions about what will be the future cash flows and what will be the risk associated with those cash flows. It will tell us what we think the equity should be worth. Now, whether or not the market agrees with us is an entirely different story.

## Valuing a Firm's Equity Directly

The "direct" discounted cash flow approach has to do with valuing equity directly; that is, using the cash flows to the equity holders and a discount rate that reflects the risk associated with those cash flows. Let's begin with the cash flows. Equity holders get two cash flows: dividends and capital gains. The assumption that is made with the direct valuation of equity is that the stock is held forever; that is, the stock is never sold, so therefore there really aren't any capital gains to worry about. Instead, the shareholders receive a steady stream of dividends in perpetuity (i.e., forever), so what matters in this valuation methodology is what are the expected dividends from now to forever and what is the required rate of return that is demanded by equity holders. The rate of return is easy: we use the cost of equity capital, $k_e$, that we just learned about in Chapter 8. However, trying to figure out what are the expected dividends from now to forever can be very difficult for a variety of reasons.

The first reason is that infinity is a very long time away and forecasting anything with great precision that far into the future is impossible; some strong assumptions have to be made. The second is that in order for this approach to yield an accurate result, firms must pay dividends optimally. However, there is no way to guarantee that the firm's management will even know how to solve for the optimal stream of dividends (it involves serious computer programming skills), and even if they did know how to do that, there is no way to force them to pay those dividends. Managers have a great deal of discretion in what they do with profit. They can buy back shares of stock, they can pay out cash dividends, or they can plow the cash back into the firm as retained earnings: management has all kinds of things that they could do instead of paying the optimal amount of dividends. We as valuators have absolutely no control over what the managers actually do. We can value the firm *assuming* that the managers will act optimally, but the fact that we cannot count on this actually happening is one of the key weaknesses of this approach and is the principal reason why it is not very popular. Another weakness, as mentioned above, is that it is very difficult to solve for the optimal stream of dividends that will maximize the value of the firm. It requires a sophisticated optimization algorithm and many strong assumptions. As a result, this method of valuation is used less often than its counterpart, the indirect approach.

So, thus far we've learned that the cash flows that we will be using are the dividends that will be paid to the shareholders and the discount rate will be the required rate of return to equity; that is, the rate of return that is required by the shareholders. Once we have these two pieces of the puzzle, then as we will see, solving for the price of equity is a relatively straightforward calculation.

## *The dividend growth (Gordon Growth) model*

The intrinsic value of any asset can be determined by taking the present value (using an appropriate discount rate) of the cash flow stream associated with that asset. If the asset is equity, then the cash flows are dividends, and the required rate of return is the cost of equity capital. So, if the stock were to pay a dividend of $\text{Div}_1$ in the first year, and the dividends were expected to grow every year at a constant rate of $g$, then the cash flows received from owning this stock would be as follows:

| Year 1 | Year 2 | Year 3 | Year 4 | ...Year $\infty$ |
|---|---|---|---|---|
| $\text{Div}_1$ | $\text{Div}_1(1+g)$ | $\text{Div}_1(1+g)^2$ | $\text{Div}_1(1+g)^3$ | $\text{Div}_1(1+g)^{\infty-1}$ |

If these are the cash flows, then using the Present Value formula, the equity can be valued as follows:

Present value of equity

$$=\frac{\text{Div}_1}{(1+k_e)^1}+\frac{\text{Div}_1(1+g)}{(1+k_e)^2}+\frac{\text{Div}_1(1+g)^2}{(1+k_e)^3}+\frac{\text{Div}_1(1+g)^3}{(1+k_e)^4}+\cdots+\frac{\text{Div}_1(1+g)^{\infty-1}}{(1+k_e)^\infty}$$

Normally, the calculation of this infinite series would be computationally impossible. But, as we learned in the Time Value of Money section, since we have a cash flow that is growing at a constant rate, then we can apply the Gordon Growth Formula, so the above infinite series converges to the following:

$$\text{Present value of equity}=\frac{\text{Div}_1}{k_e-g}$$

Thus, if the dividend growth rate is expected to be constant (as it often is, for say, utility companies), the only three things we need in order to value equity directly using the discounted cash flow method are next year's expected dividend, the cost of equity capital, and the growth rate.

For example, imagine a firm that is expected to pay out $2.5MM in dividends next year, has a cost of equity capital of 10%, and whose dividends are expected to grow at the rate of 2% in perpetuity. The present value of the equity of the firm would be calculated as follows:

$$\text{Present value of equity}=\frac{\$2{,}500{,}000}{.1-.02}=\$31{,}250{,}000$$

## *Calculating the price per share*

In the above example, if the firm has 10MM shares outstanding, then the price of the stock should be as follows:

$$\text{Stock price} = \frac{\$31,250,000}{10,000,000} = \$3.125 \text{ per share}$$

Another way of arriving at the price per share is to use next year's dividend per share rather than the total dollar amount of dividends expected next year in the Gordon Growth Formula. The firm will pay $2,500,000 in dividends and it has 10MM shares, so

$$\text{Dividend per share}_1 = \frac{\$2,500,000}{10,000,000} = \$0.25 \text{ per share}$$

We can use this next period's expected dividend per share in the Gordon Growth Formula to get the value of the price per share.

$$\text{Price per share} = \frac{\$0.25}{.1 - .02} = \$3.125 \text{ per share}$$

And if we wanted to know the present value of the equity in dollars, we would just multiply the price per share by the total number of shares

$$\$3.125 \text{ per share} \times 10,000,000 \text{ shares} = \$31,250,000$$

As we can see, the two approaches, valuing the dollar value of equity directly and valuing the price per share directly and then multiplying by the total number of shares, will yield the same answer. They are equivalent approaches.

## *What if the dividend is not growing at a constant rate?*

The above example is a useful and easy-to-calculate starting point. However, dividends usually do not grow at a constant rate. For example, how do we price the equity of rapidly growing firms like tech startups? What about firms that are expected to have some volatility in their dividends for a foreseeable period of time? Fortunately, there is an easy-to-implement approach that allows us to deal with these kinds of stocks.

That being said, in order to price these non-constant dividend growth stocks (or any non-constant growth cash flow for that matter), we still have to, at some point in the future, be able to make the assumption that eventually the firm's dividend will begin to grow at a constant growth rate. Otherwise, we will not be able to use the Gordon Growth Formula and we will be stuck with an infinite series that cannot be solved.

Our goal is to find a way to convert the infinite sequence of dividends into a finite sequence of cash flows that has an equal value. This is essential, because if the cash flows are finite, then we are able to use the present value formula to compute their present value. So, how do we do this? It actually is pretty easy once you've done it a few times. We have to forecast each of the dividends individually up until the point in time (let's call it $T$) where we can assume that thereafter the dividend growth will be stable and constant. This is important, because once the growth rate is constant, then we can use the Gordon Growth Formula at time $T$ to determine what the present value of the future dividends would be at time $T$. This value is called a *terminal equity value at time T*, sometimes just called the terminal value, for short. The terminal equity value is what the equity is expected to be worth if we were to sell it at time $T$, exactly the point in time when the dividend growth rate started to be constant. If we were sitting at time $T$, we should literally be completely indifferent between receiving the stock's remaining infinite stream of annual dividends, which are growing at a constant rate, or receiving a lump sum equal to the terminal value at time $T$. They are equivalent to each other.

Let's first walk through a hypothetical example to help develop the intuition behind what we are doing, then we will use some numbers so that you can practice on your own. Imagine if the dividends were not growing at a constant rate in years 1, 2, or 3, but we felt comfortable assuming that the growth rate would be constant beginning in year 4 and would thereafter stay that way forever (i.e., the last non-constant growth rate dividend was in year 3). To value a stock like this, we would have to individually forecast the dividend in year 1 ($D_1$), the dividend in year 2 ($D_2$), and the dividend in year 3 ($D_3$). After that, we could just assume that the dividend would start growing at a constant rate; that is, the dividend in year 4 is just $D_3(1 + g)$ and the dividend in year 5 is $D_4(1 + g)$, which is actually $D_3(1 + g)$^2, and so on. To see it in table format, the dividends would be as follows[1]:

[1]Note, to solve for the equity value, we thankfully won't actually have to calculate anything beyond year 4, since we can use the dividend in year 4 along with the dividend growth formula to get the terminal value at the end of year 3.

| Year 1 | Year 2 | Year 3 | Year 4 | Year 5 | ...Year ∞ |
|---|---|---|---|---|---|
| $D_1$ | $D_2$ | $D_3$ | $D_3(1+g)$ | $D_3(1+g)^2$ | $D_3(1+g)^{\infty-3}$ |

Our goal is to convert the infinite dividend stream in the table above to an equivalent value finite cash flow stream. Since the dividend starts to grow at a constant rate after year 3, we can use the Gordon Growth Formula to calculate the terminal value at the end of year 3, which we will call $TV_3$. Then, we can substitute $TV_3$ for the infinite sequence of dividends from year 4 to infinity and end up with a completely equivalent in value, but finite, cash flow stream that looks as follows:

| Year 1 | Year 2 | Year 3 |
|---|---|---|
| $D_1$ | $D_2$ | $D_3 + TV_3$ |

Valuing this cash flow stream is easy. We do it as follows:

$$\text{Equity value} = \frac{D_1}{1+k_e} + \frac{D_2}{(1+k_e)^2} + \frac{D_3 + TV_3}{(1+k_e)^3}$$

OK, so what we need is $TV_3$. How do we get it? Recall that the terminal value in year 3 is just the present value of all the future cash flows; that is, the dividends from year 4 to infinity.

$$TV_3 = \frac{\text{Dividend}_4}{(1+k_e)} + \frac{\text{Dividend}_5}{(1+k_e)^2} + \cdots + \frac{\text{Dividend}_\infty}{(1+k_e)^\infty}$$

Remember that, because the growth rate is constant, $D_4 = D_3(1+g)$, $D_5 = D_3(1+g)^2$, and so on, so substituting these into the above equation, we get the following:

$$TV_3 = \frac{\text{Dividend}_3(1+g)}{(1+k_e)} + \frac{\text{Dividend}_3(1+g)^2}{(1+k_e)^2} + \cdots + \frac{\text{Dividend}_3(1+g)^{\infty-3}}{(1+k_e)^\infty}$$

Lucky for us, we can use the Gordon Growth Formula to solve for $TV_3$, as follows:

$$\mathrm{TV}_3 = \frac{\mathrm{Dividend}_4}{k_e - g}$$

And because $D_4 = D_3(1 + g)$,

$$\mathrm{TV}_3 = \frac{\mathrm{Dividend}_3(1+g)}{k_e - g}$$

We then input our value for $\mathrm{TV}_3$ into the equity valuation equation and we are all set.

$$\text{Equity value} = \frac{D_1}{1+k_e} + \frac{D_2}{(1+k_e)^2} + \frac{D_3 + \mathrm{TV}_3}{(1+k_e)^3}$$

So, to value this particular stock that has non-constant dividend growth for the first 3 years, all we need is $D_1$, $D_2$, $D_3$, $k_e$, and $g$.

### *Numerical example of direct equity valuation with non-constant dividend growth rate*

Let's use some numbers to reexamine the theoretical discussion that we presented above and give us some practice using this valuation technology. Imagine we wanted to value a firm that has the following expected dividends, and the cost of equity was 10%: $D_1$ = \$100, $D_2$ = \$150, $D_3$ = \$175, and thereafter the dividend is expected to grow at a rate of 3% per year.

The cash flows would look as follows:

| Year 1 | Year 2 | Year 3 | Year 4 | Year 5 | …Year ∞ |
|---|---|---|---|---|---|
| \$100 | \$150 | \$175 | \$180.25 | \$185.66 | ??? |

Our goal is to convert this infinite cash flow stream into one that is much more manageable to compute. Since the growth rate is constant after year 3, we can use the Gordon Growth Formula to find the terminal value of the equity at the end of year 3 and use that in place of the infinite series of cash flows from year 4 to infinity.

| Year 1 | Year 2 | Year 3 |
|---|---|---|
| $D_1$ | $D_2$ | $D_3 + TV_3$ |

Since the growth rate is constant, getting the terminal value is easy: we just use the Gordon Growth Model. Recall that the cost of equity is 10%.

$$TV_3 = \frac{\text{Dividend}_4}{k_e - g} = \frac{\text{Dividend}_3(1+g)}{k_e - g}$$

$$TV_3 = \frac{\$180.25}{.10 - .03} = \$2,575$$

We should be indifferent between getting an infinite stream of dividends after year 3 growing at a 3% rate and \$2,575 at the end of year 3. So, our equivalent cash flow stream is as follows:

| Year 1 | Year 2 | Year 3 |
|---|---|---|
| \$100 | \$150 | \$175 + \$2,575 = \$2,750 |

Pricing this finite cash flow stream is relatively straightforward using the following present value formula:

$$\text{Present value} = \frac{\$100}{1+.1} + \frac{\$150}{(1+.1)^2} + \frac{\$175 + \$2,575}{(1+.1)^3} = \$2,280.99$$

## The Indirect Method of Equity Valuation/ Enterprise Value

As was mentioned above, the direct method of equity valuation is valid, but it is not used all that frequently, because we have no way of knowing whether management will actually pay out dividends optimally. Instead, practitioners usually use the indirect discounted cash flow method of valuing equity. This method determines *enterprise value* first, and then subtracts out the other financial claims against the firm to get to equity.

First, what is enterprise value? Enterprise value is the amount of money that we have to come up with in order to buy a company. If we buy a firm, we have to, of course, buy out the equity holders; after all, it is the equity that grants the claim of ownership. But, the preferred stockholders and the debt holders also have a financial claim to the firm's assets.[2] We have to buy out their claims, too. In this way, *enterprise value is the sum of all the financial claims against the firm.*

A useful analogy is when we buy a house. If the current homeowner of a home worth \$500K has a \$300K mortgage outstanding on the home, then they have \$200K in home equity. If we want to buy the home from them, they will definitely not sell us the house for just the \$200K in equity value. That isn't enough money to motivate them to sell. To make them completely satisfied, we will also have to buy out their debt obligation; otherwise, they only get \$200K, we get the house, and then they are stuck with the \$300K mortgage. That is great for us, but awful for them! So, if we want the house, we have to buy out both the equity and the debt; that is, we will have to pay \$200K + \$300K = \$500K.

We might have given you the wrong impression that enterprise value is just the market value of the firm's assets, but we need to be a little careful, because this is sometimes true, but it isn't always the case. Let us explain. If the firm has excess cash sitting on its balance sheet, then when we buy the firm, we could use that excess cash to pay off some of the firm's outstanding debt balance. So, rather than having to raise enough money to buy out all of the firm's existing debt, we just have to raise enough to buy out the *net debt*; that is, the outstanding debt balance after we have used up all of the firm's excess cash to retire as much of the existing debt as possible. Thus, enterprise value is as follows:

$$\text{Enterprise value} = \text{Equity} + \text{Preferred stock} + \text{Debt} \\ - \text{Excess cash}$$

or

$$\text{Enterprise value} = \text{Equity} + \text{Preferred stock} + \text{Net debt}$$

---

[2] Many firms do not have any preferred stock, so don't be surprised if you don't see it listed on the balance sheet.

Note, if firms have a lot of excess cash (e.g., Apple or Microsoft), then their equity will be greater in value than their enterprise value.

So, with the indirect equity valuation method, we will first directly calculate enterprise value and then we will subtract out the other financial claims in order to get equity. That is:

Equity = Enterprise value – Preferred stock – Debt
+ Excess cash

or

Equity = Enterprise value – Preferred stock
– Net debt

## *Getting estimates of cash, preferred stock, and debt*

Before we examine how to calculate enterprise value, let's first discuss how to get estimates for the values of preferred stock, debt, and cash — the other components used in the indirect valuation of equity. Cash is easy: the market value of cash and the book value of cash are identical. Cash is cash. You don't have to do anything to it in order to spend it, and a dollar is always worth a dollar in nominal terms. Consequently, we will use the book value of cash taken from the most recent balance sheet. Just be careful to exclude any restricted cash from the calculation, since that cash cannot be used for debt repayment. Examples of restricted cash include minimum cash balances required for loan agreements, refundable deposits, and minimum bank balances.

The values of preferred stock and debt are also usually taken directly from the firm's most recent balance sheet. The reason why we do this is because most preferred stocks don't actively trade in the market, so we cannot get a true market value for them. But, as long as the firm is in solid financial condition, the book value and market value of the preferred stock should be reasonably close to one another, so it is appropriate to use the book value of preferred stock as an estimate for its market value. The same is true with respect to the debt. Even though some of the firm's debt may be publicly traded, most debt isn't. And in the lucky chance that some of it is traded, it usually doesn't trade all that often, so the prices sometimes aren't all that informative. But more importantly, irrespective of the market value of the debt, the buyer will be on the hook for any outstanding principal. So, if you buy the company, that full debt obligation will likely become yours, thus using the book value of the debt makes sense.[3]

### *How to determine enterprise value*

The last piece of the puzzle necessary to indirectly value equity is enterprise value. Enterprise value is the value of all the financial claims against the firm, so to value it, we need an after-tax cash flow measure that takes into consideration the payments to all the capital providers.

This measure is called *unlevered free cash flow*, and we will explain exactly what this is shortly. We also need the required rate of return associated with the cash flows received by all the capital providers. The required rate of return to capital is easy. It is called the weighted average cost of capital (WACC). We learned about this in Chapter 8, on Risk and Return.

So, now that we know the discount rate is the WACC, how do we calculate unlevered free cash flow? It is a little complicated, but we will try to give you some intuition. We need a cash flow that is available to all of the capital providers. This cash flow can't be net income, since only the common stockholders have a claim to it. We need a cash flow measure to which all three capital providers have a claim, which means the debt holders and the preferred stockholders, too. So, that means that we have to start with a measure of cash flow that is before interest (since this is a cash outflow that goes to debt holders): a good starting point is EBIT. All the capital providers have a claim to EBIT.

Okay, so we start with EBIT, but to get to a cash flow, we need to take out tax. Here is where things get a little tricky. We will be subtracting out the tax that we would pay on EBIT. But wait, you might ask, why don't we subtract out the tax that we would pay on EBT instead? Isn't interest tax deductible? You are right, interest is tax-deductible, and if we subtract out the tax on EBIT, won't that be too large of a number? Don't we want to take advantage of the interest tax shield? Like we said, this gets a little tricky. Remember, we will be discounting this unlevered free cash flow measure by the weighted average cost of capital.

[3]Note, if the firm is not in solid financial condition, this valuation approach may not be appropriate. See Chapter 13 if you are curious about how to value firms that are in distress.

$$\text{WACC} = w_d K_d(1 - t) + w_p K_p + w_e K_e$$

Note that the benefit that comes from the tax deductibility of interest is already taken into account by the WACC when we make the $(1 - t)$ adjustment to the cost of debt. If we use EBT rather than EBIT for the calculation of tax, then we are double counting the benefit associated with the tax shield that comes from paying interest. Specifically, we would be getting the benefit of a lower tax payment (and thus higher cash flow) in the numerator of our time value of money calculation and a lower WACC in the denominator, which together will lead to an upward bias in our valuation. Double counting leads to erroneous valuations, so in order to get a valid calculation, we have to use the pre-interest EBIT rather than the post-interest EBT. The use of EBIT, rather than EBT, in the tax calculation is the reason why this cash flow measure is called an unlevered free cash flow. It yields an after-tax cash flow that is essentially equivalent to what the after-tax cash flow would be for a firm that is identical to ours but has no debt, that is, it is unlevered. If the firm didn't have any debt, then there would be no interest deduction and the tax would be paid on EBIT, since in this case EBIT and EBT would be identical.

Now that the piece of messy business is cleared up, the rest is easy. We start with EBIT and subtract out the tax that would be paid on EBIT.[4] Next, all we need to do is add back in depreciation and amortization, since these are non-cash charges, and subtract out capital expenditures and any increases in working capital, since both of these are uses of cash. When we are done, we should have unlevered free cash flow.

So, to sum things up, unlevered free cash flow, UFCF, can be calculated as follows:

$$\begin{aligned}\text{UFCF}_t = {} & \text{EBIT}_t - \text{EBIT(tax)}_t \\ & + \text{Depreciation}_t \\ & + \text{Amortization}_t \\ & - \text{Capital expenditures}_t \\ & - \text{Increase in working capital}_t \text{ or} \\ & + \text{Decrease in working capital}_t\end{aligned}$$

[4]This value is also called NOPAT (Net Operating Profit After Tax).

### *Example of the calculation of Alpha Brewing's Unlevered Free Cash Flow*

| **AB's Unlevered Free Cash Flow** (2020 Figures) | |
|---|---|
| EBIT | \$613,765 |
| Tax Rate | 21% |
| EBIT(tax) | \$128,891 |
| Depreciation & Amortization | \$85,006 |
| Capital Expenditures | — |
| Increase in Working Capital | \$6,436 |
| Unlevered Free Cash Flow | \$563,444 |

Increase in net working capital (2020) \$6,436
= Working capital (2020) \$176,843
– Net working capital (2019) \$170,407
Working capital[5] (2020) \$176,843
= AR \$174,481 + Inventory \$17,253 – AP \$14,892
Working capital (2019) \$170,407
= AR \$163,053 + Inventory \$20,173 – AP \$12,819

### *Enterprise value*

Now that we are familiar with the calculation of unlevered free cash flows, we are ready to learn how to calculate the enterprise value of a firm. Enterprise value is the present value of the firm's unlevered free cash flows discounted back at the WACC.

$$\text{Enterprise value} = \frac{\text{UFCF}_1}{(1+\text{WACC})^1} + \frac{\text{UFCF}_2}{(1+\text{WACC})^2} + \frac{\text{UFCF}_3}{(1+\text{WACC})^3} + \cdots + \frac{\text{UFCF}_\infty}{(1+\text{WACC})^\infty}$$

[5] Working capital is the difference between non-interest earning current assets minus non-interest-bearing current liabilities. Working capital is all about waiting for money to either be paid to us or by us.

Firms are infinitely lived, so similar to the challenge we had when doing the direct method of equity valuation, we have the problem of trying to take the present value of an infinite stream of cash flows. We learned that in order to price an infinite stream of cash flows, we had to be able to, at some point in time, make the assumption that the cash flow would grow at a constant rate. Otherwise, we will not be able to use the Gordon Growth Formula and we will be stuck with an infinite series that is computationally infeasible to solve.

To refresh our memory, we need to convert the infinite sequence of unlevered free cash flows into an equivalent (one that has an equal value) finite sequence of cash flows. This is crucial, because if the cash flows are finite, then the calculation becomes computationally possible. We start by forecasting each of the unlevered free cash flows individually up until the point in time, $T$, where we can make the assumption that thereafter the UFCF growth rate will be constant. Once the growth rate is constant, then we can use the Gordon Growth Formula at time $T$ to determine what the present value of the future unlevered free cash flows would be at time $T$. This value is called the *enterprise value at time T*, or sometimes, as was the case with the direct method, it is just called the *terminal value*.[6]

The terminal enterprise value is what the firm is expected to be worth if we were to buy or sell it at time $T$, exactly the point in time when the growth rate of the unlevered free cash flow started to be constant. If we were sitting at time $T$, we would be totally indifferent between receiving the remaining infinite stream of annual unlevered free cash flows, which are growing at a constant rate, or receiving a lump sum equal to the terminal enterprise value at time $T$. They are equivalent to one another.

Similar to the earlier section on the direct valuation of equity, we will first walk through a theoretical example to help develop some intuition behind what we are doing, then we will use some numbers in order to get a better feel for how it is actually done. Imagine if the UFCF were not growing at a constant rate in years 1, 2, or 3, but we felt comfortable making the assumption that the growth rate would be constant beginning in year 4 and would thereafter stay that way forever (i.e., the last non-constant growth rate UFCF was in year 3). To get the enterprise value of a firm like this, we would have to individually forecast the UFCF in year 1

[6]Be careful, because even though "terminal value" is used in both the direct and indirect methods, they refer to different things; specifically, it refers to the terminal *equity* value in the former and the terminal *enterprise value* in the latter.

($UFCF_1$), the UFCF in year 2 ($UFCF_2$), and the UFCF in year 3 ($UFCF_3$). After that, we could just assume that the UFCF would start growing at a constant rate; that is, the UFCF in year 4 is just $UFCF_3(1 + g)$ and the cash flow in year 5 is $UFCF_4(1 + g)$, which is actually $UFCF_3(1 + g)^2$, and so on. To see it in table format, the unlevered free cash flows would be as follows[7]:

| Year 1 | Year 2 | Year 3 | Year 4 | Year 5 | ...Year ∞ |
|---|---|---|---|---|---|
| $UFCF_1$ | $UFCF_2$ | $UFCF_3$ | $UFCF_3(1+g)$ | $UFCF_3(1+g)^2$ | $UFCF_3(1+g)^{\infty-3}$ |

Similar to the direct method of DCF valuation, our goal is to convert the infinite stream of UFCF in the table above into an equivalent value finite cash flow stream to which we will be indifferent.

Since the UFCF begins to grow at a constant rate after year 3, we can use the Gordon Growth Formula to calculate the terminal enterprise value at the end of year 3, which we will call $TV_3$. Then we can substitute $TV_3$ for the infinite sequence of UFCF from year 4 to infinity and end up with a completely equivalent value, but finite cash flow stream that looks as follows:

| Year 1 | Year 2 | Year 3 |
|---|---|---|
| $UFCF_1$ | $UFCF_2$ | $UFCF_3 + TV_3$ |

Valuing this cash flow stream is straightforward. We do it as follows:

$$\text{Enterprise value} = \frac{UFCF_1}{1 + WACC} + \frac{UFCF_2}{(1 + WACC)^2} + \frac{UFCF_3 + TV_3}{(1 + WACC)^3}$$

To do this calculation, we need $TV_3$. Getting it is fairly easy. Recall that the terminal enterprise value in year 3 is equal to the present value of all the future UFCF; that is, the UFCF from year 4 to infinity.

[7]To solve for the enterprise value, we won't actually have to calculate anything beyond year 4, since we can use the UFCF in year 4 along with the Gordon Growth Formula to get the terminal value at the end of year 3.

$$\text{TV}_3 = \frac{\text{UFCF}_4}{(1+\text{WACC})^1} + \frac{\text{UFCF}_5}{(1+\text{WACC})^2} + \cdots + \frac{\text{UCFC}_\infty}{(1+\text{WACC})^\infty}$$

Remember that because the growth rate is constant, $\text{UFCF}_4 = \text{UFCF}_3(1 + g)$, $\text{UFCF}_5 = \text{UFCF}_3(1 + g)^2$ and so on, so substituting these into the above equation, we get the following:

$$\text{TV}_3 = \frac{\text{UFCF}_3(1+g)}{(1+\text{WACC})} + \frac{\text{UFCF}_3(1+g)^2}{(1+\text{WACC})^2} + \cdots + \frac{\text{UFCF}_3(1+g)^{\infty-3}}{(1+\text{WACC})^\infty}$$

Since this cash flow stream is growing at a constant rate, we can use the following Gordon Growth Formula to solve for $\text{TV}_3$:

$$\text{TV}_3 = \frac{\text{UFCF}_4}{\text{WACC} - g}$$

And because $\text{UFCF}_4 = \text{UFCF}_3(1 + g)$:

$$\text{TV}_3 = \frac{\text{UFCF}_3(1+g)}{\text{WACC} - g}$$

We then input our value for $\text{TV}_3$ into the Enterprise Value equation as follows and then we are all set:

$$\text{Enterprise value} = \frac{\text{UFCF}_1}{1+\text{WACC}} + \frac{\text{UFCF}_2}{(1+\text{WACC})^2} + \frac{\text{UFCF}_3 + \text{TV}_3}{(1+\text{WACC})^3}$$

So, to obtain the enterprise value for this firm, all we need is $\text{UFCF}_1$, $\text{UFCF}_2$, $\text{UFCF}_3$, WACC, and $g$.

### *Numerical example of the calculation of enterprise value when the unlevered free cash flows do not grow at a constant rate*

Let's use some numbers to reexamine the abstract problem presented above to get a better understanding of how enterprise value is calculated.

Imagine we wanted to value a firm that has the following expected UFCF and the WACC was 10%: $UFCF_1 = \$1{,}000{,}000$; $UFCF_2 = \$1{,}500{,}000$; $UFCF_3 = \$1{,}750{,}000$, and thereafter, the UFCF is expected to grow at a rate of 3% per year.

The cash flows would look as follows:

| Year 1 | Year 2 | Year 3 | Year 4 | ...Year ∞ |
|---|---|---|---|---|
| \$1,000,000 | \$1,500,000 | \$1,750,000 | \$1,802,500 | ??? |

We need to convert this infinite cash flow stream into a finite one, so that we can actually compute the present value. Since the growth rate is constant after year 3, we can use the Gordon Growth Formula to find the terminal enterprise value at the end of year 3, and use that in place of the infinite series of cash flows from year 4 to infinity.

| Year 1 | Year 2 | Year 3 |
|---|---|---|
| $UFCF_1$ | $UFCF_2$ | $UFCF_3 + TV_3$ |

$$TV_3 = \frac{UFCF_4}{WACC - g} = \frac{UFCF_3(1+g)}{WACC - g}$$

Recall that the WACC is 10%, the growth rate is 3%, and $UFCF_4 = \$1{,}802{,}500$. So:

$$TV_3 = \frac{\$1{,}802{,}500}{.10 - .03} = \$25{,}750{,}000$$

That means that our equivalent cash flow stream is as follows:

| Year 1 | Year 2 | Year 3 |
|---|---|---|
| \$1,000,000 | \$1,500,000 | \$1,750,000 + \$25,750,000 = \$27,500,000 |

Pricing this finite stream of unlevered free cash flows is relatively straightforward using the present value formula. The Enterprise Value is as follows:

$$\text{Enterprise value} = \frac{\$1,000,000}{(1+.1)} + \frac{\$1,500,000}{(1+.1)^2} + \frac{\$27,500,000}{(1+.1)^3} = \$22,809,917$$

### *The indirect income method for valuing equity — getting equity from enterprise value*

Now that we know how to estimate a firm's enterprise value, obtaining an estimate for the value of the firm's equity can be easily done by subtracting out the book value of preferred stock and the net debt (recall that net debt is Total Debt – Excess Cash, that is, the cash that is not required for the daily operations of the business).

$$\text{Equity} = \text{Enterprise value} - \text{Preferred stock} - \text{Net debt}$$

Let's continue with the above example where the firm had the following expected UFCF: $UFCF_1 = \$1,000,000$; $UFCF_2 = \$1,500,000$; $UFCF_3 = \$1,750,000$; and thereafter, the UFCF is expected to grow at a rate of 3% per year. Recall that the firm's WACC was 10%.

We just determined that the firm's enterprise value should be \$22,809,917. Now, we would like to obtain an estimate of the value of the firm's equity. We look at the firm's most recent balance sheet and find that the firm has \$2,000,000 in excess cash, \$12,000,000 in debt, and \$2,500,000 in preferred stock. In this case, the firm's net debt is \$12,000,000 – \$2,000,000 = \$10,000,000, so the value of its equity should be as follows:

| **Equity Value from EV** | |
|---|---|
| Enterprise Value | \$22,809,917 |
| Preferred Equity | (\$2,500,000) |
| Net Debt | (\$10,000,000) |
| Equity Value | \$10,309,917 |

$$\begin{aligned}\text{Equity} &= \$22,809,917 - \$2,500,000 - \$10,000,000 \\ &= \$10,309,917\end{aligned}$$

### *Getting a better understanding of the terminal growth rate assumption*

The most often challenged assumption in a DCF analysis is the assumption of what is a reasonable terminal growth rate. For growth stocks, most of the value will come from the terminal value, so don't be surprised if the terminal value is very large relative to the UFCF that you used to calculate the terminal value. For example, in the last problem, the $UFCF_4$ was \$1,802,500 and the $TV_3$ was \$25,750,000.

| Enterprise Value Example | |
|---|---|
| Weighted Average Cost of Capital | 10.00% |
| Terminal growth rate | 3.00% |
| $UFCF_1$ | \$1,000,000 |
| $UFCF_2$ | \$1,500,000 |
| $UFCF_3$ | \$1,750,000 |
| $UFCF_4 = UFCF_3 * (1 + g)$ | \$1,802,500 |
| $TV_3 = UFCF_4/(WACC - g)$ | \$25,750,000 |

The terminal value is primarily driven by the difference between the terminal growth rate and the firm's WACC, so getting the terminal growth rate assumption right is extremely important. If the WACC and *g* are very close to one another, then the denominator in the Gordon Growth Formula

$$TV_t = \frac{UFCF_{t+1}}{WACC - g}$$

(WACC – *g*) will approach zero, and the fraction will explode toward a value of infinity. In fact, the Gordon Growth Model really isn't usable when the WACC and *g* are close to one another; fortunately, there is an alternative approach that works very well in this scenario. But, before we discuss this alternative approach, it is important that you understand the drivers of the terminal growth rate.

The reason why the growth rate assumption is so important is that the Gordon Growth Formula involves dividing the next period's UFCF by what is usually a very small number (WACC – *g* is often less than 0.10), so even minute errors in the terminal growth rate assumption can have a huge impact on the terminal value; especially when the WACC and *g* are relatively close to one another. For example, if next period's UFCF were $1,000,000, the WACC was 8%, and the actual terminal growth rate was 3%, then the terminal value would be $1,000,000/.05 = $20,000,000. But if we made the mistake and erroneously used a terminal growth rate of 3.5% instead of 3%, then the terminal value would be $1,000,000/.045 = $22,222,222. That is a difference of over $2.2MM! And, if instead of 8%, the WACC had been 6% and we had made that same mistake, then the difference would have been $1,000,000/.03 = $33,333,333 versus $1,000,000/.025 = $40,000,000, or over $6.6MM, which is huge. So, being able to defend your terminal growth rate assumption is essential. People will challenge you on it. Be prepared!

If you have not read Chapter 3, on the Income Statement, yet (specifically the section on "Factors that lead to price elastic demand and to subsequent volatility in revenues"), we encourage you to read that before you move on, since it is in that chapter that we talk about the principal driver of the terminal growth rate: sustainable competitive advantage. It is the strength and permanence of the firm's competitive advantage that drives the terminal growth rate.

A reminder of some of the factors that we discussed which create inelastic demand and sustainable competitive advantage include barriers to entry and exit, competition from substitute products, product differentiation, brand recognition and customer loyalty, absolute cost advantage, and limited access to channels of distribution. Again, please refer to Chapter 3 for a deep dive into each of these drivers of the terminal growth rate. If the firm does not have a sustainable competitive advantage, then you should expect that competition will drive down profits to the competitive level, so evaluators often use the growth rate of gross domestic product (GDP) or some industry-wide measure of growth. In the next chapter, we will explain how you can calibrate the terminal growth rate assumption.

### *What do we do if WACC and* g *are too close to one another? Or what if we are struggling to estimate the terminal growth rate? Using an EV/EBITDA multiple to get an estimate of the terminal enterprise value*

Sometimes, the WACC and *g* are too close to one another, or the valuator has too much difficulty in estimating or defending their estimate of the terminal growth rate. Fortunately, there is another approach to get an estimate of the terminal enterprise value. This second approach is to use an estimate of what you believe will be the EV/EBITDA multiple in the terminal year and multiply that by the terminal year EBITDA. We will discuss how to determine an appropriate EV/EBITDA multiple in great detail in the next chapter. For now, we will assume that it is given to us and show how it can be used to estimate the terminal value. The typical assumption is that the current EV/EBITDA multiple will be a good estimate for what the multiple will be in the terminal year; that is, that there will not likely be either an expansion or a contraction in the multiple over time. This assumption is a reasonable one unless the firm is currently growing at a much higher rate than what it is expected to grow in the future.

Let's look at an example, using the numbers in the previous section. If the firm has \$3MM of EBITDA in year 3, and a reasonable estimate (given comparable firms) for the EV/EBITDA ratio is 10x, then our estimate of the terminal enterprise value would be as follows:

$$\frac{\text{EV}_3}{\text{EBITDA}_3}\text{EBITDA}_3 = (10)(\$3\text{MM}) = \$30\text{MM}$$

### *Backing out the terminal growth rate once you have an estimate of the terminal value*

Once we have a terminal value estimate using the EV/EBITDA approach, we can back out what is the implied terminal growth rate that would give us an equivalent terminal value estimate. We know from the Gordon Growth Model that:

$$\text{EV}_3 = \frac{\text{UFCF}_3(1+g)}{(\text{WACC}-g)}$$

All that we need to do is a little algebra to solve for $g$, as follows:

$$\begin{gathered}(\text{WACC}-g)\text{EV}_3 = \text{UFCF}_3 + g(\text{UFCF}_3)\\(\text{WACC})\text{EV}_3 - g(\text{EV}_3) = \text{UFCF}_3 + g(\text{UFCF}_3)\\\text{WACC}(\text{EV}_3) - \text{UFCF}_3 = g(\text{UFCF}_3) + g(\text{EV}_3)\\\text{WACC}(\text{EV}_3) - \text{UFCF}_3 = g * (\text{UFCF}_3 + \text{EV}_3)\end{gathered}$$

$$g = \frac{\text{WACC}(\text{EV}_3) - \text{UFCF}_3}{\text{UFCF}_3 + \text{EV}_3}$$

Or, using the numbers in the example, using the EV/EBITDA method, the year 3 terminal value, $\text{EV}_3$, was estimated to be \$30MM and the WACC was equal to 10%.

$$\$30,000,000 = \frac{\$1,750,000(1+g)}{(.10-g)}$$

$$(.10 - g)\$30,000,000 = \$1,750,000(1 + g)$$
$$(.10 - g)\$30,000,000 - (g)(\$30,000,000)$$
$$= \$1,750,000 + (g)(\$1,750,000)$$
$$(.10)\$30,000,000 - \$1,750,000$$
$$= (g)(\$1,750,000) + (g)(\$30,000,000)$$
$$(.10)\$30,000,000 - \$1,750,000$$
$$= g(\$1,750,0000 + \$30,000,000)$$
$$g = \frac{(.10)\$30,000,000 - \$1,750,000}{\$1,750,0000 + \$30,000,000}$$
$$g = 3.937\%$$

And to check our work:

$$\text{EV}_3 = \frac{\$1,750,000(1+.03937)}{(.10-.03937)} = \$30,000,000$$

Thus, the implied terminal growth rate for this firm, given that it is expected to have \$1,750,000 in EBITDA in year 3 and has an expected year 3 EV/EBITDA multiple of 10x, is 3.937%.

## Application of the Direct Income Approach to Alpha Brewing Company

We will be doing a direct valuation of Alpha Brewing Company's equity; thus, we must forecast the dividends and discount them back at the firm's cost of equity capital. Alpha Brewing is an example of a company that is not growing at a constant growth rate in the near term. Thus, when valuing Alpha Brewing, we will need to forecast its financials until we reach a steady state. As you can see in what follows, this steady state revenue growth of 3.3% is expected to be reached in 2022:

| | PROFORMA 2020 | PROJECTED 2021 | PROJECTED 2022 | PROJECTED 2023 | PROJECTED 2024 |
|---|---|---|---|---|---|
| Total Revenues | $1,957,586 | $2,055,466 | $2,122,268 | $2,191,242 | $2,262,457 |
| *Revenue growth rate* | | *5.0%* | *3.3%* | *3.3%* | *3.3%* |
| Dividends | $700,438 | $512,138 | $521,574 | $541,303 | $560,234 |
| *Dividend growth rate* | | *−26.9%* | *1.8%* | *3.8%* | *3.5%* |

Although the firm is forecasted to achieve stable revenue growth in 2022, our cash flow forecasts show that the firm's dividend growth rate will not become constant until 2024, at which point the dividends are expected to grow at the rate of 3.5% per year forever. At this point the firm is a stable cash cow, meaning that the firm is expected to consistently generate more cash than it consumes, which meets the goals of the owners.

The owners of Alpha Brewing have determined that, starting in 2020, they would like to maintain a minimum cash balance of $50,000 for working capital purposes. This $50,000 cash balance is an example of restricted cash, meaning the firm faces a restriction in the amount of cash it is able to distribute, as it is required to maintain a minimum cash balance. Oftentimes, restricted cash arises from either working capital requirements (as seen here) or from bank restrictions on minimum cash balances that must be maintained in order to comply with loan terms.

The opposite of restricted cash or required cash is excess cash. Excess cash is available cash, meaning it is cash that the firm does not need to retain inside the company. The managers believe that any excess cash at the end of the year should be distributed to shareholders via an annual dividend.

In addition to learning that the firm's minimum cash balance requirement is $50,000, we have also learned that the management anticipates no additional CapEx requirements, and they confirm that all excess cash will be distributed to the owners via a dividend at the end of the year.

Using Alpha Brewing's cash flow statement, we are able to obtain the forecasted dividends for years 2020 (D1), 2021 (D2), 2022 (D3), 2023 (D4), and 2024 (D5). Assuming the firm's cost of equity capital ($K_e$) is 9.72% and the firm's terminal dividend growth rate ($g$) is 3.5%, we can use the Non-Constant Dividend Growth Rate method of valuation to directly determine the value of Alpha Brewing's equity as follows:

**Direct Method to Price Non-Constant Dividend Growth Stocks: Alpha Brewing Company**

| | | | | | |
|---|---|---|---|---|---|
| Required rate of capital (Ke): | 9.72% | | | | |
| Dividend growth rate: | 3.50% | | | | |
| Time | 1 | 2 | 3 | 4 | 5 |
| **Year** | **2020** | **2021** | **2022** | **2023** | **2024** |
| Dividend | 700,438 | 512,138 | 521,574 | 541,303 | 560,234 |
| Terminal Value (TV4) | — | — | — | 9,006,979 | — |
| Cash Flows | 700,438 | 512,138 | 521,574 | 9,548,282 | — |
| PV of CFs at Time 0 | 638,387 | 425,418 | 394,874 | 6,588,432 | |
| **Equity Value (sum of PVs)** | **8,047,111** | | | | |

## Key Takeaways

- The price of any asset can be determined by taking the present value (using an appropriate discount rate) of the cash flow stream associated with that asset.
- Valuing a firm's equity can be done either "directly" or "indirectly". The "direct" method involves taking the present value of cash flows to equity holders and discounting them back using the cost of equity capital as the discount rate. The "indirect" method involves first the calculation of enterprise value which is the present value of unlevered free cash flow discounted back at the weighted average cost of capital.

Once the enterprise value is obtained, we subtract out the net financial claims to obtain the equity value.

- The enterprise value is the sum of all the net financial claims against the firm.
- The terminal value is primarily driven by the difference between the terminal growth rate and the firm's WACC.
- If the WACC and $g$ are very close to one another, then the denominator in the Gordon Growth Formula (WACC – $g$), which is used to determine terminal growth value, will approach zero, the fraction will explode to infinity, and the Gordon Growth Model will be of no use.

# Chapter 10

# The Market Approach/Trading and Precedent Transaction Comparables

The Market Approach to valuation is based on the idea that if two things are similar (i.e., they are comparable), then they should sell at a similar price. It seems fair that rational market participants should be willing to pay a similar price for things that are comparable. In fact, this is the key advantage of the Market Approach: it makes tremendous intuitive sense. For example, if the market price is \$1.00 for a 12 oz. can of Coke®, then it makes sense that the market would be willing to pay a similar price for a 12 oz. can of Pepsi®, since the two colas are comparable. Thus, if we wanted an estimate for what should be the value of two dozen 12 oz. cans of Pepsi®, then (\$1.00 per 12 oz. can) × (24 cans) = \$24.00 would be a very reasonable answer. It seems fair.

You have probably used the market method without even realizing it; in fact, you use it pretty much anytime you make a price/value comparison between two items. Think about how you decide if an item is reasonably priced. You probably compare its features to those of its competitors and then make a value judgment about what you are getting for your money. If two things provide the same value, then it makes sense that they should have the same price. But, if two things are slightly different, then you need to make a relative value judgment about whether that slight difference should warrant a higher or lower price: this is the essence of the market approach.

Irrespective of what we are pricing, the market approach involves finding prices of things that are comparable to the thing we are trying to price, and then making reasonable and informed adjustments that reflect differences in quality, quantity, or whatever other features that might impact the relative value. For example, when using the market approach to price a firm, the "value" that we use for comparison is usually an accounting-based number (such as sales or earnings, for example). If two firms are similar — we will explain the four things that need to be similar shortly — and they have, say, the same sales or the same earnings, then it makes sense that they should probably have a similar value. Similar firms should trade at a similar multiple of Price per dollar of Sales, or Price per dollar of Earnings, or Enterprise Value per dollar of EBITDA (arguably, the most widely used comparable for acquisitions), or multiple of the market value to the book value of equity. These are just a few of the more popular examples of what we call "*comps*," which is short for *comparables*.

Two principal types of valuation comparables compose the market approach: Trading Comps and Precedent Transaction Comps. They value two different things. Trading Comps give us a measure of what should be the value of a minority (or non-controlling) share of equity, while Precedent Transaction Comps yield a measure of what should be the value if one were to own a controlling interest. There is a premium that has to be paid for owning a controlling interest, which is why using Precedent Transaction Comps will always yield a higher price than using Trading Comps.

## Trading Comparables

The Trading Comparables Method (also known as Public Company Comparables Method) uses current market prices taken from firms that are similar to the one that we are trying to price but that also happen to be publicly traded. Since the firms are publicly traded, their prices are easy to obtain and, more importantly, they accurately reflect what the market is currently willing to pay for a firm that is similar to the one that we are trying to value. Finding a perfect match is nearly impossible, though, so once we have a match, we will have to use our judgment to determine whether the firm that we are trying to value should trade at a premium or a discount to the publicly traded comparable firm. Trading comps are very useful for determining the initial public offering (IPO) price for a firm or for valuing a minority interest.

## Precedent Transactions

The Precedent Transactions Comparables and Trading Comparables methods are fundamentally similar to one another, but unlike Trading Comps, which use current market prices to determine reasonable market prices, the Precedent Transaction Method uses prices obtained from previously occurring (in this respect, they are precedent) transactions, specifically mergers and acquisitions. Remember that Precedent Transaction Comps are used to value a controlling interest in the firm, so using current market prices (trading comps) for a minority share (like a current market stock price) would not be appropriate — if you want to use such a price, then a takeover premium would have to be added.

Finding reasonable precedent transactions can be a real challenge. It is tough to find a single firm, let alone several of them, that has been recently acquired and that is an exact or even a very good fit for the firm that we are trying to price. A reasonable starting point is to find comparable firms that were recently acquired that are also in the same industry. The better the fit, the more defensible will be your price estimate. In the event that we cannot find a good industry match, we can extend our search to other industries, but we have to be very careful that we are able to defend our choices. The comp has to make sense, and you can be certain that we are going to have to defend our choices. Remember, the goal is to compare apples to apples.

The Precedent Transaction Comp method is a very good choice when we are trying to figure out what would the purchase price that should be paid in a merger or acquisition, or what might be a reasonable selling price if the firm's management were looking for an exit.

## Prerequisites for the Market Approach

### *Finding a good match*

Irrespective of whether we use Trading or Transaction comps, it is essential to find candidate firms that are as comparable as possible to the firm we want to value. In both market valuation methods discussed above, the key is searching for companies that are sufficiently comparable to the subject company under valuation. There are a lot of things that we need to think about, such as the following:

Are the companies in the same industry?
Where are they located?
Are their risks similar?
Are their growth expectations similar?
Is their profitability similar?
Are they approximately the same size?
Are their products or services comparable?
Are they competitors?
Are they both standalone companies or do they operate in several sectors? If they operate in several sectors, are those sectors comparable? Is there a sufficient overlap?
Do they have similar capital structures?
Do they use similar levels of operating leverage?
Are their tax rates similar?

These are just a few of the important questions that we might want to ask prior to moving forward with a full-blown comparable valuation analysis (this is called "spreading comps"). Later in the Chapter, when we discuss the Enterprise Value to EBITDA comp, we will show you that there are four key dimensions to finding a good match: (1) growth rate, (2) risk, (3) reinvestment rate, and (4) tax.

These are also the four dimensions that we will use to argue that any given comparable should be adjusted upwards or downwards. For example, if two firms are nearly the same, but one has a higher growth rate in its future cash flows, then it makes sense that the higher growth rate firm should generate more future cash flows and thus be more valuable; consequently, it should trade at a higher multiple of whatever measure we are using (price to sales, for example).

## *Popular comps*

Many different valuation comps are used by practitioners. Some of them are based on sales, others on net earnings or some other measure of profitability (such as EBITDA), and others on the book value of equity. There are many more besides these, but in this chapter, we will focus on those comps that are based on either sales, earnings, EBITDA, or the book value of assets. Remember that the goal of valuation is to arrive at a value that is fair and defensible: an estimate around which you can develop agreement and consensus. Each of the comps that we will be examining can either be used as a standalone valuation metric to give a single-point estimate of value or can be used together with other comps to help us obtain a range for the value we are trying to estimate.

Before we begin, it might be helpful to talk a little bit about the so-called "valid" multiples. A valid multiple is one where the cash flow in the denominator and what we are trying to value in the numerator are in agreement with one another. For example, a very popular comp is based on the price/earnings (P/E) ratio, which is price per share of stock and the earnings that accrue to one share of stock (this can also be calculated as the Market Value of Equity divided by Net Income). The shareholders are the only ones that have a claim to earnings: no one else does. So, it makes sense to compare the price of the equity claim to the cash flow obtained from that same equity claim. In this sense, the P/E multiple is a valid multiple.

But, as you will see in what follows, not all commonly used multiples are theoretically valid; note, that doesn't mean that people don't use them. For example, the multiple of Market Value of Equity/Sales (also known as Price/Sales) is an invalid multiple but is very popular. The numerator is the value of the shareholders' equity. But the denominator is Sales. The shareholders are not the only stakeholders that have a claim to the cash flows that are derived from sales. Debt holders have a claim to Sales that supersedes that of the shareholders, since interest expense is paid before the shareholders get their profit. The preferred stockholders (if there are any) also have a claim to Sales that supersedes that of equity holders, since preferred dividends get paid out prior to determining net income. The equity holders get what is left of sales, after all the costs, interests, taxes, and preferred dividends are subtracted. So, in this case, the numerator, Market Value of Equity, which is the value of the equity claim, and the denominator, Sales, which is a cash flow that is available to all capital providers, not just the equity holders, are not in agreement with one another. The Price/Sales ratio, even though it is extremely popular and used widely (especially for valuing service and software companies), is not theoretically a valid ratio (as it will cause distortions in comparable value for companies that have different capital and cost structures).

### *The last 12 months — LTM*

All of the comparables that we will be discussing, except for one (the market-to-book comp), compare either equity or enterprise value to the last 12 months (LTM) of a particular cash flow (either sales, EBITDA, or earnings). Getting the last 12 months' numbers is important in order to maintain consistency across our comps. Unfortunately, only the Form 10-K and the annual report present 12-month results for the income statement. The quarterly 10-Q report presents only (1) the income statement from the previous quarter and (2) the year-to-date (YTD) income statement. So, if we were in June, for example, the 10-Q would present the 3-month income statement for quarter two (April, May, and June) and the 6 months' YTD income statement from January to June. Unless we are lucky and happen to be valuing the firm at the end of the year, we are going to have to find some way to get the LTM results, since the most recent income statement will not provide the information that we require.

Be very careful when relying on information that comes from a 10-Q. This statement, unlike the 10-K, is not audited. So, if firms can legally take advantage of a generous accounting interpretation of a rule, they are likely to do it on a 10-Q rather than a 10-K. For example, you will notice that 10-Q reports tend to be relatively terse; that is, they don't really contain a lot of footnotes or special line items. In contrast, the annual report does often contain these things.

Again, if we are doing the valuation at the end of the firm's fiscal year, then getting LTM results is easy: all we need is the most recent annual report or 10-K, since it will give us the income statement for the current year. But, if we are doing the valuation at some other point in time, then getting a reasonable estimate for the LTM is a little more complicated, but still not all that difficult if you are using Excel to do your analysis. Follow these easy steps:

Let's say we are interested in getting the LTM estimate for Sales, and we are currently in the middle of July 2020. Our goal is to obtain the firm's sales from July 1, 2019 to June 30, 2020 and we can obtain it through the following steps:

1. Obtain the most recent annual report or 10-K and record the sales from January 1, 2019 to December 31, 2019. This will give us 12 months' worth of Sales.
2. Obtain the most recent financial statement. Since we are in July, it will be the 2nd quarter's 10-Q that comes out at the end of June. Go to the YTD results (not the quarterly results!), and again locate the cash flow that is of interest to us (in this case Sales). This will give us *this* year's

YTD sales, or the 6 months' worth of sales from January 1, 2020 to June 30, 2020.

3. Add the results of Step 1 to Step 2. This will give us the last 18 months', or a year and a half's, worth of sales from January 1, 2019 to June 30, 2020.
4. Go back to the most recent 10-Q. Obtain *last* year's 6-month YTD results for Sales from January 1, 2019 to June 30, 2019.
5. Subtract the results from Step 4 from the results obtained from Step 3. This will give us a last 12 months' estimate from July 1, 2019 through June 30, 2020. Exactly what we wanted! Perfect.

For example, we wanted the LTM revenue for a firm where the 2019 annual income statement reported $100MM in revenue, the June 2020 10-Q reports $40MM in revenue for YTD 2020, and $30MM in revenue for YTD 2019, the LTM revenue from July 1, 2019 to June 30, 2020 would be $110MM, as shown in the following table:

**LTM Example**

| | Revenue *(in MM)* |
|---|---|
| 2019 (10-K) | $100 |
| YTD 2020 (Q1 & Q2) | $40 |
| Sub-Total | $140 |
| less: YTD 2019 (Q1 & Q2) | ($30) |
| | $110 |

## *Using run-rate cash flows — how to scrub the numbers*

The market approach argues that market participants should be willing to buy and sell an asset at a price that is a fair multiple of a given LTM cash flow (it could be sales, EBITDA, or net income, for example). Thus, for any multiple to yield a reasonable price estimate, the cash flow upon which we are basing our calculation should be reliable and reproducible from year to year and should be the baseline upon which future forecasts are made. In other words, the baseline cash flow should not include any one-time charges or windfalls, since these will distort the cash flow in the current period but will not affect the cash flow as we move forward in time. This reliable and reproducible level of cash flow is called the *run-rate* cash flow; thus, there are run-rate sales, run-rate EBITDA, run-rate earnings, etc. If the reported cash flow differs from what we think should be the run-rate cash flow (say for example, because of a one-time impairment of inventory, which would negatively affect EBITDA and net income, but not sales), then we have to *scrub* the reported numbers to remove any one-time charges or windfalls that might distort the reported number from what should be the *run rate* number. We scrub the numbers by adding back in any unusual one-time charges and subtracting out any one-time windfall gains (revenues or income).

How do we spot unusual items? Both the 10-K and the 10-Q report several years of information. If a line item appears on the income statement for only 1 year, then chances are that it will be an unusual and non-recurring item, because it only happened once in the last several periods. Be careful to keenly examine the Management Discussion and Analysis (MD&A) section, along with the Footnotes to the financial reports, because unusual, non-recurring items are not always carved out separately as individual line items. Very often, though, the non-recurring items are like hidden bombs in the MD&A section, along with the Footnotes. For example, MD&A might say that the firm had a $10MM asset impairment because the firm's inventory was obsolete. This $10MM loss is definitely (we hope) non-recurring, so you should add the $10MM back into EBITDA.

When getting LTM run rate numbers, we also have to worry about things like acquisitions and divestitures. If either of these happened within the last 12 months, then there is a very good chance that the reported financial statements may not allow us to obtain accurate LTM results.

For example, in the United States, acquisitions and divestitures are accounted for using the Purchase Accounting method. That means that the acquirer (Firm A) is entitled to claim all of the target's (Firm T) net income as of the date of the acquisition. So, if the acquisition happened on January 1, 2019, then there is no problem to worry about, since the consolidated annual income statement reported on December 31, 2019 will reflect a full year's worth of the merged firm's (AT) profits, thus the LTM numbers will be correct. But, what if the acquisition happened on July 1, 2019 instead of at the beginning of the year? Now we have a problem. In this case, the December 31, 2019 consolidated income statement will still reflect a full year's worth of Firm A's net income but will only reflect 6 months' worth of Firm T's net income and only 6 months' worth of synergies between the two firms. That is, the consolidated income statement for Firm AT might tremendously understate what really should be the run rate LTM numbers.

We need to fix this. So, how do we scrub the numbers to account for an acquisition? If we are doing the valuation at the end of the acquirer's fiscal year (December 31, 2019), then it is relatively easy; in this case, we would:

1. Start with the income statement reported on the most recent 10-K.
2. Scrub the item that is of interest (let's say that for this example that item is EBITDA). This will give us not only the LTM EBITDA for Firm A, but will also include the EBITDA and any synergies obtained from Firm T from June to December.
   a. We still need to calculate the other 6 months (January–June) of EBITDA from Firm T plus related synergies.
3. To get the rest of Firm T's EBITDA, we have to obtain Firm T's financials for January 1, 2019 through June 30, 2019 and scrub that EBITDA. Note, these financials can be very difficult to obtain sometimes, in which case we have to use our best judgment to estimate what the EBITDA should have been.
4. Determine the synergies that the combined Firm AT might have hypothetically enjoyed over the period January 1, 2019 through June 30, 2019.
   a. Getting an estimate for this can sometimes be very challenging, but it is important that we make a genuine attempt to estimate it.
   b. If the firm's sales are not seasonal, then it is reasonable to assume that the synergies obtained from January–June are equal to those obtained from July–December.
5. The last step is to add the results of Step 3 and Step 4 to the results from Step 2 in order to obtain an estimate for the LTM EBITDA for the combined Firm AT.

In the last example, we were lucky. We happened to be doing the valuation at the end of the firm's fiscal year. Usually, that isn't the case, and we are doing the valuation at some point in the year other than at the end of the firm's fiscal year.

Let's say that we wanted to do it on April 1, 2020. In this case, getting the LTM results for the combined firm can get a little messy, since the most recent financial statement is a 10-Q and not a 10-K, and Firm AT has existed for 9 months and not a whole year, since it was acquired in July of 2019. In this case:

1. Use the firm AT's financial statements to calculate the LTM (April 1, 2019 through March 31, 2020) EBITDA.
   a. Note that this will include 12 months of Firm A's contribution to EBITDA and 9 months of Firm T's contribution to EBITDA and its associated synergies.
   b. We still need 3 months (from April 1, 2019 to June 30, 2019) of Firm T's EBITDA and synergies.
2. Obtain Firm T's LTM EBITDA from April 1, 2019–June 30, 2019.
3. Determine the synergies that the combined Firm AB might have hypothetically enjoyed over the period April 1, 2019 through June 30, 2019.
4. Add the results from Steps 1, 2, and 3 in order to get an LTM estimate for the EBITDA of the combined Firm AT.

Dealing with a divestiture is the mirror image of dealing with an acquisition. To accomplish this, you would use the same methodology outlined above for an acquisition, with the difference being that rather than adding the missing cash flow and synergy, you subtract them.

## Market Approach Comps

### *Comps that are based on sales*

Now that we know how to get LTM numbers, we will begin our discussion of the market approach with the comparable that is based on the ratio of the Market Value of Equity to Sales, also known as the Price-to-Sales ratio. As we mentioned above, this ratio really isn't technically a "valid" ratio, but its intuitiveness and ease of use make it extremely popular. This approach can be very useful if a firm has negative EBITDA and is especially popular when valuing firms such as service firms and software companies that don't have a lot of inventory or fixed assets; that is, most of their costs are variable ones that tend to grow proportionately with increases in sales.

### *Price/sales*

Application of a well-chosen Price/Sales comp will give us a direct estimate of the market value of equity. Using the Price/Sales comp, or any comp for that matter, is very easy. Our goal is to find a reasonable estimate of what we think a buyer would be willing to pay for the firm. So, if we want to use the market approach, we will find a similar firm (or better yet, find similar *firms* to get a better understanding of the range of price/sales ratios that exist for firms similar to ours) and calculate the ratio of its Market Value of Equity to Sales, where the Market Value of Equity is given as follows:

$$\text{Market value of equity} = (\text{Price per share}) \times (\text{Number of shares outstanding})$$

We then divide this Market Value of Equity by the LTM of Sales — see the section above for an explanation of how to get LTM numbers — in order to get an estimate for the Price/Sales comparable multiple.

Let's try it. We have been hired to value a gaming software company that currently has about $40MM in revenue and is thinking about going public in an initial public offering. Since IPOs involve the sale of lots of minority shares, we decide to use a Trading Comp, rather than a Precedent Transaction Comp. To that end, we scour the market for a reasonable comparable firm and find one that has 20MM shares outstanding at a current trading price of $15.00 per share. It also has LTM Revenues of $50MM. Let's solve for its Price/Sales multiple. The Market Value of Equity for the comparable firm is as follows:

$$\text{Market value of equity} = (20\text{MM shares})\left(\frac{\$15}{\text{Share}}\right) = \$300\text{MM}$$

So, the Price/Sales ratio for this firm is as follows:

$$\frac{\text{Price}}{\text{Sales}} = \frac{\$300\text{MM}}{\$50\text{MM}} = 6\times$$

Once we have this number, 6x, for the comparable firm, then we aren't done yet! We still have to make a value judgment about whether the multiple of 6x is a fair one. Does the gaming software firm that we are trying to value have qualities that make it more valuable than the comparable firm? Say, perhaps less risky? If so, then we might adjust the Price/Sales multiple upwards. But, if there are qualities that should make it less valuable than the comparable firm (e.g., a slightly lower growth rate), then we might want to adjust the multiple downwards. Let's assume, for now, that the comparable firm is an extremely good match, so that no adjustment is needed. In this case, using the Price/Sales comparable, a reasonable estimate for the value of our gaming software company is as follows:

$$\text{Equity} = (6)(\$40\text{MM}) = \$240\text{MM}$$

## *Price/sales — a few things to consider*

There are a few additional things to think about when using a Price/Sales comparable multiple. First, make sure that we are looking at *net revenues, rather than gross revenues.* See Chapter 3, on the Income Statement, for a discussion about the difference between these two things.

If the comparable firm is using gross revenues and we are using net revenues for our target company, then our valuation will be biased. We recommend that you always use net revenue. Also, be careful if something called *deferred revenue* appears on the firm's balance sheet as a liability. The Price/Sales comp is popular for valuing service and software companies, and it is very common for software and service companies to sell their services on a subscription basis, where the subscription is paid for in one large lump sum. If the subscription payment is made every year, then there won't likely be a problem, since our LTM revenue calculation will likely catch it. But, if the subscription payment is made, say, as a lump sum once every 2 or 3 years, then there could be a major problem between what the revenues actually should be and what is stated on the income statement. See the section on the income statement for a discussion of this issue.

## *EV/sales — Enterprise value to sales*

A slightly less used, but still reasonably popular spin on the Price/Sales multiple approach (which values equity directly), is to use enterprise value, rather than equity, in the calculation. Thus, it is an EV/Sales multiple. The EV/Sales comp will give us a direct estimate of the firm's enterprise value, from which we will subtract out preferred stock and net debt in order to obtain an estimate of the firm's equity. Unlike the Price/Sales ratio, which is not a technically valid multiple, the EV/Sales ratio is a valid multiple, since Enterprise Value is the market value of all the financial claims against the firm, and Sales is a cash flow from which all the financial claim holders (interest, preferred dividends, and net profit) will ultimately be paid.

The application of this multiple to obtain an estimate for Enterprise Value is similar to the application of the Price/Sales comparable to obtain an estimate for the value of equity. We find a similar firm and calculate the ratio of its Enterprise Value to Sales, where Enterprise Value is calculated as the Market Value of Equity plus Preferred Stock plus Net Debt, and Sales is calculated as LTM Net Revenues. Then, we take this EV/ Sales multiple and multiply it by our target's LTM Revenues (Sales) in order to obtain an estimate for its Enterprise Value. Once we have that, then we will subtract out the preferred stock and the net debt in order to obtain an estimate for the value of the firm's equity.

For example, let's continue using the previous software gaming company that we priced using the Price/Sales comp. To refresh your memory, we were hired to value a gaming software company that currently has about $40MM in revenue. The company is thinking about going public in an initial public offering, so we will be using a Trading comp, rather than a Precedent Transaction comp, to obtain a price estimate. We talk to the management team and learn that the firm has $25MM in preferred stock, $120MM in debt, and $20MM in excess cash.

We will use the same comparable firm, which was an excellent match, as in the Price/Sales example. The comparable firm has 20MM shares outstanding at a current trading price of $15.00 per share. The firm also has $150MM in debt, $50MM in preferred stock, and $30MM in cash. It also has LTM Revenues of $50MM. The important information is summarized in the following table:

**EV/Sales Example**

| | **Comparable Firm** | **Target Firm** |
|---|---|---|
| LTM Revenue | $50MM | $40MM |
| MV Equity | $300MM | ? |
| Debt | $150MM | $120MM |
| Preferred Stock | $50MM | $25MM |
| Cash | $30MM | $20MM |

Steps to price our target firm's equity:

1. Calculate the enterprise value of the comparable firm.

   EV = MV(equity) + Debt + Preferred stock – Cash
   EV = MV(equity) + Net debt + Preferred stock
   $EV_{comp}$ = \$300MM + \$120MM + \$50MM = \$470MM

2. Divide this enterprise value by the comparable firm's LTM Sales to obtain a comparable EV/Sales multiple.

   $$\frac{EV}{Sales_{comp}} = \frac{\$470MM}{\$50MM} = 9.4\times$$

3. Multiply the target firm's revenues by the comparable EV/Sales multiple to get an estimate of the target firm's enterprise value.

   $EV_{target}$ = (9.4)(\$40MM) = \$376MM

4. Subtract out preferred stock and net debt from the target's enterprise value in order to get an estimate for the value of its equity.

   $MV(equity)_{target}$ = EV – Net debt – Preferred stock
   $MV(equity)_{target}$ = \$376MM – \$100MM – 25MM = \$251MM

### *Comparables based on the market-to-book value of equity*

Another commonly used comparable is based on the ratio of the Market Value of Equity to the Book Value of Equity, also called the *Market-to-Book* ratio or the *Price to Book* ratio.

$$\frac{M}{B} = \frac{\text{Market value of equity}}{\text{Book value of equity}}$$

The market-to-book ratio measures what the market is willing to pay for a firm's equity relative to what the accountants report that equity to be worth. A relatively low M/B ratio (especially if the firm's assets are of high quality and the firm's cash flow is solid and reliable) could be a signal that the firm is potentially undervalued and might be a good deal for investors. Be careful though, a very low M/B ratio might also signify just the opposite: the firm may be experiencing difficulties and could possibly be heading into financial distress. Do your homework, so you don't get any nasty surprises. In contrast, high M/B ratios are usually associated with glamour stocks — the darlings of Wall Street. These stocks have a very high price relative to the book value of their equity, which means that the market is optimistic about their future. Be careful though. High M/B stocks are perceived by some investors to be potentially overvalued. Our job is to find a comparable firm that we believe should trade at the same M/B ratio as would our firm, so be careful if a firm you are analyzing has a very low or very high M/B multiple. We need to be sure that our comp is actually a good one.

Using the M/B multiple for comparable valuation is very straight forward:

1. Find a comparable firm.
2. Calculate the Market Value of its Equity by multiplying the number of shares outstanding by the price per share.
3. Divide this Market Value of Equity by the Book Value of Equity reported on its most recent financial statement to get an estimate of its M/B ratio.
4. Make a value judgment as to whether and why our target firm is more or less valuable than the comparable firm. Make adjustments if necessary.
5. Multiply the comparable M/B multiple by the target firm's most recently reported book value of equity in order to obtain an estimate for what should be the target's market value.

Here is an example. Assume that our target firm has 5MM shares outstanding and we want to obtain an estimate for both the value of its equity and its price per share. We search carefully and find a comparable firm that has 10MM shares outstanding at a price of $10 per share. The comparable firm has a book value of equity of $80MM.

**M/B Example**

| | Comparable Firm | Target Firm |
|---|---|---|
| MV Equity | $100MM | ? |
| BV Equity | $80MM | $70MM |

So, let's follow our procedure:

1. Find a comparable firm. Done!
2. Calculate the Market Value of its Equity.

   MV(Equity) = ($10 per share)(10MM shares) = $100MM

3. Divide this Market Value of Equity by the Book Value of Equity reported on its most recent financial statement to get an estimate of its M/B ratio.

$$\frac{M}{B} = \frac{\$100MM}{\$80MM} = 1.25\times$$

4. Make a value judgment as to whether and why our target firm is more or less valuable than the comparable firm. Let's assume that the comparable firm is a great match, so no adjustment is needed.
5. Multiply the comparable M/B multiple by the target firm's most recently reported book value of equity.

   MV(Equity) = (1.25)($70MM) = $87.5MM

And to get an estimate for the price of the stock, we would divide the $87.5MM by the number (5MM) of the target's shares outstanding.

$$\text{Price per share} = \frac{\$87.5MM}{5MM} = \$17.50 \text{ per share}$$

## *Comparables based on the price-to-earnings multiple*

Another popular, and widely used, valuation multiple is the venerable price/earnings ratio, also known as the P/E ratio. The P/E multiple can either be expressed as follows:

$$\frac{P}{E} = \frac{\text{Price per share of stock}}{\text{Earnings per share of stock}}$$

or as follows:

$$\frac{P}{E} = \frac{\text{Market value of equity}}{\text{LTM net income}}$$

The P/E multiple is a gauge of how optimistic the market is about a firm's future earning power. A high P/E multiple means that the market is optimistic about the firm's future. The opposite is true for firms with low P/E multiples. Here is an example that will help us to get a better understanding of the optimism.

Junior's Rock and Bowl's stocks cost $10 per share and the firm currently generates $1 in annual profit. Thus, it has a P/E ratio of 10x. Julietta's Bowlarama's stocks cost $15 per share and also generate $1 in annual profit. Julietta's P/E ratio is 15x. Why would the market pay 1.5x more per dollar of Julietta's earnings than they would per dollar of Junior's? Perhaps the market believes that Julietta's Bowlarama will be generating a lot more earnings in the future than will Junior's Rock and Bowl, and that is why the market is willing to pay a premium for it today. Be careful: a high P/E multiple could also mean that the firm is a glamour stock and that it is potentially overvalued.

When finding a comparable P/E multiple, we have to be very careful to ensure that the comparable firm's earnings have not been manipulated in some fashion (perhaps through the use of accruals, misstating doubtful receivables, or some other earnings management tool) to make the firm look like it is performing better than is actually the case. Note, we also have to make sure that not only does the comparable firm have good earnings quality (that means that their reported earnings accurately reflect the real earnings), but also that our target firm is accurately reporting earnings. If either firm is misstating earnings, then this method will yield inaccurate results.

The nice thing about using a P/E multiple is that it allows us to obtain a direct estimate for the value of a firm's equity and it is widely used by investment and portfolio managers, so it is fairly easy to explain to a client. In fact, chances are that they will already have heard of this multiple. Like all the other comps we will be discussing, the P/E multiple can be used either as a trading or transaction comp.

Using the P/E multiple to value equity is just as easy as it is to use any of the other multiples that we have discussed:

1. Find a comparable firm.
2. Calculate the Market Value of its Equity.
3. Divide it by the firm's LTM of Net Income.
4. Make a value judgment as to whether and why our target firm is more or less valuable than the comparable firm. Make adjustments if necessary.

5. Multiply the comparable P/E multiple by the target firm's FTM net income to obtain an estimate for the target's stock price.

Let's do an example. Uncle Joe's Bowlaplex is interested in getting an estimate for the value of its equity. Its LTM of net income is $5MM. Following our procedure…

1. Find a comparable firm.

We scour the market for comps and find Junior's Rock and Bowl and Julietta's Bowlarama. Junior's has a P/E multiple of 10x and Julietta's has one of 15x. After interviewing Uncle Joe and the rest of his management team, we learn that Uncle Joe is looking to aggressively expand his Bowlaplex brand, similar to the way in which Julietta has grown the Bowlarama. Consequently, we believe that Julietta's Bowlarama might be a good comp for Uncle Joe's Bowlaplex. We will completely ignore Junior's Rock and Bowl, since it is not a growth company and after doing our due diligence, we learn that the firm has no plans for further expansion.

2. Calculate the Market Value of Julietta's Equity.

Julietta's Bowlarama trades at $15 per share.

3. Divide it by Julietta's LTM Net Income.

The firm's LTM net income is $1, so its P/E ratio is 15x.

4. Make a value judgment as to whether and why our target firm is more or less valuable than the comparable firm.

We think that Julietta's and Uncle Joe's are comparable to one another, so we will not be making any adjustments because we do not think that they are needed. Consequently, we will use a P/E multiple of 15× to value the Bowlaplex.

5. Multiply the comparable P/E multiple by the Bowlaplex's LTM net income to obtain an estimate for its stock price.

Uncle Joe's Bowlaplex has $5MM in LTM net income. So, if we multiply $5MM by a multiple of 15x, we obtain the following estimate for the value of the equity of Uncle Joe's Bowlaplex:

$$\text{Market value of equity} = (\$5\text{MM})(15\text{x}) = \$75\text{MM}$$

And if the Bowlaplex has, for example, 10MM shares outstanding, then the estimated value of his price per share would be as follows:

$$\text{Price per share} = \frac{\$75\text{MM}}{10\text{MM}} = \$7.50 \text{ per share}$$

Note that the P/E multiple can also be used (and is very often used) as a "forward" P/E multiple; that means that we calculate the forward P/E ratio by taking the comparable firm's current stock price and dividing it by the firm's next year's predicted earnings. Then, we would use this forward P/E multiple by multiplying it by the target firm's 1-year forward forecasted earnings (rather than LTM earnings) in order to obtain a future price estimate.

## Comparables Based on Enterprise Value to EBITDA

The last valuation multiple we will examine — although there are many more that you might encounter — is the EV/EBITDA multiple, which is arguably the most important and among the most widely used for business valuation. See Chapter 3, on the Income Statement, for a detailed discussion of EBITDA. Most of the deals that we (the authors in our professional capacity) have done have ultimately closed around a negotiated value that was based on an EV/EBITDA comparable. EBITDA provides a relatively clean representation of the operating profitability of a company, since it excludes non-cash costs like depreciation and amortization, and non-operating items such as interest expense and taxes; that means that using EBITDA makes it easier for us to compare companies without having to worry about confounding differences attributable to capital structure, tax domiciles, and the way in which we account for assets.

The problem with EBITDA, however, is that it ignores capital expenditures and increases in working capital, both of which can be substantial uses of cash. This means that when we use an EV/EBITDA multiple to value firms with a lot of capital expenditures or year after year increases in working capital, this market valuation metric will tend to overstate the true value of the firm. Also, when scrubbing EBITDA, please be mindful that sometimes accountants choose to bundle depreciation in with Cost of Goods Sold and amortization in with Selling, General and Administrative Expenses. Please be careful, as most firms have at least some depreciation or amortization. So, if you don't see either of these on the income statement, always be sure to check the statement of cash flows. The information about depreciation and amortization that appears on the statement of cash flows will dominate that found on the income statement for the purposes of calculating LTM EBITDA.

The EV/EBITDA comp will give us a direct estimate of the firm's enterprise value, from which we will subtract out preferred stock and net debt in order to obtain an indirect estimate of the firm's equity. Similar to the EV/Sales ratio, the EV/EBITDA ratio is a valid multiple, since enterprise value is the market value of all the financial claims against the firm, and EBITDA is a cash flow from which all the financial claim holders (interest, preferred dividends, and net profit) will ultimately be paid.

The EV/EBITDA multiple can be applied in the same way as the EV/Sales multiple to obtain an estimate for the value of equity:

1. Find a comparable firm.
2. Calculate its Enterprise Value, where Enterprise Value is calculated as the Market Value of Equity plus Preferred Stock plus Net Debt.
3. Calculate its LTM EBITDA, where LTM EBITDA is calculated as LTM EBIT plus LTM Depreciation and LTM Amortization.
4. Calculate the comparable EV/EBITDA multiple by dividing the results of Step 2 by the results of Step 3.
5. Calculate our target firm's LTM EBITDA.
6. Multiply the target's LTM EBITDA by the comparable EV/EBITDA multiple; that is, multiply the results of Step 4 by the results of Step 5 to obtain an estimate of the target firm's enterprise value.
7. Subtract out the target firm's Preferred Stock and the Net Debt in order to obtain an estimate for the value of the target's Equity.

For example, let's use the same software gaming company that we priced using the Price/Sales and the EV/Sales comps. To refresh your memory, we were hired to value a gaming software company that currently has about $40MM in LTM Revenue and $25MM in LTM EBITDA. The company is thinking about going public in an initial public offering, so we will be using a Trading comp, rather than a Precedent Transaction comp, to obtain a price estimate. We talk to the management team and learn that the firm has $25MM in preferred stock, $120MM in debt, and $20MM in cash.

We will use the same comparable firm that we used in the Price/Sales example, which we deemed to be an excellent match. The comparable firm has 20MM shares outstanding at a current trading price of \$15.00 per share. The firm also has \$150MM in debt, \$50MM in preferred stock, and \$30MM in cash. It also has LTM Revenues of \$50MM and LTM EBITDA of \$37MM. The important information is summarized in the following table:

**EV/EBITDA Example**

| | Comparable Firm | Target Firm |
|---|---|---|
| LTM Revenue | \$50MM | \$40MM |
| LTM EBITDA | \$37MM | \$25MM |
| MV Equity | \$300MM | ? |
| Debt | \$150MM | \$120MM |
| Preferred Stock | \$50MM | \$25MM |
| Cash | \$30MM | \$20MM |

Steps using the EV/EBITDA multiple to price our target firm's equity:

1. Calculate the enterprise value of the comparable firm.

   $$EV = MV(\text{equity}) + \text{Debt} + \text{Preferred stock} - \text{Cash}$$
   $$EV = MV(\text{equity}) + \text{Net debt} + \text{Preferred stock}$$
   $$EV_{comp} = \$300MM + \$120MM + \$50MM = \$470MM$$

2. Divide this enterprise value by the comparable firm's LTM EBITDA to obtain a comparable EV/EBITDA multiple.

   $$\frac{EV}{Sales_{comp}} = \frac{\$470MM}{\$37MM} = 12.7\times$$

3. Multiply the target firm's EBITDA by the comparable EV/EBITDA multiple to get an estimate of the target firm's enterprise value.

   $$EV_{target} = (12.7)(\$25MM) = \$317.5MM$$

4. Subtract out preferred stock and net debt from the target's enterprise value in order to get an estimate for the value of its equity.

$MV(equity)_{target}$ = EV – Net debt – Preferred stock
$MV(equity)_{target}$ = \$317.50MM – \$100MM – 25MM = \$176.5MM

Our estimate for the market value of equity using the EV/EBITDA multiple comps is \$176.5MM.

## Application of the Market Approach to Alpha Brewing Company

Now let's use the EV/EBITDA method to value our Alpha Brewing Company example:

**Brewery EV/EBITDA Example**

| | **Andrew's Pale Ales** | **B&B's Boston Brews** | **Kelly's Malt Lagers** | **Alpha Brewing Co.** |
|---|---|---|---|---|
| LTM Revenue | \$1,700,000 | \$2,387,500 | \$2,955,000 | \$1,829,520 |
| LTM EBITDA | \$825,000 | \$955,000 | \$985,000 | \$611,473 |
| MV Equity | \$9,100,000 | \$12,950,000 | \$14,250,000 | ? |
| Debt | \$420,000 | \$650,000 | \$775,000 | \$483,888 |
| Preferred Stock | \$100,000 | \$200,000 | \$0 | \$0 |
| Cash | \$120,000 | \$50,000 | \$300,000 | \$266,507 |
| EV | \$9,500,000 | \$13,750,000 | \$14,725,000 | ? |
| EV/EBITDA | 11.52x | 14.40x | 14.95x | ? |
| EV/EBITDA Average | **13.62x** | | | |

| **Alpha Brewing's EV & MV of Equity** | |
|---|---|
| LTM EBITDA | \$611,473 |
| Comp Average EV/EBITDA | 13.62x |
| Target Firm's EV | \$8,328,263 |
| Preferred Stock | \$0 |
| Net Debt | \$217,381 |
| Target Firm's MV of Equity | **\$8,110,882** |

AB's LTM EBITDA = $526,467 (2019 EBIT) + $85,006 (2019 Dep & Amort) = $611,473.

Let's assume that we are looking to determine the value of Alpha Brewing Company's equity on January 1, 2020 and that we have found three solid comps for Alpha Brewing: Andrew's Pale Ales, B&B's Boston Brews, and Kelly's Malt Lagers. The average EV/EBITDA ratio for these three firms is 13.62x, and we will use this as an initial estimate of what the market might be willing to pay for Alpha Brewery's EBITDA. Since Alpha has $611,473 in EBITDA, the implied enterprise value is $611,473 times 13.62, which equals $8,328,263. If we take out the net debt, which is $217,381, we arrive at an equity value estimate of $8,110,882.

## *The four drivers of value in an EV/EBITDA multiple valuation*

The goal of this section is to help you better understand the four drivers of value when using the EV/EBITDA methodology: (1) growth, (2) taxes, (3) risk, and (4) reinvestment. As you will see, these are the characteristics that we need to match in order to find a good comparable firm. They are also the dimensions on which we can argue for more or less value when we are negotiating price with a buyer or seller.

Anytime we do a market valuation that is based on an EV/EBITDA multiple — or any multiple for that matter — we are implicitly assuming that the characteristics of the cash flow generating process for that firm will be similar to that of the comparable firm. For example, if we are using an EV/EBITDA multiple, then we would try to find a comparable firm whose EBITDA is growing at a rate that is similar to that of the firm we are trying to price.

In these next few paragraphs, we will derive the EV/EBITDA multiple from the basic principles of the income-based approach to valuing enterprise value. Bear with us as we slog through this derivation — we don't want you to lose the forest for the trees. Our goal here is to have you understand where the EV/EBITDA multiple comes from and what the factors are that impact its value. We didn't just pull the four factors out of our hats.

Let's begin with enterprise value. We have learned that enterprise value is the market value of the financial claims against the firm; that is, what it would literally cost you out of pocket to purchase the firm.

Recall that:

$$\text{EV} = \text{Market value of equity} + \text{Preferred stock} + \text{Debt} - \text{Excess cash}$$

To keep this derivation simple, let's assume that the business is growing its unlevered free cash flow at a constant rate. If that is the case, then we learned in the income approach section that we can price the firm's enterprise value as follows:

$$\text{EV} = \frac{\text{UFCF}(1+g)}{\text{WACC}-g}$$

where:

UFCF = This year's Unlevered Free Cash Flow,
WACC = Weighted Average Cost of Capital, and
$g$ = Annual growth rate of the unlevered free cash flows.

So, if the current UFCF can be written as follows:

$$\text{UFCF} = \text{EBITDA} - \text{Tax(EBIT)} - \text{Capex} - \Delta\text{WC}$$

Then, if we substitute:

$$\text{EBIT} = \text{EBITDA} - \text{Dep} - \text{Amort}$$

into the previous equation, we get the following:

$$\text{UFCF} = \text{EBITDA} - \text{Tax(EBITDA} - \text{Dep} - \text{Amort)} - \text{Capex} - \Delta\text{WC}$$

We insert this into the Gordon Growth equation to get

$$\text{EV} = \frac{(1+g)\left[\text{EBITDA} - \text{Tax}\left(\text{EBITDA} - \text{Dep} - \text{Amort}\right) - \text{Capex} - \Delta\text{WC}\right]}{\text{WACC}-g}$$

Dividing both sides of the equation by EBITDA yields the following:

$$\frac{\text{EV}}{\text{EBITDA}} = \frac{(1+g)\left[1 - \text{Tax} + \text{Tax}\left(\dfrac{\text{Dep} + \text{Amort}}{\text{EBITDA}}\right) - \dfrac{\text{Capex}}{\text{EBITDA}} - \dfrac{\Delta\text{WC}}{\text{EBITDA}}\right]}{\text{WACC} - g}$$

Simplifying this equation (yeah, we know, it is still a mess) yields a representation for the EV/EBITDA multiple, as follows:

$$\frac{\text{EV}}{\text{EBITDA}} = \frac{(1+g)\left[1 - \text{Tax}(1 - \left(\dfrac{\text{Dep} + \text{Amort}}{\text{EBITDA}}\right) - \dfrac{\text{Capex}}{\text{EBITDA}} - \dfrac{\Delta\text{WC}}{\text{EBITDA}}\right]}{\text{WACC} - g}$$

It is a little complicated-looking, but we can still learn a lot from examining this relationship. Don't let the number of different parts throw you off. This equation shows that there are four factors that impact the value of the EV/EBITDA multiple: (1) growth, (2) tax, (3) risk, and (4) reinvestment. Let's examine how each of these factors impacts the EV/EBITDA multiple.

We will begin with **Growth**. Growth is represented by $\boldsymbol{g}$ in the equation. The higher the growth rate, the higher will be the firm's terminal value. The higher the terminal value, the more we will be willing to pay for the firm. We know that $g$ appears in both the numerator and the denominator of the fraction, but, believe us, if you increase $g$, then the fraction will always go up in value. For those of you that have had calculus, the derivative of the EV/EBITDA multiple with respect to $g$ is everywhere positive.

The next factor is **Tax**. As long as the sum of depreciation and amortization is less than the firm's EBITDA (which is very often the case), then increasing the tax rate should decrease the value of the EV/EBITDA multiple. This makes intuitive sense, since if we increase the tax rate, then the firm will pay more tax and consequently have lower unlevered free cash flow.

**Risk** is the next factor that affects the EV/EBITDA multiple. The factor that represents risk is the weighted average cost of capital (WACC). The riskier the firm, the higher will be its WACC. The higher the WACC, the lower will be the present value of the future cash flows, and hence the lower will be the firm's price. The derivative of the EV/EBITDA multiple with respect to the WACC is everywhere negative. The higher the risk, the lower the EV/EBITDA multiple.

The final factor is **reinvestment**, as measured by capital expenditures and changes in working capital. Both of these expenses are uses of funds and have the effect of reducing unlevered free cash flow. So, all other things held equal, firms that have to reinvest a greater percentage of their funds into CAPEX or changes in working capital should trade at a lower EV/EBITDA multiple.

To summarize, relative to our comparable firm, the target firm's EV/EBITDA multiple should be higher if it has:

1. A higher terminal growth rate
2. Lower capital expenditures and working capital requirements relative to its EBITDA
3. Less risk (a lower WACC)
4. Lower tax rates

### *Calibrating the terminal growth rate assumption using the implied EV/EBITDA multiple*

We touched on this somewhat in the last chapter but will present a different spin on it here. One of the most convincing ways to defend your terminal growth rate assumption is by using the EV/EBITDA multiple to calibrate your terminal enterprise value estimate. You have to understand what is and how to use an EV/EBITDA multiple prior to being able to calibrate a terminal growth rate estimate with it.

We can make a very powerful argument in support of our terminal growth rate assumption for the DCF method by showing that the EV/EBITDA multiple that is implied by the terminal growth rate makes sense given what EV/EBITDA multiples are for firms that are similar to the one that we are valuing.

Let us explain by continuing with the numerical example that we used in the last chapter where the WACC is 10% and the terminal growth rate is 3%, which meant that since $UFCF_3$ = \$1,750,000, $UFCF_4$ is \$1,750,000x (1.03) = \$1,802,500, which led to $TV_3$ = \$25,750,000. See the following panel for the calculation.

| Enterprise Value Example | |
|---|---|
| Weighted Average Cost of Capital | 10.00% |
| Terminal growth rate | 3.00% |
| $UFCF_1$ | $1,000,000 |
| $UFCF_2$ | $1,500,000 |
| $UFCF_3$ | $1,750,000 |
| $UFCF_4 = UFCF_3 {*} (1 + g)$ | $1,802,500 |
| $TV_3 = UFCF_4/(WACC–g)$ | $25,750,000 |

To see whether the 3% terminal growth rate is reasonable, we will

1. Determine the firm's EBITDA in year 3, $EBITDA_3$
2. Divide the terminal enterprise value, $TV_3$ by $EBITDA_3$ to get the EV/EBITDA multiple that is implied by our growth rate assumption.

   For example, if the firm had $3MM of EBITDA in year 3, then the implied EV/EBIDTA multiple would be as follows:

$$\frac{EV_3}{EBITDA_3} = \frac{\$25,750,000}{\$3,000,000} = 9.25x$$

3. Compare the 9.25x multiple with that of similar firms that are currently trading in the market. If similar firms are trading in the 9–9.5 range, then our assumption of 3% for a terminal growth rate is well supported. But, if similar firms are trading at EV/EBITDA multiples of around 5x, rather than somewhere around 9.25x, then a growth rate of 3% is probably too high, since it implies too high of a multiple. Alternately, if similar firms are trading at EV/EBITDA multiples around 15x, then the 3% terminal growth rate assumption is too low, since it yields an implied multiple that is just too low relative to that of similar firms.

While being relatively easy, this very powerful and convincing calibration will save you a lot of headaches at the negotiating table.

## Key Takeaways

- The market approach relies upon the value of comparable firms to establish a competitive market price.
- Trading comparables provide an estimate of what should be the value of a minority (or non-controlling) equity stake in the firm. In contrast, precedent transaction comparables provide an estimate of the value if one were to own a controlling equity stake in the firm.
- The key to the successful use of the market approach is to identify companies that are sufficiently comparable to the subject company under valuation.
- Cash flows over the last 12 months (LTM) are commonly used in the market approach to maintain consistency across comparables.
- The baseline cash flow should not include any one-time charges or windfalls since these will distort the cash flow in the current period but will not affect the cash flow as we move forward in time and this reliable and reproducible level of cash is called the *run rate* cash flow.
- A high P/E multiple means that the market is optimistic about the firm's future. The opposite is true for firms with low P/E multiples. High P/E multiple firms are often called glamour stocks and low P/E multiple firms are often called value stocks.
- The EV/EBITDA comparable gives a direct estimate of the firm's enterprise value, from which preferred stock and net debt are subtracted to obtain an indirect estimate of the firm's equity.
- There are four drivers of the EV/EBITDA multiple: growth, risk, taxes, and reinvestment.

# Chapter 11

# The Asset Valuation Approach

The previous two methods of valuation, the market and income approaches, are widely used in the profession. They rely primarily on the firm's income and cash flow statements for their inputs. But, an alternative and also acceptable approach is the asset valuation approach, which is primarily based on the balance sheet. Although perhaps not as popular or as widely used as either the income or market approaches, the asset-based approach should, at the very minimum, at least be considered as a part of any business valuation. In a nutshell, the asset valuation approach calculates the difference between the fair market value of the assets and the firm's liabilities in order to obtain an estimate of the value of the firm's equity.

There are two commonly used asset valuation approaches: the Adjusted Net Asset Valuation Method and the Asset Accumulation Valuation Method. They are similar and, in fact, the two names are often (and erroneously) used synonymously, but the difference lies in the way in which the net assets' fair market value is determined. The Asset Accumulation Method is the harder and more arcane of the two, since it involves the painstaking identification and valuation of each individual category of the company assets (that includes all of the tangible and intangible assets, even the ones that are not reported on the balance sheet). This approach is often employed when a firm does not have a steady history of generating positive profit, is not likely to generate positive profit in the near future, or is in the process of or contemplating liquidation. In contrast, the Adjusted Net Asset Value is often used when the firm is still a going concern, and the method typically does a single, overarching valuation of the entirety of the firm's net assets.

## The Adjusted Net Asset Value Method

We will begin with a discussion of the Adjusted Net Asset Value Method (ANAV) since it is easier to do and more frequently encountered than the Asset Accumulation Method. A good place to start is the company's most recent balance sheet, prepared in accordance with the appropriate accounting standards for your country. Next, we identify any non-operating assets, such as those that are used primarily for the owners' benefits (country club memberships, time-shares, jets, gym memberships, etc.) and ones held for investment reasons, such as investment property and securities. We will be putting these non-operating assets aside for now, because they really don't add very much, if anything, to the going concern value of the firm. Not that they aren't valuable; just that they don't impact the going concern value and we don't expect them to contribute to the firm's operating income.

Next, we will carefully examine the remaining assets and one by one revalue (adjust) them to their current market values. This includes cash and marketable securities (whose market value and book value will likely be identical), accounts receivable, inventory, prepaid assets; any long-run, tangible assets (property, plant, and equipment); identifiable intangible assets (patents, trademarks, copyrights, franchises); and other identifiable assets that might add value (e.g., deferred income taxes and investments).

With respect to revaluing accounts receivable, the most we could ever hope to collect is the invoice amount (customers would not be happy to pay more than what they owe); that is, the market value of a receivable will never be more than the book value. Thus, if none of the accounts receivable are doubtful, then the value that we use for accounts receivable will be equal to the book value. For example, after examining each *individual* account receivable (one by one) we decide that 5% of them may never be collected, then the adjusted value of accounts receivable would be 95% of the book value.

In contrast, the adjusted value of the rest of the firm's assets, like inventory and PP&E, can be significantly higher than their book value. These assets are recorded at the lesser of historical cost or market value; that is, their book value never goes up, it can only go down. Thus, if, for example, the market value of a firm's PP&E tripled, its book value would not change.

So, how would we do this in practice? To obtain the adjusted value of assets like inventory and PP&E, we would do our best to find the current price in the market for each *individual* asset comprising the balance sheet account. For example, if the firm has a thousand different items in inventory, then we have to estimate the current market price for each item in inventory. Same for PP&E; for instance, if we had a parcel of real estate on the books, we would need to call a real estate appraiser to obtain the estimate for its current market value. Imagine how time-consuming this would be if we had seven hundred and eighty parcels of real estate on the books. No fun at all. The potential laboriousness of this process is one of the reasons why the asset approach is less popular than the market or income approaches.

Once we have adjusted the value of each of the individual balance sheet asset accounts, we then sum them up to obtain what is called the firm's *adjusted* operating assets. From these, we will subtract all the non-interest-bearing liabilities, such as accounts payable and accrued liabilities — but not the current portion of long-term debt or notes payable. This difference is called the firm's *adjusted net operating assets* because they are the adjusted operating assets net of the non-financial liabilities. The adjusted net operating assets are those assets that are funded only with debt, preferred stock, and equity and thus have a funding cost associated with them. Another way of saying this is that adjusted net operating assets are those assets that are not free to finance.

Let us explain more fully what we mean by this. Accounts payable and accrued liabilities are non-interest-bearing liabilities: we don't pay explicit interest on them. So, the portion of our total assets funded by these liabilities don't have any explicit interest expense or opportunity cost of equity capital associated with them. They are essentially free to finance. What we need for the Adjusted Net Asset Value Method is the dollar value of assets that are NOT free to finance; that is, total operating assets *net* of accounts payable, accrued liabilities, or any other non-interest-bearing liability.

Thus, an initial estimate of the market value of the firm's equity can be obtained as follows:

$$\text{MV(Equity)} = \text{Adjusted net operating assets} - \text{BV(Debt)}$$

But how good is this estimate? After all, it relies on all the assets actually being reported on the balance sheet. What if there are hidden assets attributed to intangible goodwill (brand, trade secrets, human capital) that were not reported and thus not included in the calculation of our adjusted net operating assets? This associated hidden goodwill, if it were to exist, would certainly increase the value of the equity.

A popular way to capture the value of any hidden intangible assets is to use the *Cumulative Excess Earnings Method*. This value is commonly referred to as the *intangible value in the nature of goodwill*, that is, the value of goodwill that isn't reflected in the financial statements. This additional intangible goodwill component is then added to the adjusted net operating assets in order to obtain an estimate of the firm's *total adjusted net operating assets*. We then subtract out the total debt and preferred stock to obtain an estimate of the value of the firm's equity.

So, in summary, the Adjusted Net Asset Value Method involves doing a complete redetermination of the market value of the firm's net operating assets (one by one) and a Cumulative Excess Earnings Method valuation of any additional business value that might be attributable to the firm's unreported assets. The sum of these two things is the Total Adjusted Net Asset Value. From this, the total debt and preferred stock are subtracted in order to get an estimate for the market value of equity.

## *How to implement the cumulative excess earnings method?*

The intuition behind the Cumulative Excess Earnings Method is that the firm's net assets should generate a fair return on the capital that is used to fund those assets. So, we will compare what the capital tied up in those assets "should" be earning to what it is forecasted to earn. If the adjusted net operating assets are forecasted to earn more than what is required, we say that the firm will generate *Excess Earnings*; that is, there exists hidden value above and beyond that which is represented by the adjusted net operating assets.

So how do we actually do the calculation? We multiply the firm's adjusted net operating assets by a required rate of return (usually the weighted average cost of capital because this is the required return on invested capital) to get an estimate of what should be next year's required earnings on those net operating assets:

$$\text{Required earning}_{t+1} = \text{Adjusted net operating Assets}_t * \text{WACC}$$

We then compare the required earnings to what the firm actually earned. We typically use EBIT as a measure of the actual earnings. Thus:

$$\text{Excess earnings}_{t+1} = \text{EBIT}_{t+1} - (\text{Adjusted net operating assets}_t * \text{WACC})$$

If next year's actual earnings exceed the required earnings, then the company will generate excess earnings. But, why is the firm generating excess earnings? We will answer this question shortly. Let's figure out how to value these excess earnings first.

When we value the excess earnings, we typically make the assumption that the firm will earn these excess earnings every year from now on, so we can take their present value as if we were valuing a zero-growth annuity (i.e., a perpetuity) using the Gordon Growth formula.[1] This present value is called the Cumulative Excess Earnings.

$$\text{Cumulative excess earnings}_t = \frac{\text{Excess earnings}_{t+1}}{\text{WACC}}$$

The Cumulative Excess Earnings is an indicator of the hidden value associated with the unreported *intangible value in the nature of goodwill* for the firm we are valuing; that is, things like brand, human capital, trade secrets, etc. It is these assets that are generating the excess earnings. This *intangible value in the nature of goodwill* is then added to the adjusted net operating assets in order to obtain the total adjusted net operating assets, which is an estimate of the market value of the firm's operating assets that are financed with debt, preferred stock, and equity. Now we are close. One more step and we are done.

Once we have the total adjusted net operating assets, then the market value of equity can be estimated as follows:

$$\begin{aligned}\text{MV(Equity)} &= \text{Total adjusted net operating assets} \\ &\quad - \text{BV (Debt)} - \text{BV (Preferred stock)}\end{aligned}$$

## *Example of using cumulative excess earnings and the adjusted net asset value method*

In the following example, we expect that the firm will generate \$100MM in EBIT next year, and that the firm has a WACC of 10%. Further, we assume that the operating assets have already been revalued (i.e., their value has already been adjusted). Note that it is very common that

[1]Note, you could also assume that these excess earnings will grow at a constant rate, in which case you would use the Gordon Growth formula, but with your growth rate instead of zero growth. Use your judgment and pick which is the most appropriate. The zero-growth method is the most conservative.

adjustments will have to be made when obtaining the market value of adjusted net operating assets, especially for things like fixed assets where the book value and market value may differ substantially, accounts receivable[2] if there are outstanding balances associated with customers that are not likely to pay, inventory that should be impaired or potentially written up in value, and, of course, potential contingent liabilities like lawsuits and unreported legal judgments or settlements.

Non-interest-bearing liabilities, such as accounts payable and accrued liabilities, are never worth more than book value. Contingent liabilities are extremely difficult to price as they are probabilistic in nature and are very often associated with a lack of information. To value these potential liabilities, we often must obtain the advice of legal counsel or other relevant experts as to the likelihood of losing and the potential damages and what might be the spillover effects on future examples. For example, if a patent infringement lawsuit is lost, this could significantly impact future cash flows.

Let's solve an example to better understand the estimate for the market value of the equity, using the Adjusted Net Asset Value method.

The given adjusted Balance Sheet looks as follows:

| **Adjusted Operating Assets** | | **Adjusted Liabilities and Equity** | |
|---|---|---|---|
| Cash | $100 | Accounts Payable | $150 |
| Accounts Receivable | $200 | Accrued Liabilities | $100 |
| Inventory | $250 | Taxes Payable | $100 |
| Pre-paid Expenses | $100 | Long-Term Debt | $350 |
| PP&E | $300 | Equity | $450 |
| Intangibles | $200 | | |
| Adjusted Op. Assets | $1,150 | Adj. Total L&E | $1,150 |

[2] This is especially true if there is no allowance for doubtful receivables or if the allowance is too small. Be sure to check the aging schedule to get a better idea of the quality of the receivables.

| **Required Earnings Calculation** | | **Excess Earnings Calculation** | |
|---|---|---|---|
| Adj. Net Op. Assets | $800 | Next Year's EBIT | $100 |
| WACC | 10% | Required Earnings | ($80) |
| Required Earnings | $80 | Excess Earnings | $20 |

| **Cum. Exc. Earnings Calculation** | |
|---|---|
| Excess Earnings | $20 |
| WACC | 10% |
| Cum. Exc. Earnings | $200 |

The firm has $1,150 in Adjusted Operating Assets and $350 in Adjusted Operating Liabilities (Accounts Payable, Accrued Liabilities, and Taxes Payable), so Adjusted Net Operating Assets is $1,150 – $350 = $800. Since the Weighted Average Cost of Capital is 10%, the Required Earnings are $800 * 0.1 = $80. Next year's EBIT is forecasted to be $100, so the Excess Earnings are $100 – $80 = $20. We make the assumption that these Excess Earnings will continue forever, so their present value can be calculated by taking the present value of a perpetuity, as follows:

$$\text{Cumulative excess earnings}_t = \frac{\text{Excess earnings}_{t+1}}{\text{WACC}} = \frac{\$20}{0.1} = \$200$$

Thus, $200 is our estimate of the Intangible Assets in the Nature of Goodwill.

Now that we know the value of the Intangible Assets in the Nature of Goodwill ($200), we can do the final adjustment to the balance sheet and use it for asset-based valuation purposes. The Adjusted Balance Sheet looks as follows:

| **Adjusted Operating Assets** | | **Adjusted Liabilities and Equity** | |
|---|---|---|---|
| Cash | $100 | Accounts Payable | $150 |
| Accounts Receivable | $200 | Accrued Liabilities | $100 |
| Inventory | $250 | Taxes Payable | $100 |
| Pre-paid Expenses | $100 | Long-Term Debt | $350 |
| PP&E | $300 | Equity | $650 |
| Intangibles | $200 | | |
| Intangible Assets in Nature of Goodwill | $200 | | |
| Adjusted Op. Assets | $1,350 | Adj. Total L&E | $1,350 |

Notice that the Total Adjusted Operating Assets is now $1,350, rather than $1,150. There is $200 of hidden value in Intangible Assets in the Nature of Goodwill that we are now capturing. This means that our market value estimate for the equity ($450) that we obtained by doing the initial market value adjustment of the firm's operating assets and liabilities was too low. It did not include the non-reported value associated with the Intangible Assets in the Nature of Goodwill. A better estimate for the market value of the equity, using the Adjusted Net Asset Value method ($1,350 – $350 – $350), is $650MM.

### *Dealing with "negative goodwill"*

The Adjusted Net Asset Value Method is very intuitive if the firm has positive Intangible Assets in the Nature of Goodwill — there is hidden value not reflected in the most recent balance sheet — but what do we do if the cumulative excess returns are negative? Can there be a negative Intangible Assets in the Nature of Goodwill? Not really. In this case, we say that the firm has an *economic obsolescence*. This means that when we adjusted our assets to their market values, one or more of the assets was probably overstated and will need to be adjusted downward.

Let's use the previous example, but this time, rather than expecting that next year's EBIT will be $100, we expect it to be only $70.

| Excess Earnings Analysis | | Calculation of Present Value | |
|---|---|---|---|
| Next Year's EBIT | $70 | Capitalization Rate | 10% |
| Required Earnings | ($80) | Excess Earnings | ($10) |
| Excess Earnings | ($10) | Cum. Exc. Earnings | ($100) |

In this case, the cumulative excess earnings are negative, so the firm is expected to experience economic obsolescence. That means that we blew it! One or more of the assets that we marked to market is probably overstated. Our adjusted balance sheet currently looks as follows:

| Adjusted Operating Assets | | Adjusted Liabilities and Equity | |
|---|---|---|---|
| Cash | $100 | Accounts Payable | $150 |
| Accounts Receivable | $200 | Accrued Liabilities | $100 |
| Inventory | $250 | Taxes Payable | $100 |
| Pre-paid Expenses | $100 | Long-Term Debt | $350 |
| PP&E | $300 | Equity | $450 |
| Intangibles | $200 | | |
| Adjusted Op. Assets | $1,150 | Adj. Total L&E | $1,150 |

We need to figure out where we made our mistake. So, we CAREFULLY reexamine each of the assets and liabilities (if any) that we marked to market, and verify the values for cash, accounts receivable, inventory, and pre-paid expenses. Unfortunately, imagine that when we did the initial adjustment, while we were able to get a fair appraisal for the firm's land and buildings, we were not able to get an accurate appraisal for either the firm's capital equipment or its intangible assets. Thus, we suspect that the overstatement is likely coming from one or both of these two balance sheet items.

So, we do research to see if we can get a more accurate appraisal of the actual value of these two asset categories. We start with the capital equipment, since PP&E is likely a lot easier to value than are the intangible assets. Assume that, after a lot of digging, numerous phone calls, and a lot of Internet searching, that we find that the capital equipment seems to be correctly valued. That means that the overstatement is likely coming from the intangible assets; that is, those assets don't seem to be contributing enough EBIT given what we thought they were worth. They have experienced some economic obsolescence and are worth less than what we thought. How much less? Well, according to our calculation of (–$100M) for the firm's Cumulative Excess Earnings, they are worth about $100MM less. So, we will adjust their value to reflect the economic obsolescence. Note, the equity will have to be adjusted, too, since it is the difference between total Net Adjusted Assets and Long-Term Debt.

When we make those changes, the properly adjusted balance sheet looks as follows:

| **Assets** | | **Liabilities and Equity** | |
|---|---|---|---|
| Cash | $100 | Accounts Payable | $150 |
| Accounts Receivable | $200 | Accrued Liabilities | $100 |
| Inventory | $250 | Taxes Payable | $100 |
| Pre-paid Expenses | $100 | Long-Term Debt | $350 |
| PP&E | $300 | Equity | $350 |
| Intangibles | $100 | | |
| Adjusted Op. Assets | $1,050 | Adj. Total L&E | $1,050 |

Unfortunately, the equity is worth $100MM less than what was recorded on the original balance sheet.

## The Asset Accumulation Method

The Asset Accumulation method is very easy to understand; in fact, it is easier to understand and explain to others than the Adjusted Net Asset Valuation Method. Unfortunately, it is much harder to implement. To implement this approach, first we will identify ALL the assets and liabilities (even the ones that are off-balance sheet, like brand and human capital), and then we will assign a *fair market* value to each of them individually. Literally ALL the assets and ALL the liabilities. Then, we calculate the value of the firm's equity by taking the difference between the fair market value of its assets and liabilities.

On the surface, the Asset Accumulation Method seems very intuitive. So, what is the catch? Well, whereas the methodology seems easy to explain, this approach actually requires painstaking and oftentimes excruciating attention to detail: every single asset and liability matters and must be individually identified and valued. Note, not all of the assets and liabilities are that easy to value; for example, trademarks, patents, copyrights, customer lists and customer relationships, trade secrets (just to name a few assets), and some liabilities that can be difficult to spot, like contingent liabilities (such as pending nasty lawsuits or tax audits). Moreover, the Asset Accumulation Method can become extremely complicated because many firms lack the necessary level of detail and granularity about what they own and owe, and thus it can be a real challenge to get the information required to accurately determine the value of the equity.

## *How to apply the asset accumulation method*

To apply this methodology, we begin with the firm's most recently prepared balance sheet. It hasn't happened to us all that often in our professional capacity, but there is the possibility that the firm may not have a proper balance sheet, which means that we have to start from scratch and identify the firm's assets and liabilities on our own. Next, we first identify and then assign a value to all of the firm's assets (and we do mean ALL of the assets), even the intangible ones that don't appear on the balance sheet. This includes not only all the usual operating assets, like accounts receivable, inventory, property, plant and equipment, and patents, but also intangible things like brand, trade secrets, customer lists, and other things that add value, even though they can often be very difficult to value with precision.

After we have identified and assigned a value to all the assets, we will do the same thing for the liabilities. Again, we want them ALL, including any contingent liabilities (like lawsuits and other contingent obligations) that may not appear on the balance sheet. This method can become a real chore: we have to identify every single asset and liability and then price them. It is important to not miss a single one. Once we have identified all the assets and liabilities and have assigned values to them, the last thing to do is to subtract the total liabilities from the total assets in order to get an estimate for the value of the firm's equity.

The Asset Accumulation Method is very useful for pricing firms that rely heavily on the use of their assets to create value, such as an oil and gas company or a firm that has a lot of real estate/property holdings. It is also useful in asset purchases when allocating the purchase price across the firm's assets. Even if we choose not to utilize this approach in making a recommendation to our client, doing the analysis can still be extremely useful, since it forces us to identify and assign a value to each and every asset and then do the same for every claim against those assets. Because of the tremendous challenges associated with implementing the Asset Accumulation Method, in most situations where an Asset-based Valuation is desirable, we usually end up using the Net Asset Value Method.

## Application of the Asset Approach to Alpha Brewing Company

Now let's use the Adjusted Net Asset Value method to value our Alpha Brewing Company example:

| Adjusted Net Asset Value Method Outline |
|---|
| (1) Remove Non-Operating Assets<br>(Unnecessary for firm's operations or going concern status) |
| (2) Revalue remaining Assets to current market values<br>Result is "Adjusted Operating Assets" |
| (3) Subtract from (2) all Non-Interest Bearing Liabilities<br>Result is "Adjusted Net Operating Assets" |
| (4) Apply Cumulative Excess Earnings method to discover Int. Assets in the Nature of GW & add to Adjusted Net Operating Assets for Total ANOA |
| (5) Subtract Total Debt from Total Adjusted Net Operating Assets<br>Result is "Market Value of Equity" |

| Adjustments to Assets |
|---|
| (A) Inventory & PP&E adjusted up to current market values<br>Assumption is that the owner leveraged his extensive business network to obtain below-market prices. |
| (B) Accounts Receivable was adjusted down<br>Assumption is a lack of allowance for doubtful accounts<br>Normally just writes it off if missed collections. |
| (C) Cash & Security Deposit left unadjusted. |

Balance Sheet (Pre-Cumulative Earnings)

| Assets | Original | Adjusted | Adjustments | Adjusted Liabilities & Equity | Adjusted |
|---|---|---|---|---|---|
| Cash | $266,507 | $266,507 | Same | Accounts Payable | 12,819 |
| Accounts Receivable | $163,053 | $146,748 | 10% Down | Current Portion of Long-Term Debt | 56,893 |
| Inventory | $20,173 | $25,216 | 25% Up | Long-Term Debt | 426,995 |
| Security Deposit | $20,000 | $20,000 | Same | Owners' Equity | 939,743 |
| PP&E | $814,982 | $977,979 | 20% Up | | |
| Total | $1,284,715 | $1,436,449 | | Total | $1,436,449 |

| **Adjusted Net Operating Assets** | | **Required Earnings** | |
|---|---|---|---|
| Adjusted Operating Assets | $1,436,449 | Adjusted Net Operating Assets | $1,423,630 |
| Non-Financial Liabilities | ($12,819) | WACC | 7.66% |
| Adjusted Net Operating Assets | $1,423,630 | Required Earnings | $109,062 |

| **Excess Earnings** | | **Cumulative Excess Earnings** | |
|---|---|---|---|
| Next Year's EBIT | 613,765 | Excess Earnings | 504,703 |
| Required Earnings | ($109,062) | WACC | 7.66% |
| Excess Earnings | 504,703 | Cumulative Excess Earnings | $6,588,095 |

| **Total Adjusted Net Operating Assets** | | **MV of Equity (Post-Cumulative)** | |
|---|---|---|---|
| Adjusted Net Operating Assets | $1,423,630 | Total Adj. Net Op. Assets | $8,011,726 |
| Cumulative Excess Earnings | $6,588,095 | BV(Debt) | ($483,888) |
| Total Adj. Net Op. Assets | $8,011,726 | MV(Equity) | $7,527,838 |

Looking at the unadjusted (original) balance sheet we see that Alpha Brewing has an equity book value of $0.75MM (total assets of $1.28MM less total liabilities of $0.5MM). Next, we adjust the value of the assets and liabilities to reflect their market values. Cash requires no adjustment because $1 is worth $1: no more, no less.

With respect to accounts receivable, we carefully examined each of the outstanding invoices individually and had some concerns about a large invoice that was already 90-days overdue. Upon discussion with the owners, we decided to value that receivable as uncollectable and therefore zero. The result was a 10% reduction in accounts receivable (ouch!). A closer examination of the firm's inventory revealed a 25% increase in its market value relative to its book value reflecting the recent market price increase in hops. The security deposit value is unchanged as it represents a cash deposit. Lastly, we reviewed the firm's PP&E with certified real estate and equipment appraisers. In doing so we learned that the market value of the building and the brewery equipment was accurately stated at book value, however, the market value of the land was substantially higher than its historical cost. This led to a 20% upward adjustment in the value of PP&E. We make all of these adjustments and create an adjusted version of the balance sheet.

Regarding the adjusted value of the firm's liabilities — we have no reason to believe that the firm's vendors or lenders would accept any less than what they are owed, which is the book value of these liabilities. Alpha Brewing is in good financial condition, hence its liabilities were unadjusted.

Now that we have the Adjusted Operating Assets and Liabilities, we are able to calculate the total Adjusted *Net* Operating Assets that we will use to calculate the Cumulative Excess Earnings, which will be our estimate of the Intangible Value in the Nature of Goodwill. Let's do it. The firm has $1.436MM in Adjusted Operating Assets from which we will subtract the $12.8k of non-financial liabilities to obtain $1.424MM of Adjusted Net Operating Assets.

Recall that

$$\text{Excess earnings}_{t+1} = \text{EBIT}_{t+1} - (\text{Adjusted net operating assets}_t * \text{WACC})$$

To get Excess Earnings, we will begin with forecasted EBIT. Next year's forecasted EBIT is $613.8k. Alpha Brewing's Weighted Average Cost of Capital is 7.66% and the Adjusted Net Operating Assets amount to $1.424MM, so the required earnings are (0.0766) ∗ ($1.424MM) = $109.1k. Thus, the Excess Earnings are

$$\$613.8k - 109.1k = 504.7k$$

The firm has a lot of excess earnings, implying there could be some substantial value hidden in the Intangible Value in the Nature of Goodwill. We next assume that we will receive these Excess Earnings every year in perpetuity and then take the present value of the infinite stream of $504.7k per year. Recall that the present value of a perpetuity is

$$\text{PV(Perpetuity)} = \text{CF/(Discount rate)}$$

So, the Cumulative Excess Earnings are $504.7k/0.0766 = $6.588MM. Note, this is our estimate of the adjusted value of the Intangible Value in the Nature of Goodwill.

We are almost there. Next, we add our $6.588MM estimate of the Intangible Value in the Nature of Goodwill to our total of $1.424MM for Adjusted Net Operating Assets to obtain our Total Adjusted Net Operating Assets, which equals $6.588MM + $1.424MM = $8.012MM. From this, we will subtract out the book value of debt ($484k) to obtain an estimate of the market value of the Alpha Brewing Company's equity.

MV of equity = Total adj. net operating assets – Debt
= $8.012MM – $0.484MM = $7.528MM.

| **Adjusted Net Operating Assets** | | **Required Earnings** | |
|---|---|---|---|
| Adjusted Operating Assets | $1,436,449 | Adjusted Net Operating Assets | $1,423,630 |
| Non-Financial Liabilities | ($12,819) | WACC | 7.66% |
| Adjusted Net Operating Assets | $1,423,630 | Required Earnings | $109,062 |
| **Excess Earnings** | | **Cumulative Excess Earnings** | |
| Next Year's EBIT | $613,765 | Excess Earnings | $504,703 |
| Required Earnings | ($109,062) | WACC | 7.66% |
| Excess Earnings | $504,703 | Cumulative Excess Earnings | $6,588,095 |

(*Continued*)

(*Continued*)

| **Total Adjusted Net Operating Assets** | | **MV of Equity (Post-Cumulative)** | |
|---|---|---|---|
| Adjusted Net Operating Assets | $1,423,630 | Total Adj. Net Op. Assets | $8,011,726 |
| Cumulative Excess Earnings | $6,588,095 | BV(Debt) | ($483,888) |
| Total Adj. Net Op. Assets | $8,011,726 | MV(Equity) | $7,527,838 |

**Balance Sheet (Post-Cumulative Earnings)**

| **Adjusted Operating Assets** | | **Adjusted Liabilities & Equity** | |
|---|---|---|---|
| Cash | $266,507 | Accounts Payable | $12,819 |
| Accounts Receivable | $146,748 | Current Portion of LTD | $56,893 |
| Inventory | $25,216 | Long-Term Debt | $426,995 |
| Security Deposit | $20,000 | Owners' Equity | $7,527,838 |
| PP&E | $977,979 | | |
| Int. Assets in Nature of GW | $6,588,095 | | |
| Total | $8,024,545 | Total | $8,024,545 |

Using the Asset-Based Approach, we are able to estimate the market value of Alpha Brewing's equity to be $7.528MM. Note that the firm's original adjusted book value of equity was only $0.93MM; this is a huge difference! Alpha Brewing is an excellent example of a firm where the lion's share of its value cannot be captured by GAAP accounting. The brewery has a great reputation for selling high-quality craft beer and it has loyal customers. Unfortunately, GAAP accounts for neither, thus the tremendous disparity between the original adjusted book value of the equity and the estimate for the market value of equity.

## Key Takeaways

The Adjusted Net Asset Valuation method is used when the firm is still a going concern. The method typically does a single, overarching valuation of the entirety of the firm's Net Assets.

- The Asset Accumulation approach is often used when a firm does not have a steady history of generating positive profit, is not likely to yield positive profit in the near future, or is in the process of or contemplating liquidation.

- The market value of an accounts receivable will never be more than the book value, because the most we could ever hope to collect is the invoice amount.
- Non-interest-bearing liabilities, such as accounts payable and accrued liabilities, are never worth more than book value.
- The adjusted value of inventory and PP&E can be significantly higher than their book value because they are recorded at the lesser of historical cost or market value; that is their book value never goes up, it can only go down.
- Adjusted Net Operating Assets are all of the adjusted assets minus the dollar value of the non-financial liabilities such as accounts payable and accrued liabilities. The adjusted net operating assets are funded only with debt, preferred stock, and equity and thus have a funding cost associated with them.
- The Cumulative Excess Earnings indicate the hidden value associated with the unreported *Intangible Assets in the Nature of Goodwill* for the firm we are valuing.

# Chapter 12

# Forecasting EBITDA and Unlevered Free Cash Flow

Thus far in this handbook, we have learned several popular methodologies for business valuation: the income approach, the asset valuation approach, and the market approach. At the heart of the former is the forecasting of Unlevered Free Cash Flows (UFCF). At the heart of the latter is an understanding of firm's run rate EBITDA and the comparable EV/EBITDA multiple. As we will see, EBITDA is a core component of Unlevered Free Cash Flow, so by discussing UFCF, we cover both methods.

Before we get started looking at the flow of a forecasting model and assessing the usefulness of the historical financials, it is important for us to consider information that can be found in the Footnotes to the historical financial statements and the Management Discussion and Analysis (MD&A) section of the financial statements. The Footnotes explain the accounting techniques that were employed in preparing the financial statements (such as LIFO or FIFO, for example). They can also provide more detailed explanations of the line items reported on the financial statements. MD&A provides a discussion of the financial results and further clarifies what happened to the firm in the previous period. The MD&A offers the management's "story" and contains information that cannot be found anywhere else on the financial statements. That being said, the MD&A is the management team's "spin" on the numbers, so read this section carefully and make your own judgment on to what extent you want to believe what you read.

## How to Forecast UFCF?

All three of the valuation approaches (Market Comparable Approach, Income Approach, and Asset Valuation Approach) rely critically on EBIT. The Market Approach uses the ratio of Enterprise Value to the firm's current run-rate EBITDA, which is EBIT plus Depreciation and Amortization. The Asset Valuation approach relies on Cumulative Excess Earnings, which compares required earnings on the firm's current Net Assets to the firm's current EBIT. Thus, neither of these two approaches really involves all that much forecasting: we forecast run-rate EBIT one period ahead in the case of the Asset Valuation approach and we determine contemporaneous run-rate EBIT for the Market value approach. The Income Approach, in contrast, does rely critically on forecasting future cash flows. For example, to determine Enterprise Value, we would take the present value of the firm's unlevered free cash flows, which are given as follows:

$$\begin{aligned} \text{UFCF}_t = {} & \text{EBIT}_t - \text{EBIT(tax)}_t + \text{Depreciation}_t \\ & + \text{Amoritization}_t - \text{Capital expenditures}_t \\ & - \text{Increase in working capital}_t \end{aligned}$$

Thus, we need to forecast EBIT, which includes Depreciation and Amortization, the tax rate, CAPEX, and Changes in Working Capital.

Our goal is to create forecasts that are as accurate as possible and defensible to challenges from the counterparty on the other side of the transaction. That means that our revenue growth assumptions and other key operating assumptions have to make sense, given what we believe will happen in the future. Most financial forecasting models will have a section that includes a few years (three is usually enough) of historical income statements, from which we can obtain a solid understanding of the firm's historical operating relationships. Such relationships include the year-over-year sales growth rate, gross profit margin, relative spending on SG&A, etc. These historical relationships are often the starting reference points for forecasting our future Operating Assumptions, so getting a better understanding of them is very important. Please note that the historical relationships are useful only if the status quo is maintained; that is, if the past truly is indicative of what we expect will happen in the future. For example, in 2018 no one would have expected the catastrophic impact of Covid-19 on the revenues of airlines or restaurants.

## Forecasting EBIT

### *Forecasting revenues*

Forecasting EBIT begins with forecasting Revenues. The assumptions that we make when we forecast Revenues are perhaps the single most important assumptions in a forecasting model. To get good revenue estimates, it is helpful to understand what happened in the past and see to what extent the past is representative of the future. Do the historical revenue numbers and growth trajectory make sense? Is the growth trajectory sustainable? Is the past indicative of the future? What do we know about the product market? Are there any anticipated big changes coming that could impact revenues? If so, then these changes need to be reflected in our revenue estimates.

For a balance sheet-driven firm, revenue is the total amount that is generated from the sale of inventory to the firm's consumers. In contrast, service-oriented firms generate their revenues by charging clients for their services. The key issue with revenue is when exactly it is recognized for accounting purposes, so be sure to understand whether the historical statements are prepared using the cash basis or the accrual basis of accounting. The good thing is that revenues are additive. If the firm has more than one product, then we can just take a sum of the individual revenues for each of its products. For example, if you were trying to determine the total revenues for the Gap®, you might separately estimate the revenues for Banana Republic®, Gap®, and Old Navy®, and then add them together to achieve Gap's total revenues.[1]

Sometimes it is easier to use growth rates to forecast revenues, rather than estimating the cash flows directly; this is especially true for diversified firms that are in multiple product markets, where estimating revenues for each of their product lines and then aggregating them might not be feasible. In this case, thinking of future revenue in terms of revenue growth rates, rather than directly as raw dollars, means that the growth rates will be the inputs into our valuation model. We use these growth rates to calculate the future revenues.

Once we have our revenue estimates, it is often helpful to use the Market Share that is implied by our revenue estimate to calibrate whether

[1]Note that as of the date of publication of this book, Banana Republic®, Gap®, and Old Navy® were all owned by the Gap®.

our numbers make sense. To do this, we would calculate the market share implied by our revenue forecasts; that is, take the firm's revenues and divide them by total industry-wide revenues. Given the implied market share, are our sales assumptions reasonable? For example, if the largest player in the market only has a 10% market share, and our revenue estimates imply that our firm would have a 25% share of the market, then, unless our firm was in some way very disruptive of the market, our revenue estimates were probably too high.

## *Forecasting cost of goods sold*

After we have our revenue forecasts, the next income statement item that we will forecast is Cost of Goods Sold. Cost of Goods Sold (COGS) is, for the most part, a variable cost. Variable Costs (e.g., raw materials and labor) fluctuate proportionally with the quantity of what we are selling (be it a product or a service). Consequently, we typically forecast COGS as a percentage of sales, which makes a lot of sense, as long as the price of the firm's goods or services doesn't fluctuate wildly. So, if on average COGS were 75% of sales historically, we might use this as a baseline forecast. Thus, if our sales next year are $100MM, then we would forecast COGS to be $75MM.

We have to be careful when looking at the historical relationship of COGS to Sales and then relying on that to forecast the future. Some firms include depreciation in COGS. Most firms have some depreciation. If we don't see any on the income statement, but we see it on the statement of cash flows, then we know that depreciation has been bundled in with COGS. In this case, we need to break depreciation out of COGS, so that we can get its proper historical value. We should expect that COGS should be relatively stable with respect to Sales. If it isn't, then we need to do some research to understand what happened. For example, if in 1 year COGS increased substantially relative to Sales, say from 50% to 75%, then we might discover that the reason why is because the firm had to impair some of its assets. For example, if the firm had to write off the value of obsolete inventory, inventory would be reduced, and that reduction would be reflected dollar for dollar as an increase in COGS. In this case, the 75% ratio of COGS to Sales is not useful for making future forecasts, since it doesn't represent what would be the normal ratio of COGS to Sales.

## *Forecasting selling, general, and administrative expenses*

Once we have forecasted COGS, the next income statement item that we will forecast is Selling, General, and Administrative Expenses (SG&A), which are the non-direct costs associated with running our business. Think of these as the operating costs that we had to incur so that we could do the labor and buy the raw materials. These include things like marketing, advertising, R&D, and corporate overhead. Be careful, similar to the way that some firms bundle Depreciation into COGS, they can also bundle Amortization of intangible assets in their SG&A numbers, and thus there is no separate line item for Depreciation and Amortization. Always check with the statement of cash flows to see if the firm has any Amortization. If it does, then subtract that Amortization number from the bundled SG&A figures in order to get historical cash SG&A. It is these historical cash SG&A figures that we will use for forecasting purposes.

Although, SG&A often gets labeled as overhead and is thought of as a fixed cost, at least a part of SG&A (the Selling Expense) is a variable cost. Selling expenses include the commissions paid to the firm's sales personnel, and these are usually tied to either sales or gross profit. Unlike Selling Expenses, General and Administrative Expenses (G&A) typically have a very high fixed component. They include things like brand marketing expenses, advertising, R&D, corporate overhead, and entertainment costs. A very high G&A expense as a percent of sales can be a signal of a bloated cost structure. Because of this, G&A is often one of the first areas an acquirer looks to cut costs in the event of a merger or acquisition. That being said, a certain amount of G&A is necessary.

In standard financial models, SG&A is typically forecasted very conservatively as a percentage of sales. Note that this usually overstates SG&A, thus understates profit, and thus understates the value of equity. We might want to change this assumption if we have access to detailed data about the firm's future administrative costs.

## *Forecasting EBITDA*

Now that we have Revenues, COGS, and SG&A expenses forecasted, we can use these values to obtain an estimate for future EBITDA. Note that if both COGS and SG&A expenses are estimated as a percentage of sales, then EBITDA will be a fixed percentage of sales as well. In other words, the common assumption made is that the EBITDA margin is constant over time. Again, we can change this assumption if we believe it to be appropriate.

## *Forecasting CAPEX, depreciation, and amortization*

Our forecasts for Depreciation and Amortization will be driven by their associated Depreciation and Amortization schedules. Depreciation is driven by additions to Property, Plant, and Equipment (PP&E), which in turn are driven by Capital Expenditures, so we will discuss CAPEX first.

CAPEX has two components: Maintenance CAPEX and Expansion CAPEX. Maintenance CAPEX is the level of Capital Expenditures required to sustain a base level of growth. It is intended to ensure that a company is competitive and operating efficiently in its product market. Maintenance CAPEX includes things like upgrading obsolete technology (such as computers and phone systems) or replacing an outdated manufacturing equipment with the latest and greatest market offerings. Maintenance CAPEX reflects the use of the PP&E, it wears out over time. The more units you make, the greater the wear and tear on the asset. Consequently, Maintenance CAPEX grows with the quantity of things that are sold and thus is most closely tied to COGS.

Expansion CAPEX is different: it is the additional Capital Expenditure necessary to add significant amounts of capacity to accommodate future revenue growth. Examples of Expansion CAPEX include things like buying another warehouse, or new machines in order to handle an increase in capacity required by an increase in revenues. When the firm reaches a point where it needs to acquire more manufacturing capacity, the expense associated with that acquisition typically tends to be very large when compared to its Maintenance CAPEX. For example, imagine that the firm expects a massive, steady increase in revenues (e.g., it has started marketing internationally), and thus needs to buy a new building and also purchase all the equipment necessary to handle the additional demand. This type of investment can be enormous and represents a tremendous use of cash, so we need to be very careful when we forecast this kind of CAPEX.

So, how do we forecast it? Expansion CAPEX is driven by capacity constraints. If the firm has excess manufacturing capacity, then it will not need any Expansion CAPEX; however, if the firm will run out of capacity over the course of the period that we are trying to forecast, then we need to carefully think about not only the amount of the Expansion CAPEX required to handle an increase in sales but also the timing of the Expansion CAPEX.

If Revenue growth is high, be sure to keep an eye on the firm's capacity utilization to make sure that we aren't missing any large potential required Expansion Capital Expenditures. If you are looking at a model with hefty growth in sales and no increase in CAPEX, be suspicious. In all cases, we have to ensure that our CAPEX forecasts make sense and afford sufficient capacity to satisfy the demand implied by our Revenue forecasts.

So, in summary, when forecasting CAPEX, we typically deconstruct it into its two components: Maintenance and Expansion CAPEX. Maintenance CAPEX is driven by the quantities of things that the firm is producing. If we make more stuff, we will tend to wear out our equipment more quickly. Consequently, we typically forecast Maintenance CAPEX continuously as a percentage of COGS.

Expansion CAPEX is not forecasted continuously but is instead forecasted in discrete increments as management recognizes the need to expand capacity to support forecasted sales growth. Thus, we would expect to see some years with zero Expansion CAPEX and other years with perhaps significant investment in Expansion CAPEX.

### *Forecasting the changes in working capital*

The last component of Unlevered Free Cash Flow is Change in Working Capital. We define Net Working Capital as non-interest-earning Current Assets (Accounts Receivable, Inventory, and Pre-Paid Expenses) minus non-interest-bearing Current Liabilities (Accounts Payable and Accrued Expenses).

Net Working Capital provides a summary measure of the amount of Cash that is "tied up" in the firm's Working Capital accounts. If Net Working Capital is positive, that means that for the firm to generate its sales it required more funds in Accounts Receivable, Inventory, and Pre-Paid Expenses than were generated by the firm's Accounts Payable and Accrued Liabilities associated with that level of sales. If Net Working Capital is negative, that means that for the firm to generate its sales it required less funds in Accounts Receivable, Inventory, and Pre-Paid Expenses than were generated by the firm's Accounts Payable and Accrued Liabilities associated with that level of sales.

While most firms have positive Net Working Capital requirements, in which case Net Working Capital is a use of funds, it is possible for a firm to have a Negative Net Working Capital requirement, in which case Net Working Capital becomes a source of funds. Negative Net Working Capital requirements can be found in firms such as Apple Inc. that are able to exercise great market power in their purchasing and payment terms.

Working Capital assets and liabilities tend to grow with the firm's revenues and costs, thus as the firm's revenues increase, the firm will require more accounts receivable, need more inventory to satisfy customer demand, and will owe more money to its suppliers and employees. As a result, working capital items are typically forecasted as either a percentage of sales (accounts receivable) or a percentage of COGS (everything else).

### *Forecasting accounts receivable*

To forecast the Change in Working Capital, we begin by forecasting Accounts Receivable. Accounts Receivable represent Sales that have not yet been collected, so it makes sense to forecast A/R as a percentage of sales. Sometimes people use Days Sales Outstanding, which represents the average number of days of Sales that are tied up in Accounts Receivable, calculated as (AR * 365)/Sales. For example, we expect that the firm will get paid in 30 days. So, Accounts Receivable would be forecasted as being 30 days' worth of Sales, or (Annual Sales/365 days) * 30 days. Thus, if the firm had $365,000 in annual sales, we would forecast Accounts Receivables as being ($365,000/365 days) * 30 days = $30,000 in forecasted Accounts Receivable.

### *Forecasting inventory*

Inventory is expensed to COGS when it is finally sold, so Inventory should technically be expressed as a percentage of COGS and not as a percent of sales. But, if you make the assumption that COGS is growing with Sales, then Inventory would also be forecasted as a percentage of Sales. Sometimes, people prefer to use Inventory Turnover (aka, Inventory Turns) to drive Inventory. Inventory Turns measure the number of times the company cycles through its Inventory, on average, through the year. It is calculated by dividing (Total COGS)/Average inventory.[2] So, if the historical inventory turns are 3x per year, and COGS is equal

[2]Average inventory = (Beginning + Ending)/2.

to $300MM, then the firm will be forecasted to have $100MM in inventory.

### *Forecasting Pre-paid Expenses*

When forecasting Pre-paid Expenses, it is typical to forecast them as a percentage of Cost of Goods Sold (COGS). The idea is that COGS is typically driven one for one by the quantities of things sold by the firm, so if we make more things, we likely need more of the Pre-paid Expenses that go along with making more things. To forecast Pre-paid Expenses, we typically look at the historical relationship of Pre-paid Expenses/COGS and see if it is stable over time. If it is, then we assess whether we believe it will continue to be stable. If it is, then we typically use this historical relationship to forecast future Prepaids. If not, then we will make whatever adjustments we deem necessary.

### *Forecasting accounts payable*

Note that Accounts Payable are technically driven by purchases, but since purchases are a key component of COGS and COGS is a variable cost, Accounts Payable are often forecasted as a percentage of COGS. Don't be surprised if you see payables forecasted that way.

### *Forecasting accrued liabilities*

When forecasting Accrued Liabilities (AL), we tend to see them grow in proportion to COGS, since COGS is driven by the quantity of what we are selling. If we sell more things, we will need more of the items that are typically reported as AL (payroll, utilities, phone bills, etc.). Look at the historical ratio of AL/COGS. If this ratio is stable, then ask the question of whether we think this relationship will remain stable over the forecasting horizon. If so, then we can use the historical ratio as the driver for AL. If not, then we will make any appropriate changes.

### *Forecasting net working capital*

Once we have forecasted all of the Working Capital assets and liabilities for each of the years that are of interest to us, we then calculate the annual Net Working Capital.

Net Working Capital is defined as follows:

$$\text{Net working capital}_t = \text{Accounts receivable}_t + \text{Inventory}_t + \text{Pre-paid Expenses}_t - \text{Accounts payable}_t - \text{Accrued liabilities}_t$$

To obtain the *Change in Net Working Capital*, we subtract last period's Net Working Capital from this period's forecasted Net Working Capital:

$$\text{Change in net working capital}_t = \text{Net working capital}_t - \text{Net working capital}_{t-1}$$

If the Change in Working Capital is positive, that means that the firm had to use up additional cash in order to grow its Revenue line; that is, it has even more cash tied up in Net Working Capital this year than it did last year, and in this case, Net Working Capital was a use of Cash.

## Forecasting the tax rate

Forecasting the Federal Tax rate in the United States is relatively easy, since the Federal Tax rate is a fixed 21%. State corporate tax rates vary tremendously, so be sure to do your homework so that you include the appropriate State tax rate as well. Also, certain municipalities, such as NYC for example, charge a corporate income tax. Be mindful of these differences in tax rates between cities and states, because they can have a substantial impact on your final post-tax estimates.

## Forecasting unlevered free cash flow

Now that we know how to forecast all of the component parts, we can easily sum them up to determine Unlevered Free Cash Flow (UFCF):

$$\text{UFCF}_t = \text{EBIT}_t - \text{EBIT(tax)}_t + \text{Depreciation}_t + \text{Amortization}_t - \text{Capital expenditures}_t - \text{Increase in working capital}_t$$

The following table summarizes the various drivers used to forecast the line items necessary for calculating Unlevered Free Cash Flow.

| Forecasting Drivers | |
|---|---|
| Revenues | Year over Year % |
| COGS | % of Sales |
| SG&A | % of Sales |
| EBITDA | % of Sales |
| D&A | % of PP&E |
| Maintenance Capex | % of Sales |
| Expansion Capex | Lump-sum/Discrete |
| Accounts Receivable | % of Sales |
| Inventory | % of COGS |
| Pre-paid Expenses | % of COGS |
| Accounts Payable | % of COGS |
| Accrued Liabilities | % of COGS |
| Tax Rate | 21% + State Tax |

The following example calculates the unlevered free cash flow for our hypothetical Firm BBA. The calculation is based on our forecasts for the year 2020, with the various growth assumptions listed.

| UFCF Forecasting Example (Firm BBA) | |
|---|---|
| **Annual Growth Assumptions** | |
| **I/S** | |
| Revenues | 20% Increase |
| COGS | 40% of Revenues |
| SG&A | 5% of Revenues |
| Deprecation | 15% of PP&E |
| Amortization | None for this firm |
| Taxes | 21% of EBIT |
| **B/S** | |
| Cash | 0% Change |
| A/R | 10% of Revenues |
| Inventory | 20% of COGS |
| Pre-paid Expenses | 15% of COGS |
| PP&E | Increase = to CapEx |
| Accounts Payable | 5% of COGS |
| Accrued Liabilities | 10% of COGS |
| **S/CF** | |
| CapEx | 10% of Revenues |

| **BBA Income Statement (Partial)** | | |
|---|---|---|
| | **2019** | **2020** |
| Revenues | 1,000 | 1,200 |
| COGS | 400 | 480 |
| Gross Profit | 600 | 720 |
| SG&A | 50 | 60 |
| Depreciation | 60 | 78 |
| Amortization | 0 | 0 |
| EBIT | 490 | 582 |
| Taxes | 103 | 122 |

| **BBA Balance Sheet (Partial)** | | |
|---|---|---|
| | **2019** | **2020** |
| Assets | | |
| Cash | 100 | 100 |
| Accounts Receivables | 100 | 120 |
| Inventory | 80 | 96 |
| Pre-paid Expenses | 60 | 72 |
| Total Current Assets | 340 | 388 |
| PP&E | 400 | 442 |
| Total Assets | 740 | 830 |
| Liabilities | | |
| Accounts Payable | 20 | 24 |
| Accrued Liabilities | 40 | 48 |
| Total Current Liabilities | 60 | 72 |

| **BBA Statement of Cash Flows (Partial)** | | |
|---|---|---|
| | **2019** | **2020** |
| Investing Activities | | |
| Capital Expenditures | 100 | 120 |

| **UFCF Calculation** | |
|---|---|
| | **2020** |
| EBIT | 582 |
| EBIT(Taxes) | (122) |
| Depreciation | 78 |
| Amortization | 0 |
| Increases in WC | (36) |
| CapEx | (120) |
| UFCF | 382 |

Let's walk through this forecast of UFCF. Remember,

$$\begin{aligned} \text{UFCF}_t = \text{EBIT}_t - \text{EBIT(tax)}_t &+ \text{Depreciation}_t \\ &+ \text{Amortization}_t - \text{Capital expenditures}_t \\ &- \text{Increase in working capital}_t \end{aligned}$$

First, we need to forecast the firm's EBIT; to do that, we need Sales, COGS, SG&E, and Depreciation and Amortization. Looking at our drivers, we see that Sales is forecasted to grow at a rate of 20% next year. Since sales amounted to $1MM last year, we expect them to be worth $1.2MM next year. COGS are expected to be 40% of sales and SG&A are 5% of sales, so they are expected to be $480k and $60k, respectively. Getting Depreciation is a little tougher because it's dependent on forecasted PP&E. Depreciation is forecasted to be 15% of whatever is the forecasted PP&E, so we need to forecast the PP&E first. PP&E grows with CapEx, and our assumption is that CapEx will be 10% of Revenues. Since Revenues are expected to be $1.2MM million and CapEx is forecasted to be 10% of that, we hence expect CapEx to be $120k. We add the $120k to the firm's 2019 PP&E to get $400k + $120k = $520k. Depreciation is assumed to be 15% of PP&E, so it is (.15) * ($520k) = $78k. The firm doesn't have any amortization, so we don't have to worry about that. This means that we are all set to forecast EBIT. It is Sales ($1.2MM) – COGS ($480k) – SGA ($60k) – Depreciation ($78k), which equals $582k.

Next, we estimate what the tax on the EBIT will be. The corporate tax rate was assumed to be 21%, so the tax payable on the EBIT will be (.21) ($582k) = $122k.

Now we need to forecast our Net Change in Working Capital so we will need to forecast our Current Asset and Current Liability accounts. Since the Cash account is not a part of Working Capital, we can ignore this account in our calculation. Accounts Receivable has historically been 10% of Revenues. Since Revenues are forecasted to be $1,200k, we forecast Receivables to be $120k. Inventory has historically been 20% of COGS, since COGS is forecasted to be $480k, Inventory should be $96k. The last Working Capital asset is Prepaid Expenses, which has historically been 15% of COGS or $72k. Thus, the Working Capital assets increased by $48k ($288k in 2020 – $240k in 2019).

Next, we need to forecast the Working Capital liabilities. Accounts Payable and Accrued Liabilities have historically been 5% and 10% of COGS, respectively, thus we forecast them to be $24k and $48k, respectively. Which leads to an increase in Working Capital liabilities of $12k ($72k in 2020 – $60k in 2019). To calculate the net increase (or decrease) in Net Working Capital, we subtract the increase in Working Capital liabilities from the increase in Working Capital assets, or $48k minus $12k equals a forecasted increase in Net Working Capital of $36k for 2020. To get Unlevered Free Cash Flow, we need to subtract any increase in Net Working Capital, because an increase in Net Working Capital is a use of funds.

Finally, to get forecasted Unlevered Free Cash Flow, we need to calculate CapEx for 2020. Historically, CapEx has been 10% of Revenues, which equals (.10)($1,200k) = $120k.

We are now ready to calculate Unlevered Free Cash Flow. We begin with our forecasted 2020 EBIT of $582k. Next, we multiply our forecasted EBIT by the tax rate of 21% to obtain our forecasted tax on EBIT of $122k. Taxes on EBIT are subtracted. Then we add back our 2020 Depreciation and Amortization of $78k and $0k, respectively. Finally, we subtract out our forecasted $36k increase in Net Working Capital and our forecasted $120k in CapEx, giving us Unlevered Free Cash Flow (UFCF) of $382k for 2020.

## Key Takeaways

- Market Comparable Approach, Income Approach, and Asset Valuation Approach rely critically on EBIT.
- The historical relationships are useful only if the status quo is maintained; that is, if the past truly is indicative of what we expect to happen in the future.
- The key issue with forecasting revenues is when exactly are they recognized for accounting purposes, so be sure to understand whether the historical financial statements are prepared using the cash basis or the accrual basis of accounting.
- Sometimes accountants will bundle depreciation into COGS and the amortization of intangible assets into SG&A. They do this to present a cleaner looking income statement. Most firms have depreciations, so in the event you do not see depreciation on the Income Statement, be sure to look at the statement of cash flows. If the firm has depreciation, it will always appear in the operating activities section. If this is the case, all you need to do is subtract this depreciation from the bundled COGS to get the actual COGS. And do similarly for amortization and SG&A.
- In standard financial models, SG&A is typically forecasted very conservatively as a percentage of sales, which usually overstates SG&A, and thus understates profit and understates the value of equity.
- A positive change in working capital means that the firm had to use up additional funds in order to grow its revenue line; that is, it has even

more funds tied up in net working capital this year than it did last year, and in this case, net working capital was a use of funds.

- The formula for Unlevered Free Cash Flow (UFCF) at time *t*: $UFCF_t = EBIT_t - EBIT(tax)_t + Depreciation_t + Amortization_t - Capital\ expenditures_t - Change\ in\ working\ capital_t$

# Chapter 13

# Special Cases in Valuation

This chapter will examine some special cases in valuation, including firms with cyclical cash flows and firms that are in financial distress.

## Dealing with Cyclical Cash Flows

Valuing firms with cyclical cash flows (perhaps from cyclical revenue or cyclical costs) presents a challenge for the standard valuation methodologies that we have discussed thus far. Regardless of which approach we try to use (asset-based, market-based, or income-based), the valuation of firms with cyclical cash flows can be problematic. This is because if the valuation is being done at a point in time when it happens to be a boom (recession) period, then the firm's cash flows will be temporarily inflated (depressed).

For example, if we are using the discounted cash flow-based income approach to value a cyclical firm, then we would typically forecast the firm's cash flows and then assume a terminal growth rate to calculate the terminal value. But when we apply the terminal growth rate, depending on where the firm is in its business cycle (boom or bust, for example), the resulting terminal value may be either too large or too small, depending on whether we are in a boom or a recession. This leads to valuations that are incorrect, given what we believe will actually happen to the firm in the future.

The same is true for the market approach. Imagine if we were using an EV/EBITDA multiple to value a firm, but the firm just happened to be reaching the nadir of its business cycle. In this case, the firm's EBITDA would be much lower than what we would expect it to be in the future. In fact, the EBITDA would be at its lowest value and not at all representative of what we think should be the firm's run-rate EBITDA. Thus, if we multiply the current depressed EBITDA by the comparable multiple, we will end up with a value that would be unfairly and incorrectly low. We need a better estimate for the run-rate EBITDA.

Even the asset-based approach has problems with cyclical cash flows. Imagine if we are doing an Adjusted Net Asset Value calculation when the firm is at the peak of a business cycle. We would compare the firm's required earnings based on its WACC and Net Assets to its EBIT. At the peak of the firm's business cycle, its EBIT would be at its maximum, which would lead to large Capitalized Excess Earnings and a large increase in the firm's Intangible Value in the Nature of Goodwill. Consequently, the estimate of the firm's equity value would be too high, given what we believe will happen to the firm's EBIT moving forward.

So how do we get a good estimate for the value of a firm that has cyclical cash flows? Some people erroneously just take the average of the historical cash flows, but this only makes sense if the cash flow's growth rate over that historical period of interest was equal to zero, and that we expect the status quo to be maintained; that is, that we don't really expect any significant changes to happen in the firm's product market moving forward. For most firms, taking an average of the historical cash flows will downwardly bias the calculation of the terminal cash flow, which will downwardly bias your terminal value and hence your entire valuation.

A better way of dealing with cyclicality is to use Normalized Cash Flows, rather than the firm's actual cash flows. See the following figure to get a better idea of what we mean by Normalized Cash Flows.

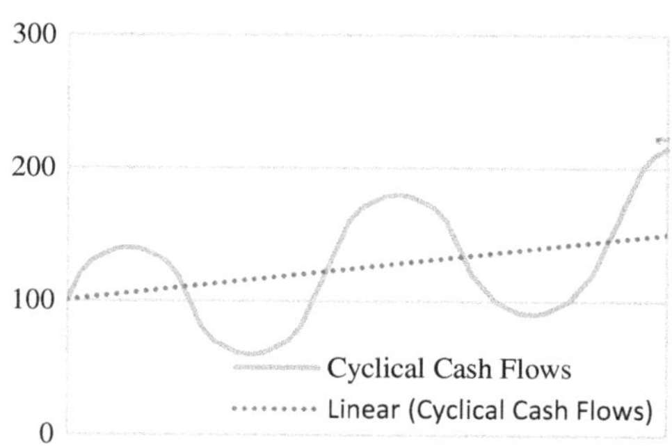


To obtain a Normalized Cash Flow forecast, we use the following process:

1. Using our historical and forecasted cyclical numbers as inputs, we run an ordinary least squares regression to find the line that gives us the best estimate.
    a. The regression line is the one that minimizes the sum of the squared errors ("the best estimate") between the line itself and the actual cash flows.
2. Use the regression line to forecast the Normalized Cash Flow in whatever terminal year we choose.
3. Use two points on the line to determine the normalized growth rate.

While it is helpful to know the basics of ordinary least squares (OLS) regression analysis to thoroughly understand the Normalized Cash Flows concept, actually calculating them is fairly easy to do in Excel. So, do not worry too much if you have never studied regression analysis; we will walk you through what you need to know.

## Using Excel for Cyclical Cash Flows

### *Getting a normalized forecast*

Let's say that we wanted to value a company that has the following forecasted unlevered free cash flows and a weighted average cost of capital of 11%. Note, that although we stopped our forecasts in 2029, the unlevered free cash flows are expected to maintain their growth trajectory and cyclicality into the future.

| **Forecasted UFCF** | |
|---|---|
| **Year** | **Cash Flow** |
| 2020 | $100 |
| 2021 | $200 |
| 2022 | $300 |
| 2023 | $400 |
| 2024 | $350 |
| 2025 | $250 |
| 2026 | $150 |
| 2027 | $275 |
| 2028 | $375 |
| 2029 | $425 |

As we can see, the unlevered free cash flows seem to follow a 6-year cycle. If we made the mistake and just went ahead and used the cash flow in year 5 (2024) to calculate our terminal value, then the value that we'd obtain would be way too high, given our expectations of the future cash flows.

Our goal is to take this cyclical forecast and normalize it; that means, convert it from a cash flow stream that is cyclical into an estimated one that is linear. Fortunately for us, Excel has a very useful function ("FORECAST") that will do this for us. FORECAST uses linear regression analysis to report an estimate of the normalized cash flow that we will use in our terminal value calculation. Using it is easy, but first we have to load Excel's Data "Analysis ToolPak." This tool package allows us to use Excel's regression-related functionality. To enable the "Analysis ToolPak," first open Excel, then:

Excel → Tools → Excel Add-Ins → Enable "Analysis ToolPak" by clicking on the check box → OK.

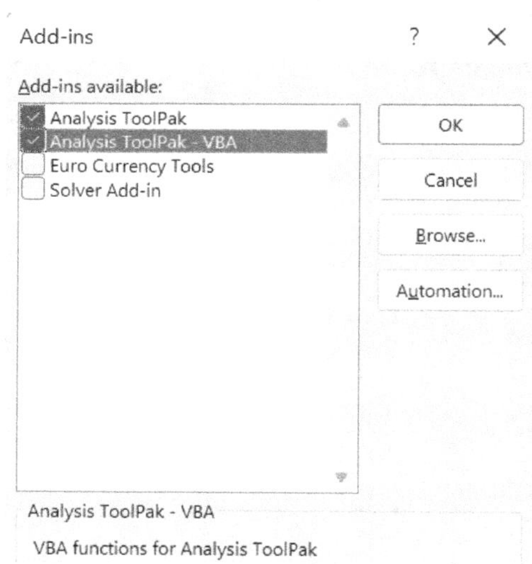


Once the Analysis Toolpak is installed, we input the data into two columns (just like we did in the example above), and then use the following command:

= FORECAST(*x, known_y's, known_x's*)

Those are Excel's desired inputs, so translated into our language:

= FORECAST(The year in which we want the terminal cash flow, the actual forecasted cash flows themselves, the years over which the forecast occurs).

So, if we want to use year 5 (2024) as the year in which we will be calculating the terminal value, then we would use the following formula to get the normalized cash flow in year 5:

= FORECAST (2024, B3: B12, A3: A12)

| | A | B | C | D |
|---|---|---|---|---|
| 1 | Forecasted UFCF | | | |
| 2 | YEAR | CASH FLOW | | |
| 3 | 2020 | \$100 | | |
| 4 | 2021 | \$200 | | |
| 5 | 2022 | \$300 | | |
| 6 | 2023 | \$400 | | |
| 7 | 2024 | \$350 | | |
| 8 | 2025 | \$250 | | |
| 9 | 2026 | \$150 | | |
| 10 | 2027 | \$275 | | |
| 11 | 2028 | \$375 | | |
| 12 | 2029 | \$425 | | |
| 13 | $UFCF_5$ | =FORECAST(2024,B3:B12,A3:A12) | | |

| | A | B |
|---|---|---|
| 1 | Forecasted UFCF | |
| 2 | YEAR | CASH FLOW |
| 3 | 2020 | \$100 |
| 4 | 2021 | \$200 |
| 5 | 2022 | \$300 |
| 6 | 2023 | \$400 |
| 7 | 2024 | \$350 |
| 8 | 2025 | \$250 |
| 9 | 2026 | \$150 |
| 10 | 2027 | \$275 |
| 11 | 2028 | \$375 |
| 12 | 2029 | \$425 |
| 13 | $UFCF_5$ | 272.88 |

where cells B3:B12 contain forecasted cyclical cash flows from 2020 to 2029, and cells A3:A12 contain the corresponding years. The result of this

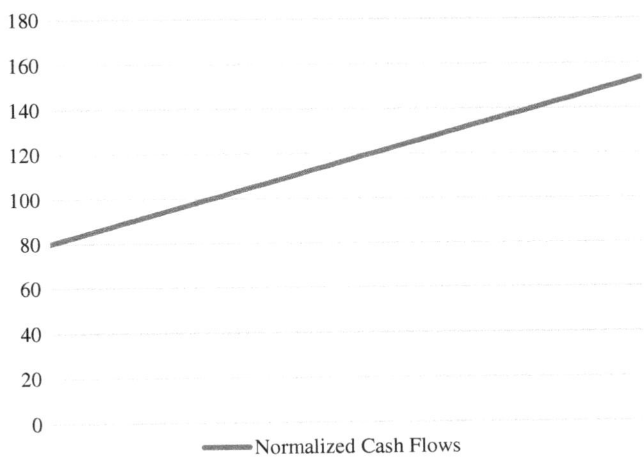

FORECAST calculation is \$272.88, which is the normalized estimate of what the cash flow should be in 2024.

## *Getting a normalized growth rate*

Now that we have the terminal year's normalized cash flow, in order to use the Gordon Growth Model to calculate the terminal value, we next have to obtain an estimate for the normalized growth rate. Doing this is relatively easy in Excel. Here is how we do it:

1. Use the FORECAST function to estimate both the terminal cash flow in year $T$ (2024) and in year $T + 1$ (2025).
   So, in this case, we want:

$$\text{UFCF}_5 = \text{FORECAST}(2024, \text{B3: B12, A3: A12}) = \$272.88$$

and

$$\text{UFCF}_6 = \text{FORECAST}(2025, \text{B3: B12, A3: A12}) = \$292.12$$

| | A | B | C | D |
|---|---|---|---|---|
| 1 | Forecasted UFCF | | | |
| 2 | YEAR | CASH FLOW | | |
| 3 | 2020 | \$100 | | |
| 4 | 2021 | \$200 | | |
| 5 | 2022 | \$300 | | |
| 6 | 2023 | \$400 | | |
| 7 | 2024 | \$350 | | |
| 8 | 2025 | \$250 | | |
| 9 | 2026 | \$150 | | |
| 10 | 2027 | \$275 | | |
| 11 | 2028 | \$375 | | |
| 12 | 2029 | \$425 | | |
| 13 | $\text{UFCF}_5$ | 272.8788 | | |
| 14 | $\text{UFCF}_6$ | =FORECAST(2025,B3:B12,A3:A12) | | |

| | A | B |
|---|---|---|
| 1 | Forecasted UFCF | |
| 2 | YEAR | CASH FLOW |
| 3 | 2020 | \$100 |
| 4 | 2021 | \$200 |
| 5 | 2022 | \$300 |
| 6 | 2023 | \$400 |
| 7 | 2024 | \$350 |
| 8 | 2025 | \$250 |
| 9 | 2026 | \$150 |
| 10 | 2027 | \$275 |
| 11 | 2028 | \$375 |
| 12 | 2029 | \$425 |
| 13 | $\text{UFCF}_5$ | 272.88 |
| 14 | $\text{UFCF}_6$ | 292.12 |

2. Next, we will use our point estimates for $\text{UFCF}_5$ and $\text{UFCF}_6$ to solve for the compound growth rate that will grow $\text{UFCF}_5$ to be equal to $\text{UFCF}_6$.

   $\text{UFCF}_5 = \text{UFCF}_5(1 + g)$

Solve for $g$ as follows:

$$g = \frac{\text{UFCF}_6}{\text{UFCF}_5} - 1$$

And substituting in our estimates from Step 1, we get the following:

$$g = \frac{\$292.12}{\$272.88} - 1 = 0.0705 = 7.05\%$$

We are almost there. We have the terminal cash flow. We have the terminal growth rate. All we need now is a discount rate. Using normalized terminal cash flows solves part of the cyclicality problem, but what about the increased risk? Doesn't cyclicality increase the firm's riskiness? If so, then what about the firm's weighted average cost of capital? Don't we have to make some corrections for that too?

### *Valuing a cyclical firm*

The answer is no. Luckily for us, the cyclicality will likely be captured by beta. Cyclical firms have higher betas than non-cyclical firms. So, we are all set. We don't have to do anything to the firm's WACC (11%), since it already captures that increased volatility. It looks like we have everything that we need in order to value this cyclical firm.

Step 1. Calculate the terminal value in year 5.

$$\text{TV}_5 = \frac{\text{UFCF}_5(1+g)}{\text{WACC}-g} = \frac{\$272.88(1+0.0705)}{0.11-0.0705}$$
$$= \$7{,}330.44$$

Step 2. Restate the infinite stream of cyclical cash flows with an equivalent finite stream of cash flows.

| **Forecasted UFCF** | | |
|---|---|---|
| **Year #** | **Actual Year** | **Cash Flow** |
| 1 | 2020 | \$100 |
| 2 | 2021 | \$200 |

*(Continued)*

*(Continued)*

| Forecasted UFCF | | |
|---|---|---|
| **Year #** | **Actual Year** | **Cash Flow** |
| 3 | 2022 | \$300 |
| 4 | 2023 | \$400 |
| 5 | 2024 | \$350 + \$7,330.44 |

Step 3. Take the present value of this cash flow stream using a WACC = 11%.

$$\begin{aligned} \text{EV} &= \frac{\$100}{1.11} + \frac{\$200}{1.11^2} + \frac{\$300}{1.11^3} + \frac{\$400}{1.11^4} + \frac{\$7,680.44}{1.11^5} \\ &= \$5,293.23 \end{aligned}$$

## Firms in Financial Distress

Another challenge that we sometimes face is how to value a firm that is in financial distress. Financial distress poses an interesting challenge, since we may face great uncertainty about the future viability of the firm; thus, it could be very difficult to get a reliable run-rate number for a market-based valuation or to forecast a defensible terminal growth rate for an income-based valuation. As the financial distress becomes more severe and the firm approaches bankruptcy, its going concern value will continue to erode. When the going concern value finally reaches zero, the firm will cease to be a going concern and instead will just be a pile of stuff to be valued at its liquidation value. Liquidation value is the total value of the assets if they are sold immediately (net of transactions and legal costs, of course) minus the book value of the debt. If this is positive, then the equity holders will end up with some value. If this is negative, then the equity holders will usually end up with nothing.

Neither the market-based nor the income-based approach is particularly well-suited for valuing firms that are deeply in financial distress. These approaches are better suited for valuing firms that generate reliable, forecastable cash flows, and for which we can get run-rate numbers. Fortunately for us, however, the asset-based approach is a solid choice for valuing firms that are well on their way to becoming piles of stuff.

The way in which we tackle the valuation of a firm that is in distress depends on whether we believe the distress is temporary or fatal. We will examine both cases in this chapter.

## *Do we believe that the distress will not be fatal?*

If we do not believe that the distress will be fatal to the firm, then the way in which we value the firm depends on our beliefs about how quickly the firm will recover from the distressed state. If the distress is temporary (say from a temporary supply chain disruption) and we sincerely believe that the cash flows will quickly revert to "normal," then we might want to consider using normalized cash flows (along with the income approach) to obtain the enterprise value, and then back out the value of equity (see the section above on using normalized cash flows). We might even think about excluding the abnormal period from the normalization regression, so as to not unfairly and negatively distort the firm's long-term outlook and its terminal growth rate.

Alternately, we might want to use the Adjusted Net Asset Value method to get an estimate of the firm's equity. Just realize that the firm's current EBIT is not representative of what the firm's run-rate EBIT will be once things have stabilized. So, in this case, we might want to use a normalized EBIT figure instead when calculating the cumulative excess earnings that will determine the Intangible Value in the Nature of Goodwill.

In the case where the distress is temporary, but we believe that it will take several years before the firm becomes "normal" again, then we have to tread even more carefully. Here, there may be substantial risk that our forecasts may not pan out, and that the firm will end up in bankruptcy. We can still use the income approach to value the firm's enterprise value, but we must very carefully and meticulously forecast the cash flows throughout the entire hyper-risky transition phase. It is always important to do a thorough sensitivity analysis as part of any valuation assignment, but the importance of sensitivity analysis is further amplified when a firm is in prolonged financial distress. Sometimes even a small hiccup can throw the distressed firm into a tailspin and completely invalidate our assumptions. Our advice is to focus keenly on the bad case scenarios, and make sure that the firm always has adequate liquidity to meet its financial obligations. If it doesn't, then we should consider abandoning the income-based approach and instead using an asset-based approach. The closer the firm gets to bankruptcy, the stronger becomes the case for using an asset-based approach relative to the other choices.

### *Do we think that the distress is fatal?*

If we believe the distress is potentially fatal, then neither the income approach nor market approach is likely a good choice, since both of these approaches are based on the notion that the firm is a solid going concern (i.e., it is going to generate cash flows well into the future). If the distress is likely but not absolutely certain to be fatal, then the asset-based approach can be a very good choice; especially the Asset Accumulation approach (see Chapter 11, on Asset-Based Valuation), which will carefully value each and every asset (including ones that are not on the balance sheet, such as brand, customer lists, trade secrets, etc.) and each working capital liability.

If, however, the distress is very likely to be fatal and we believe that the liquidation value of the assets exceeds the book value of the debt, then we recommend moving straight to the Liquidation Value approach, which we will describe in what follows. However, if the liquidation value of the assets is less than the book value of the debt, then in the event of bankruptcy there will be no liquidation value leftover for the shareholders. The thing is, the firm isn't bankrupt YET, so there is still some chance of the firm's situation improving, and equity still has some value. In this case, we should think about applying a Real Options Valuation Approach (which we will discuss shortly), but the assumptions required for this approach are fairly draconian, so be wary of the estimates that are obtained using this method.

### *The liquidation value method*

The Liquidation Value Method is our recommended choice when (1) the firm is approaching bankruptcy and (2) we believe that the liquidation value of the firm's assets will be greater than the book value of the firm's debt; that is, there will actually be some positive liquidation value available to the shareholders after everyone else is paid. The Liquidation Value of equity is calculated as the difference between the total value of the firm's assets if they were to be sold today (i.e., liquidated) minus the book value of the liabilities. Do not forget to subtract out any legal and transaction costs that the firm might incur, since those have to get paid prior to the shareholders getting any residual value.

Equity = Liquidation value of assets
– Book value of total debt
– Transaction costs – Legal fees

How different is an asset's liquidation value from its market or wholesale value? The answer is: it depends. If the asset is highly liquid, then it can be sold fairly quickly at or close to its wholesale price (to another dealer, for example), but if the asset is not highly liquid, then it will be sold at a price that could potentially be much lower than its wholesale price (sometimes literally pennies on the dollar). For example, imagine if you had 2 months to sell your automobile. You are in no rush whatsoever to sell, so at what price would you list the car? But, what if, instead, you had to sell your automobile today, as in right now. What would the price be then? It is easy to sell an automobile quickly. Here in the US, pretty much any car dealer will be happy to offer you the low end of the Kelly Blue Book trade-in value for your car, in cash, today. The difference between the current fair market value and the wholesale value for your car can potentially be substantial; especially if the car is painted in an unpopular color or has idiosyncratic modifications made to it.

The Liquidation Value approach resembles the Asset Accumulation Approach but has one very important difference: it uses liquidation values for the assets and book values for the liabilities, rather than fair market values for assets and liabilities. To refresh your memory, the Asset Accumulation Approach identifies all the firm's assets and liabilities, and then assigns a *fair market* value to each of them individually. It is a painstaking and time-consuming process because we have to identify every single asset, even those that are not reported on the balance sheet. Then, the value of equity is calculated by taking the difference between the fair market value of the assets and liabilities. In contrast, although Liquidation Value Approach also goes through the painstaking task of identifying all the firm's assets and liabilities, it instead assigns a *liquidation* value to each of the assets individually and uses the book value of liabilities in the equity calculation.

## *Valuing distressed equity as a call option on the assets of the firm*

*(Note, this section requires some knowledge of Precalculus.)*

If the Liquidation Value of Assets is less than the book value of debt, then the Liquidation Model would predict that the value of the equity is zero, since shareholders have limited liability. Limited liability means that the equity of a corporation cannot be negative because the shareholders cannot be sued directly for losses incurred by the firm; that means, the least that equity can ever be worth is zero. So, in the event that the firm is indeed liquidated, due to the existence of limited liability, the value of the firm's equity can be written as follows:

Equity = Max (Liquidation value of assets
− Book value of total debt
− Transaction costs − Legal fees, 0)

But, in reality, as long as the firm is not actually dead and is still operating, there will always be some positive equity value — even if the current market value of the assets is less than the book value of the liabilities. The firm can keep running until it actually defaults on an obligation. The equity is bounded below by zero; that means, that as long as the firm is still alive, there is always a "chance," no matter how slim, that the market value of the assets might recover enough to cover the liabilities, thus the Liquidation Model approach (which would erroneously predict a value of zero) is not appropriate. In this case, the only meaningful valuation approach left for us is to use real option pricing models. We want to share a very important word of warning here. Although we have done our best to write this section as clearly and as comprehensibly as possible, option pricing is relatively complicated and requires at least a basic proficiency in Precalculus to implement effectively.

For those readers who are not familiar with options, they give the holder the right, but not the obligation, to do something; in this case, either buy or sell an asset at a predetermined price, which is called the *strike price*. A call option gives the right to buy at the strike price, while a put option gives the right to sell at the strike price. For the purposes of this chapter, we will focus on call options.

For example, assume that we are holding a call option to buy 100 shares of stock at a strike price of $20 per share. If the current stock price is less than \$20, we would not choose to exercise our right to buy the stock. Why pay \$20 per share when the current price is lower than that? Doing that would be silly, since we would be losing money. It is better to just let the option expire worthlessly. But, what if, instead, the current price of the stock was \$25? In this case, the right to buy it at a strike price of \$20 is very valuable. We would certainly exercise that right (called exercising the option) and buy 100 shares at \$20 per share for a total price of \$2,000. We could then instantly turn around and sell those same 100 shares in the market at a market price of \$25 per share, or a total of \$2,500, and pocket a healthy \$500 profit.

A call option's value at maturity can be written as follows:

$$\text{Call option value} = \text{Max (Asset price} - \text{Strike price, 0)}$$

Note, that just like equity, a call option can never be worth less than zero. It either has value and we exercise the option, or we choose to allow it to expire worthlessly.

There is some options-related terminology that you should be familiar with. If the current price of the stock is greater than the strike price, then we say that the option is *in the money*; that is, there is money to be made right now if we exercise the option. If the current price of the stock is equal to the strike price, then we say that the option is *at the money*, and there is no money to be made right now if we exercise the option. Lastly, if the current price of the stock is less than the strike price, then we say that the option is *out of the money*; in which case, we would lose money if we exercised the option. Options for which the current price of the stock is much lower than the strike price are called *deep out of the money* options.

Why all this talk about options? Because, the equity of firms where the market value of the assets is less than the book value of debt can be thought of as a deep out of the money call option. In this case, the underlying asset is the market value of the firm's assets and the strike price is the book value of the firm's debt. For example, if the firm is solvent, then equity holders get the difference between assets and liabilities. However, if the firm is bankrupt, then the equity holders get zero. Since in our case the underlying asset (what you get if you pay the strike price) is the market value of the assets and not a financial security, the option is called a *real option*. The payoff to equity of this real option is as follows:

$$\text{Equity value} = \text{Max (MV of assets} - \text{BV of debt, 0)}$$

Note that the formula for the payoff to equity is very similar to the formula for the payoff to a call option:

$$\text{Call option value} = \text{Max (Asset price} - \text{Strike price, 0)}$$

This means that we can value the equity of a distressed firm exactly as if it were a real call option, where the underlying asset is the market value of the firm's assets and the strike price is the book value of the firm's debt.

Option valuation has been well understood since the early 1970s. In 1973, Fischer Black and Myron Scholes published a fundamental paper on how to price call options. Their now famous solution is called the Black–Scholes formula.[1] The same year, Robert Merton also published a model that arrived at a similar solution, but he approached the problem from a completely different perspective.[2] Merton and Scholes shared the 1997 Nobel Prize for their efforts. Unfortunately, Fischer Black had passed away so he could not officially receive the award.

## *The Black–Scholes option pricing formula*

The Black–Scholes formula for pricing a call option is as follows:

$$\text{Equity} = \text{Assets} * N\left(\frac{\ln\left(\frac{\text{Assets}}{\text{Debt}}\right) + \left(k_{rf} + \frac{\sigma^2}{2}\right)t}{\sigma\sqrt{t}}\right)$$

$$- \text{Debt} * e^{-k_{rf}t} * N\left(\frac{\ln\left(\frac{\text{Assets}}{\text{Debt}}\right) + \left(k_{rf} + \frac{\sigma^2}{2}\right)t}{\sigma\sqrt{t}} - \sigma\sqrt{t}\right)$$

---

[1] Fischer Black and Myron Scholes, "The Pricing of Options and Corporate Liabilities," *Journal of Political Economy* 81, no. 3 (1973): 637–54.

[2] Robert C. Merton, "Theory of Rational Option Pricing," *Bell Journal of Economics and Management Science* 4, no. 1 (1973): 141–83.

where:

Assets is the Market Value of the firm's assets,
Debt is the Book Value of the firm's debt,
$k_{rf}$ is the risk-free rate of return,
$\sigma$ is the standard deviation of the firm's rate of return to assets, and
$t$ is the maturity of the debt.

We will explain exactly how to estimate these inputs into the Black–Scholes model later in this chapter. What about $e$, $\ln(x)$ and $N$? For the readers that are not familiar with this mathematical notation, $e$ is a number that is roughly equal to 2.71828184. To be precise, $e$ is the number whose natural logarithm is exactly equal to 1; that is, $\ln(e) = 1$, where $\ln(x)$ is the natural logarithm of the value $x$.[3] Excel can easily calculate the value of natural logarithms. Just use the Excel function = LN(value). For example, $\ln(2.50) = 0.916290732$.

$N(x)$ is the standard normal distribution function evaluated at the value $x$. In Excel, it is written as NORMSDIST($x$). NORMSDIST($x$) calculates the value of the standard normal distribution function evaluated at the value $x$; that is, it tells us the probability, assuming that the underlying probability distribution is a normal distribution with mean equal to zero and standard deviation equal to one, and that the actual value of a random draw from the distribution will be less than the value $x$. For example:

$$\text{NORMSDIST}(0.00) = 50.00\%$$

That means that if the underlying distribution is distributed normally with a mean of zero and a standard deviation of one, then you have a 50% probability of getting a random draw that has a value less than zero. Similarly:

$$\text{NORMSDIST}(1.00) = 84.13\%$$

[3]The standard logarithm, written as $\log(x)$, is said to be in base 10. In this case, $\log(10) = 1$, since $10^1 = 1$, that is ten to the power one is equal to ten. Similarly, $\log(1) = 0$, since $10^0 = 1$; $\log(100) = 2$, since $10^2 = 100$; $\log(1{,}000) = 3$, since $10^3 = 1{,}000$; $\log(0.1) = -1$, since $10^{-1} = 1/10 = 0.1$; $\log(0.01) = -2$, since $10^{-2} = 1/(100) = 0.01$; and so on. The logarithm that we will be using is called the natural logarithm and is in base $e$, where $\ln(e) = 1$, or $\ln(2.71828184) = 1$, and $\ln(1/e) = -1$.

This means that you have an 84.13% chance of getting a random draw that is less than 1.00.

The Black–Scholes model requires many very strong assumptions in order to yield an accurate price for a call option. As you will see, many of these assumptions are violated when using the model to price equity as a real option; especially if the real option is deep-out-of-the-money. Consequently, we have to interpret the results of our Black–Scholes calculations with great care.

The Black–Scholes formula requires the following:

1. There can be no opportunities for arbitrage. This means that the underlying asset has to be actively traded in the market. Arbitrage opportunities will be traded away in an active market, so the market value of the asset that is used in the model will be an equilibrium value. Unfortunately, here is where we encounter our first problem. Although a firm's equity might be publicly traded, its assets are definitely not publicly traded. Moreover, some of the firm's assets (things like brand and trade secrets) can be challenging to value.
2. The asset's price process has to be continuous; that means that there can be no unexpected price jumps. Unfortunately, this assumption is usually violated in real options models, which tends to cause the Black–Scholes model to systematically underprice deep-out-of-the-money options. We can compensate for this by using a higher value for the standard deviation of the asset's return.
3. The standard deviation is known and remains constant over the life of the option. Unfortunately, the variance of the rate of return to assets, and hence its standard deviation (which is the square root of the variance), is unknown and is very likely to change over the life of the option. Moreover, this variance can be extremely challenging to estimate with any kind of precision.
4. The option can be exercised instantaneously at maturity. Unfortunately, this assumption is also violated, since bankruptcy is not instantaneous: it can take months before the equity holders receive their piece of the pie.
5. The firm has only one debt issuance, and that debt has to be a bond with a zero-coupon rate. Again, this is almost never the case.

With all these caveats in mind, we will first demonstrate how to use the Black–Scholes formula to obtain an estimate for the value of distressed equity, then we will explain how we actually obtain the model's inputs.

In the following example, we have:

- MV(Assets) = $6 million
- BV(Debt) = $9 million
- Life of option = 10 years
- Standard deviation of return to MV(Assets) = 40%
- Risk-free rate = 10%

$$\text{Equity} = \$6\text{MM} * N\left(\frac{\ln\left(\frac{\$6\text{MM}}{\$9\text{MM}}\right)+\left(.1+\frac{.4^2}{2}\right)(10)}{\sigma\sqrt{t}}\right)$$

$$-\$9\text{MM} * e^{-.1(10)} * N\left(\frac{\ln\left(\frac{\$6\text{MM}}{\$9\text{MM}}\right)+\left(.1+\frac{4^2}{2}\right)t}{.4\sqrt{10}} - .4\sqrt{10}\right) = \$3.75\text{MM}$$

Recall that our estimate of the market value of the firm's assets is $6MM. So, if we know that the equity still has a value of $3.75MM (it is surprising how value still remains, isn't it?), that means that even though the book value of debt might be $9MM, its market value is the difference between the market value of the assets and the estimated value of the equity; specifically, $6MM – $3.75MM = $2.25MM. This is definitely not good news for the debtholders.

Now that we know how to use the Black–Scholes formula and interpret its results, we will discuss how we obtain estimates for the inputs to the model.

### *Getting the market value of the assets*

- Use an asset-based approach (we usually use the asset accumulation approach, but the adjusted net asset value approach can be used, too) to estimate the market value of the firm's assets.
- Sum these up to get an estimate of the total market value of the firm's assets.

### *Getting an estimate for the book value of debt/strike price*

- This will be taken directly off of the Balance Sheet.
- Be sure to include short-term debt in your calculation.

### *Getting an estimate of the exercise date/duration*

Most firms have complicated capital structures that include multiple debt issuances, most of which are not zero-coupon bonds (e.g., term loans, notes, and coupon bonds). Given that there might be numerous different kinds and maturities of debt, we need to find a good proxy for the average debt maturity. Although this is a little complicated, we can do this by calculating the *duration* of the firm's debt portfolio. Duration is the weighted average time to maturity of the firm's debt, using the relative present values as weights. Duration is calculated as follows:

$$\text{Duration} = \frac{\sum_{t=1}^{N} \text{PV}(\text{CF}_t) * t}{\sum_{t=1}^{N} \text{PV}(\text{CF}_t)}$$

For example, the duration of a $1,000, 6-year Eurobond[4] that has an 8% coupon (so the annual interest payment is $80) and an 8% discount rate (note that Eurobonds pay interest annually) is as follows:

**Eurobond Duration**

| Year # | CFt | PVt | PVt*t |
|---|---|---|---|
| 1 | 80 | 74.07 | 74.07 |
| 2 | 80 | 68.59 | 137.18 |
| 3 | 80 | 63.51 | 190.53 |
| 4 | 80 | 58.80 | 235.20 |
| 5 | 80 | 54.45 | 272.25 |
| 6 | 1,080 | 680.58 | 4,083.48 |
| | | 1,000.00 | 4,992.71 |

[4]Eurobonds are bonds that pay annual interest.

So, using the formula above, D = 4,992.71/1,000 = 4.993 years.

A word of warning: most corporate bonds pay interest on a semi-annual basis. So, if we wanted to calculate the duration of a $1,000, 2-year bond that pays 8% semi-annual interest (that means $80/2 = $40 every 6 months), with a 12% semi-annual (which means 6% every 6 months) discount rate, it would be as follows:

**Corporate Bond Duration**

| Year # | CFt | PVt | PVt*t |
|---|---|---|---|
| 0.5 | 40 | 37.74 | 18.87 |
| 1.0 | 40 | 35.60 | 35.60 |
| 1.5 | 40 | 33.58 | 50.37 |
| 2.0 | 1,040 | 823.78 | 1,647.56 |
| | | 930.70 | 1,752.40 |

So, using the formula above, Duration for this semi-annual bond would be 1,752.4/930.70 = 1.88 years.

Calculating the duration of a zero-coupon bond is easy: its duration is equal to its maturity.

### *Getting an estimate for the risk-free rate*

As our proxy for the risk-free rate of return, we usually use the interest rate of a US government treasury bond that has a maturity that is as close as possible to the weighted average duration of the firm's debt. You can easily get this on Bloomberg or by just Googling "US Treasury bond rates."[5]

### *Getting an estimate for the annualized variance (standard deviation) of the rate of return to assets*

This part is not going to be easy. It is extremely difficult to estimate the annualized variance of the rate of return to assets with any kind of

[5] https://www.bloomberg.com/markets/rates-bonds/government-bonds/us.

precision. However, if both the equity and debt are publicly traded, then things get a little easier for us.

Since MVA = MVDebt + MVEquity, then:

$$\sigma_A^2 = w_e^2\sigma_e^2 + w_d^2\sigma_d^2 + 2w_e w_d \rho_{e,d}\sigma_e\sigma_d$$

where:

- $w_e$ and $w_d$ are the market value weights of debt and equity,
- $\sigma_e$ and $\sigma_d$ are the historical annualized standard deviations of the rate of return to the firm's stocks and bonds, respectively, and
- $\rho$ is the correlation between stock and bond returns.

What do we do if the firm's bonds are not publicly traded? In this case, the best we can do is to try and find a reasonable proxy for the standard deviation of the return to the firm's bonds. It is common to use the standard deviation of the return on similarly rated bonds as a proxy for $\sigma_d$ and the correlation between the similar bonds and the firm's stock as a proxy for $\rho_{e,d}$.

## Summary of Approaches When Firm Is in Distress

The following is a table that summarizes which approach will most likely yield the best results depending on the severity of the financial distress.

| Belief About Severity of Distress | Recommended Valuation Approach |
|---|---|
| Distress is temporary and things should improve quickly | Income approach → forecast through the challenging period or use normalized cash flows<br>or<br>Adjusted net asset value approach → using normalized EBIT |
| Distress is temporary but it might take a long time for things to improve | Adjusted net asset value approach → using normalized EBIT<br>Note that the closer the firm gets to bankruptcy, the stronger becomes the case for using an asset-based approach relative to the other choices |

| Belief About Severity of Distress | Recommended Valuation Approach |
|---|---|
| Distress is likely but not absolutely certain to be fatal | Asset accumulation approach |
| Distress is very likely to be fatal and the liquidation value of the assets exceeds the book value of the debt | Liquidation value approach |
| Distress is very likely to be fatal and the liquidation value of the assets is less than the book value of the debt | Real options approach |

## Key Takeaways

- This chapter deals with two special cases in valuation: firms with cyclical cash flows and firms in financial distress.
- One must be careful when dealing with a cyclical firm. The point at which you calculate the firm's terminal value (peak versus trough) could have a profound impact on your estimated value. For example, at the peak of the firm's business cycle, its EBIT would be at its maximum, which would lead to significant Capitalized Excess Earnings and a large increase in the firm's intangible value like goodwill. Consequently, the firm's equity value estimate would be too high.
- Liquidation value is the total value of the assets if they are sold immediately (net of transactions and legal costs, of course) minus the book value of the debt.
- It is always important to do a thorough sensitivity analysis as part of any valuation assignment, but the importance of sensitivity analysis (we will discuss this more in Chapter 14) is further amplified when a firm is in prolonged financial distress.
- If the liquidation value of the assets is less than the book value of the debt, then in the event of bankruptcy there will be little to no liquidation value leftover for the shareholders.
- A firm's equity has similar characteristics as a call option on the assets of the firm where the strike price is the book value of the firm's debt.

# Chapter 14

# Arriving at a Final Price Estimate — The Football Field and Sensitivity Analysis

This handbook has examined several different valuation methods, including the Income Approach, Market Approach, and Asset-Based Approach. We have tried to give some indication of which valuation approach might be best suited to the firm's financial condition and when each approach might be most appropriate. Each of these methodologies, when combined with an intelligent sensitivity analysis, will yield a range of price estimates. But how do we decide what should be the final price estimate? For example, just the market approach alone has many different pricing multiples, such as Price/Sales, EV/Sales, Book Value/Market Value, Price/Earnings, and EV/EBITDA (just to name a few). Do we choose just one method? Do we take an average of all the approaches? Do we simply close our eyes and throw a dart? Obviously, we don't just throw a dart!

Our goal is to come up with a price estimate that is reasonable, as accurate as possible, and, of critical importance, defensible. The defensibility of our price estimate is crucial if we intend to convince other people about the validity of our valuation. One way that we can help convince others is by doing a *sensitivity analysis* and demonstrating the sensitivity (or even better, the lack thereof) of our calculated price estimate to changes in key valuation inputs; for example, the growth rate, cost of capital, assumptions about working capital or CAPEX, among other things. But, once we have done a sensitivity analysis, then what? Does that affect our point estimate in any way? The short answer is probably not too much. BUT... it does affect the confidence interval around our point estimate and, hence, not only the point estimate's defensibility, but also the likelihood of being able to actually transact at that point estimate.

At the end of the day, an asset's market value depends on the supply and demand conditions in the market; specifically, what an arms-length buyer and seller end up negotiating to be the final transaction price. Our goal is to search for the truth, and then prepare and present our honest valuation in a convincing and defensible way. The purpose is to convince our counterparty that our price estimate is fair and truthful. If the sensitivity analysis yields a tight confidence interval around our point estimate (i.e., there is little variation in the estimated price), then we are far more likely to convince our counterparty to buy or sell the asset at our point estimate.

## Sensitivity Analysis

Each of the valuation methodologies discussed thus far relies on a given set of inputs, such as EBITDA, Unlevered Free Cash Flows, CAPEX, growth rates, working capital assumptions, etc. Each set of inputs will yield a specific point estimate for the value that we are trying to estimate (e.g., price). Our confidence in the point estimate is only as good as the precision with which we can forecast the inputs. You know the old saying, "garbage in, garbage out." How sensitive is our point estimate to changes in our input assumptions? We will start with an overarching theoretical discussion (not too technical) of what a sensitivity analysis tries to achieve, and then walk you through how you might actually approach doing one. Remember, the goal is to be able to defend the validity of our point estimate to a potential buyer or seller.

The bottom line is that we are going to be making changes to the inputs of our model and seeing the impact of those changes on the model's output. Is the output sensitive to reasonable changes in the assumptions? That is, does our estimate change tremendously if we make a reasonable change to one or more of our inputs? Or, is our model's output relatively inert to these changes? The less sensitive the output is to reasonable changes to the inputs, the more confident we are in our point estimate and the more defensible it will be to a potential buyer or seller.

So, what do we mean by the word "confident?" Most people tend to think of inputs as having a symmetric probability distribution (e.g., a normal distribution) of values evenly centered around a mean, which is the *expected value* of the distribution. Note that the mean and the median (the 50th percentile, where half of the possible outcomes are higher than the median, and the other half are lower than it) are identical to each other when a distribution is symmetrical. Since the mean is the expected value of a distribution (trust us on this if you haven't had a statistics class), many people think that it is a reasonable starting point and use the mean value as their input; for example, what do we expect will be the growth rate next year, or CAPEX next year? Well, the growth rate could potentially be 1%, or 3%, or 5%, or whatever, but given what we know right now, what do we "expect" it to be? There is a certain intuitive "fairness" to using an expected value, hence the expected value is what will be the input that we would use in our model. As a result, since the inputs of our model are all expected values, then the output of our valuation model will also be an *expected value*.

But how confident are we that this expected value output of our calculation is a reasonable point estimate upon which we can base a transaction? After all, we have to convince someone to agree with our valuation, so that they actually pay our price. The answer to how confident we are in our point estimate depends on the confidence that we have in, and hence our ability to defend, our forecasts of the inputs into our valuation model. The valuation model is just a mathematical algorithm. Mathematical algorithms don't lie, they don't think, they just take the inputs that we provide them and crank out a value. The more precise our ability to estimate the inputs, the greater our confidence in our computed value will be. Enter the concept of *sensitivity analysis*.

For those of us that have had a basic statistics class (don't worry if you haven't, we won't be going that deep into statistics here), we were introduced to the concept of a *confidence interval*. The confidence interval has to do with how likely it is that in the future we will realize an actual outcome for an input (e.g., revenue growth) that is close to our expected value for that input. People tend to think of confidence as a probability; for example, the weather announcer says that they are 95% confident that it is going to rain tomorrow. Will it rain for sure? They don't know. Nobody knows. But, given the conditions that they see out there right now, such as the movement of the clouds and all the other factors, historically when these conditions have been present, 95% of the time it ended up raining the next day. Similarly, we might expect next year's revenue growth to be 4.0%. Note, this is what we expect, but we really don't know what exactly will actually happen. That being said, even though we don't know for sure, imagine if we have 95% confidence that the actual realized value of next year's revenue growth will be between 3.2% and 4.8%.[1] That means that we honestly believe that, given the information that we have available to us right now, the actual growth rate next year should fall outside of the 3.2% to 4.8% of the range only 5% of the time. A tighter confidence interval, say for example, 3.9–4.1% rather than 3.2–4.8% for our 95% confidence interval, means that we have greater confidence in our 4.0% point estimate, since we would expect that only 5% of the time would next year's growth actually be either less than 3.9% or more than 4.1%; that is a tighter range. As an extreme example, imagine if we could perfectly predict the future and thus, we knew *for sure* that the next year's growth rate would actually be 4.0%. In this case, the range would be 4.0–4.0%, and we would not only be extremely confident in the quality of our forecast, but we would also be absolutely certain about it!

Now that you (we hope) understand the spirit of what we are trying to do with a sensitivity analysis, we can discuss how one might actually go about conducting a sensitivity analysis. Remember, our goal with a sensitivity analysis is to help us better understand just how much our point estimate varies as we make what we think are reasonable changes to our model's inputs. What if we expect that next year's revenue growth rate will be 4.0%, but since we don't know it for sure, we honestly believe that with a high degree of likelihood it will be somewhere between the worst case scenario of 3.9% and the best case scenario of 4.1%? Is our point estimate very sensitive to changing the growth rate to 3.9% or 4.1%? How much does this change impact our valuation? That is exactly the reason why we do a sensitivity analysis.

In summation, sensitivity analysis forces us to challenge the key assumptions that drive our valuation. Our counterparty will certainly be challenging our valuation, so we have to be ready to defend not only our assumptions, but also the reliability of our point estimate.

---

[1] We do not want to go deep into the statistical discussion of how to establish or why one would choose a 90% versus 95% versus 99% or any other confidence interval. That would require a lot of data and a lot more background in statistics than we deem necessary for this handbook. The goal here is to give you an idea of what a sensitivity analysis tries to accomplish, which is to make ourselves and other people feel good about the transactability of our point estimate.

## *Sensitivity analysis and the income approach*

The income approach (DCF) requires us to estimate unlevered free cash flows and then discount them back at the firm's weighted average cost of capital. The resulting calculation will yield an estimate of the firm's enterprise value; from this, we subtract out net debt and preferred stock to obtain an estimate of the value of the firm's equity. The key inputs to this type of approach are the unlevered free cash flow and the weighted average cost of capital; consequently, these will be the starting points for our sensitivity analysis.

It is important to note that there is no "standard" amount by which we adjust an input value when doing a sensitivity analysis. Instead, we should be thinking about the future distribution of the input, and what might be a reasonable range of values that may potentially occur. Note, it is very difficult to estimate an actual 95% confidence interval around a future forecast value (such as revenue growth); there are just too many factors that are out of our control. Instead, we have to use our knowledge of the firm, the nature of competition in the product market, anticipated changes in the macroeconomy and regulatory environment, and anything else we might be able to learn to come up with reasonable ranges for each of our inputs. Remember, in situations of litigation or negotiation your counterparty will be doing this for sure, so you have to be able to defend yourself.

So where to start? Many people come up with three alternative scenarios: (1) the base case, (2) the upside case (also called the "management" case, because sometimes the management team preparing the forecasts is a little too "optimistic" with their estimates), and (3) the downside case. Others just do a base case and several downside cases, because they are not worried about things being better than expected, they are worried about things being worse than expected; if things go really wrong, what does the forecast look like? Still, others use the expected case, the worst case, and the best case. There are endless possibilities. For the purposes of this chapter, we will be doing three cases: (1) a base case, (2) an upside case, and (3) a downside case.

Let's begin with doing a sensitivity analysis on unlevered free cash flow.

$$\begin{aligned}\text{UFCF}_t = {} & \text{EBIT}_t - \text{EBIT(tax)}_t + \text{Depreciation}_t + \text{Amortization}_t \\ & - \text{Capital expenditures}_t - \text{Increase in working capital}_t\end{aligned}$$

Although we could change the values of all the components of UFCF, the most common assumption to challenge is the growth rate in revenues (especially the terminal growth rate), because almost everything (certainly EBIT) is in some way driven by the quantity component of revenues. The three cases that we use should reflect what our reasonable expectations would be (1) if everything goes as we expect it to go, (2) if revenues are much less than expected — our worst case scenario, and (3) if revenues are greater than expected — our best case scenario.

Once we have the three different scenarios for the revenue growth rates, then the rest is relatively easy, since COGS, SG&A, and the working capital items are all typically forecasted as a percentage of either sales or COGS. For example, as we have discussed earlier in this book, the working capital items (accounts receivable, inventory, prepaid expenses, accounts payable, and accrued liabilities) should grow in direct proportion to the quantity component of revenue (with the exception of accounts receivable, which are driven by both price and quantity). The intuition is simple: to sell more stuff, we need more stuff. The historical relationships between working capital accounts and quantity sold tend to be very stable over time, and the proportions are relatively invariant to reasonably small changes in scale. So, as sales change, the working capital items will change, too, but in a steady proportion relative to sales. Consequently, unless we anticipate a major change in the firm's supply chain policies, we should not expect these model inputs to vary much from our expectations, thus many analysts do not toggle the working capital assumptions. But, if we wanted to challenge them, we would do so by creating three cases, just like we did for the revenue line.

The same is true for challenging the assumptions with respect to COGS. The relationship between COGS and sales is typically very stable over time, unless there are unexpected warranty repairs, impairments, or other similar things that might change the relationship. Similar to the working capital items, because the relationship between COGS and sales is stable and relatively insensitive to scale, thus as revenues grow, so does COGS. Many analysts do not challenge this relationship when they are doing a sensitivity analysis.

SG&A expense is an interesting item because it often has a large, relatively fixed component that isn't directly tied to sales growth. If you haven't read the chapter on forecasting unlevered free cash flow, please do so and you will see what we mean. If the fixed component is an overwhelmingly large part of the SG&A expense, then it really doesn't make much sense to toggle that number. This is because if something is fixed, that means that it doesn't change, irrespective of what happens to sales: it is pretty much a constant. If, instead, most of the SG&A expense comes from selling expense or brand marketing expenditures, then one would model it as a percentage of sales. As we learned above in our discussion of COGS, if the relationship between SG&A expense and sales is fairly stable, which would be the case if a lion's share of SG&A expense were variable, then there might not be much benefit to challenging the SG&A assumptions.

So far, pretty much the only assumption that seems to universally get challenged is the one about sales growth. We hope that you have a good understanding of why that is the case. Sales drives pretty much everything, so when sales are off, so is pretty much everything else (except your fixed costs).

You might ask, what about the CAPEX assumption (especially expansion CAPEX), because that can be a huge expense when we run out of capacity? That is a good question, but the answer is a little complicated. Let's start with maintenance CAPEX, because that one is easy. Maintenance CAPEX typically grows in line with the quantity sold. In addition, the ratio of maintenance CAPEX to sales is normally very stable, irrespective of the level of sales (in the same way that COGS or inventory have a stable relationship to sales), so many people do not run a sensitivity analysis on it. But expansion CAPEX is a whole different story. It is smart to challenge the expansion CAPEX assumptions up until the point in time that the firm reaches a steady state of cash flow growth. We need to be especially wary if, in the upside case, the increase in revenues causes the firm to run out of manufacturing or service capacity. If so, then there might be additional expansion CAPEX that has to be invested in order to accommodate the additional revenues. This means that, in the upside case, expansion CAPEX might potentially be much larger than in the base case and, hence, unlevered free cash flow would be much less than what we might otherwise expect.

Things change a bit once we reach our terminal year. The income approach requires us to use the Gordon growth model to solve for the firm's terminal value at the point in time when the firm's terminal growth rate is stable (see Chapter 9, on the Income Approach). In order for that to happen, not only does the revenue growth rate have to be constant, but CAPEX has to equal depreciation; if not, then the formula cannot be applied. If CAPEX equals depreciation, then that means that pretty much all of our CAPEX from that point on will be maintenance CAPEX.

It is possible to run a sensitivity analysis on the tax rate, but tax rates are set by state and federal statutes, so these tend to not change randomly. Unless we believe that there is a very good reason to challenge the tax assumptions, like if there is some uncertainty over whether the tax rate will change in the future, the tax rate is usually an assumption that we tend to leave alone.

The last piece of the puzzle is the Weighted Average Cost of Capital. It is very common to run a sensitivity analysis on the firm's WACC. Recall that the WACC represents the required return on the capital that has been invested in the firm. The two most challenged assumptions in a valuation model are the terminal growth rate and the WACC. Both are subjective and both can potentially have a very large impact on value; especially when the growth rate is relatively close to the WACC. To understand why, remember that the terminal value is calculated as follows:

$$\text{Terminal enterprise value}_t = \frac{\text{UFCF}_{t+1}}{\text{WACC} - g}$$

So, when $g$ is close to the WACC, the denominator in the fraction approaches zero and the fraction starts to explode in value, which means in this case even small errors in the estimate of either of these inputs can make a big difference in value. Consequently, it is very important that we carefully examine the sensitivity of our price estimate to reasonable changes in these important inputs.

To this end, analysts often create a two-dimensional table with growth on one axis and WACC on the other axis. The table reports what the value would be if the growth rate and WACC were to vary at the same time. For example, imagine that we had a firm that generated no cash flow for the first 4 years, but then in year 5 generated \$100MM in unlevered free cash flow, and we expect that the cash flow will grow at a constant rate of 4%. We also expect that the firm will have a WACC of 10.0%. How much should we be willing to pay for this firm? The calculation of value is very easy:

$$\text{Value} = \frac{\text{TV}_5}{(1+\text{WACC})^5} = \frac{\left(\dfrac{100\text{MM}(1+g)}{\text{WACC}-g}\right)}{(1+\text{WACC})^5}$$

If we input our expected values for the terminal growth rate and the WACC, we get the following:

$$\text{Value} = \frac{\left(\dfrac{100\text{MM}(1+.04)}{.1-.04}\right)}{(1+.1)^5} = \$1,076\text{MM}$$

But how comfortable are we with this price estimate? How sensitive is it to changes in our inputs? We can create a sensitivity analysis table that reports the output of our valuation for different, but still reasonable (as in potentially likely to happen) values of the growth rate and the WACC.

**Sensitivity Analysis Table**

| | | Growth Rate | | | | |
|---|---|---|---|---|---|---|
| | | 3.6% | 3.8% | 4.0% | 4.2% | 4.4% |
| | 9.8% | $1,047 | $1,084 | $1,124 | $1,166 | $1,211 |
| WACC | 9.9% | $1,026 | $1,061 | $1,099 | $1,140 | $1,184 |
| | 10.0% | $1,005 | $1,040 | $1,076 | $1,116 | $1,158 |
| | 10.1% | $985 | $1,018 | $1,054 | $1,092 | $1,132 |
| | 10.2% | $966 | $998 | $1,032 | $1,069 | $1,108 |

As we can see, although our expected value is $1,076MM, the value could potentially range between $966MM and $1,211MM. The tighter this range, the more comfortable we are — and the more likely we are to convince our counterparty — that our expected value is a good point estimate of value.

To show you just how sensitive to inputs the value can get when the growth rate and the WACC are close to one another, let's repeat the sensitivity analysis we did above, but where the expected growth rate is 9.0% and the base case WACC is 10.0%.

| Sensitivity Analysis Table | | | | | | |
|---|---|---|---|---|---|---|
| | | Growth Rate | | | | |
| | | 8.6% | 8.8% | 9.0% | 9.2% | 9.4% |
| | 9.8% | $5,671 | $6,817 | $8,537 | $11,404 | $17,137 |
| WACC | 9.9% | $5,211 | $6,169 | $7,554 | $9,731 | $13,648 |
| | 10.0% | $4,817 | $5,630 | $6,768 | $8,476 | $11,321 |
| | 10.1% | $4,475 | $5,173 | $6,125 | $7,500 | $9,660 |
| | 10.2% | $4,176 | $4,782 | $5,589 | $6,719 | $8,414 |

First of all, the value under the base case is HUGE: over $6.7 billion! Second, the range of possible values is also huge: $4.176 to $17.137 billion. Because the growth rate is so close to the WACC, this valuation is extremely sensitive to even very small changes in inputs.

### *Sensitivity analysis and the market approach*

If you haven't read the chapter on the market approach, please do so.

Doing a sensitivity analysis within the market approach is simple since there are only two inputs: the multiple and the cash flow. The good thing is that many times we know the cash flow with certainty: it is literally the last twelve months (LTM) of whatever cash flow we are using. For example, if we were doing a valuation based on the EV/EBITDA multiple, then we would use the LTM EBITDA. There is no uncertainty about that. So, where does the uncertainty lie? It lies in the comparable multiple.

When we "spread" our comps, we typically get a range of values that are associated with the firms that we are using as our comparable firms. For example, if we find three comparable firms, then we will get three different comparable multiples. Many analysts use the high to low range of the comparable firm multiples as the upside and downside cases in their sensitivity analysis. For example, imagine if we had the following EV/EBITDA comps for the firm that we are trying to value:

| Market Comps | |
|---|---|
| | **EV/EBITDA** |
| Firm A | 12.3 |
| Firm B | 12.45 |
| Firm C | 12.6 |

The firm we are valuing might be closest to Firm B with respect to its growth rate, tax rate, reinvestment rate, and risk. So, we decide upon a base case EV/EBITDA multiple of 12.45x, which we think is defensible. If the firm's LTM EBITDA is $40MM, then our estimated value would be 12.45 * $40MM = $498MM. That will represent our base case for the sensitivity analysis. So, how sensitive is this base case price estimate to reasonable changes in the EV/EBITDA multiple? To answer this question, we might consider using the low end of the range (12.3x) as our downside case, and the high end (12.6x) as our upside case. When we do that, we obtain the following results. Note that it is common to report such results in a tabular format.

**Sensitivity Analysis Cases**

| Case | EV/EBITDA | Value |
|---|---|---|
| Downside | 12.3x | $492 |
| Base | 12.45x | $498 |
| Upside | 12.6x | $504 |

Our sensitivity analysis shows that although our base case point estimate is $498MM, a reasonable range of values could potentially be between $492MM and $504MM. Now, it is up to us to build the arguments to support the case as to why the appropriate point estimate should be $498MM.

## The Football Field

A popular way to visually present price estimates and their associated sensitivity analysis in a way that is easy to understand is to graph them on a "football field." A football field (see Figure 1) allows for easy comparison across approaches, and to find ranges of intersectionality. Remember, not all approaches are well suited for every type of valuation. For example, if the firm is not generating positive cash flows (e.g., negative EBITDA), then market approaches based on these cash flows (e.g., EV/EBITDA) are not appropriate, in this case we might use a multiple based on Revenues instead.

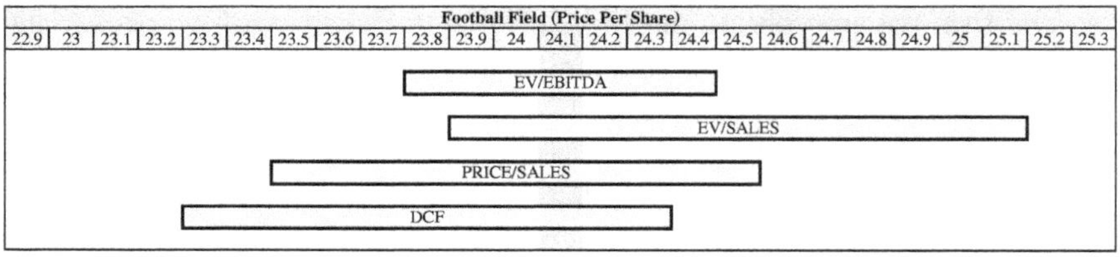


Figure 1. Sample Football Field

## *Football field example*

Imagine that we have done a valuation of a minority share of stock using the market and income approaches, and get the following value estimates for the price of a minority share:

- EV/EBITDA = \$24.1 *per share* with a sensitivity analysis that yields a range of \$23.8–24.4.
- EV/Sales = \$24.5 *per share* with a sensitivity analysis that yields a range of \$23.9–25.1.
- Price/Sales = \$24.0 *per share* with a sensitivity analysis that yields a range of \$23.5–24.5.
- DCF indirect approach = \$23.9 *per share* with a sensitivity analysis that yields a range of \$23.3–24.3.

A common way to present this information is on a Football Field, where the ranges are juxtaposed against one another.

## *Arriving at a final point estimate*

The Football Field makes it very easy to visually compare the results of the four different valuation approaches, but the critical question remains: how do we use all this information to determine a single-point estimate? If we were to give each of the approaches the same weight, then a reasonable point estimate might be \$24.1 per share. However, and this is very important, we might have a strong reason to prefer one approach over the others. For example, if the firm had a lot of operating leverage (fixed costs relative to variable costs), then the EV/EBITDA multiple would be a much better choice than Price/Sales or even EV/Sales — these multiples work very well for companies where most of their costs are variable or when EBITDA is negative but are less appropriate when there is a lot of operating leverage.

So, as much as we wish there were an easy solution for the determination of the singular point estimate, the bottom line is that one must use one's best judgment to arrive at an estimate that is defensible. Some analysts prefer to provide a range of values rather than a specific point estimate. For example, using the football field above, we might be comfortable arguing for a price that is between \$24.0 and \$24.2 per share. Other analysts create their own weights for each of the approaches, based upon which they think are the most appropriate and defensible, and take a weighted average. For example, an analyst (note, we are not advocating for this scheme, just using it for an example) might choose to use the following hypothetical weighting scheme:

| **Method** | **Weight** | **Mean** |
|---|---|---|
| EV/EBITDA | 60% | \$24.15 |
| EV/Sales | 20% | \$24.45 |
| Price/Sales | 10% | \$24.0 |
| DCF | 10% | \$23.8 |

This would yield a weighted average point estimate of

$$(.6 \times \$24.15) + (.2 \times \$24.45) + (.1 \times \$24.0) + (.1 \times \$23.8) = \$24.16$$

In our experience, the EV/EBITDA multiple is the one that is used most often (not that the others aren't popular or useful) for acquisition-related transaction purposes. Sometimes the analyst will use other valuation approaches to calibrate whether the estimate provided by the EV/EBITDA method is reasonable. For example, imagine if in the example above the EV/EBITDA approach yields a mean estimate of \$35 a share (rather than the actual \$24.15), then given the other valuations presented at the football field, one might be suspicious about the defensibility of such a high price estimate. It is possible that something is wrong or that there is an error. Note, it might also be possible that the EV/EBITDA approach is the most appropriate approach and that the others are not as appropriate; in that case, it is up to us to make that argument. Be ready though, we will likely get push back from our counterparty. Always be ready to defend your point estimate.

So, the bottom line is that there is no easy one-size-fits-all solution to getting a defensible point estimate. We must use our judgment, sound reasoning, and build a solid case to support our estimate. We must prepare our arguments for why we chose a particular method or weighting scheme. For example, why did we choose that particular growth rate or WACC or comparable multiple? BE PREPARED: our counterparty is likely to push back irrespective of our level of care in conducting the analysis ... and if you are going to court and there is a litigator (with their own expert witness in tow) cross-examining you, then you can count on it.

## Alpha Brewing Company Valuation — Putting It All Together

In the previous chapters, we applied three valuation methods to Alpha Brewing Company, each method provided a different estimate of value, summarized in the following table.

| **Alpha Brewing Co.'s Three Approaches** | |
|---|---|
| Income Approach [Ch.9, DDM] | \$8,047,111 |
| Market Approach [Ch.10, EV/EBITDA] | \$8,110,882 |
| Asset Approach [Ch.11, NAVM] | \$7,527,838 |

Let's quickly review how we utilized each of the valuation methodologies to arrive at Alpha's value.

### *Chapter 9's income approach exhibit*

| Direct Method to Price Non-Constant Dividend Growth Stocks: Alpha Brewing Company | | | | | |
|---|---|---|---|---|---|
| Required rate of capital (Ke): | 9.72% | | | | |
| Dividend growth rate: | 3.50% | | | | |
| Time | 1 | 2 | 3 | 4 | 5 |
| **Year** | **2020** | **2021** | **2022** | **2023** | **2024** |
| Dividend | 700,438 | 512,138 | 521,574 | 541,303 | 560,234 |
| Terminal Value (TV4) | – | – | – | 9,006,979 | – |
| Cash Flows | 700,438 | 512,138 | 521,574 | 9,548,282 | – |
| PV of CFs at Time 0 | 638,387 | 425,418 | 394,874 | 6,588,432 | |
| Equity Value (sum of PVs) | **8,047,111** | | | | |

Recall that we can use the Income Approach to obtain an intrinsic value estimate. There were two income approaches: the direct and the indirect approach. The indirect approach involves taking the unlevered free cash flows and discounting them back at the firm's WACC. This approach yields an estimate for enterprise value from which we deduct net debt and preferred stock in order to obtain an estimate for the firm's equity value. In contrast, the direct method of valuing the firm's equity involved taking the present value of the firm's forecasted dividends and discounting those back at the firm's cost of equity capital. It is this approach that we used above.

### *Chapter 10's market approach exhibit*

| Brewery EV/EBITDA Example | | | | |
|---|---|---|---|---|
| | **Andrew's Pale Ales** | **B&B's Boston Brews** | **Kelly's Malt Lagers** | **Alpha Brewing Co.** |
| LTM Revenue | $1,700,000 | $2,387,500 | $2,955,000 | $1,829,520 |
| LTM EBITDA | $825,000 | $955,000 | $985,000 | $611,473 |
| MV Equity | $9,100,000 | $12,950,000 | $14,250,000 | ? |
| Debt | $420,000 | $650,000 | $775,000 | $483,888 |

| Brewery EV/EBITDA Example | | | | |
|---|---|---|---|---|
| | **Andrew's Pale Ales** | **B&B's Boston Brews** | **Kelly's Malt Lagers** | **Alpha Brewing Co.** |
| Preferred Stock | $100,000 | $200,000 | $0 | $0 |
| Cash | $120,000 | $50,000 | $300,000 | $266,507 |
| EV | $9,500,000 | $13,750,000 | $14,725,000 | ? |
| EV/EBITDA | 11.52x | 14.40x | 14.95x | ? |
| EV/EBITDA Average | **13.62x** | | | |

| Alpha Brewing's EV & MV of Equity | |
|---|---|
| LTM EBITDA | $611,473 |
| Comp Average EV/EBITDA | 13.62x |
| Target Firm's EV | $8,328,263 |
| Preferred Stock | $0 |
| Net Debt | $217,381 |
| Target Firm's MV of Equity | **$8,110,882** |

The Market Approach involves using relative values in order to estimate the price of Alpha Brewing's equity. Relative values were found by searching for comparable firms that were a reasonable match to Alpha Brewing on four factors: risk, growth, reinvestment rate, and tax. Our search yielded three similar firms whose financials are summarized in the above chart. We calculated each of the three comparable firms' enterprise values (EV) to EBITDA multiple, and used these multiples to determine what would be a reasonable and defensible EV/EBITDA multiple for AB. We, then, use this reasonable multiple to calculate the AB's Enterprise Value and then subtract out the net debt and preferred stock to obtain an estimate for the value of its Equity.

## *Chapter 11's asset approach exhibit*

**Adjusted Net Asset Value Method** (because brewery is still a going concern)

(1) Remove non-operating assets (unnecessary for firm's operations or going concern status)

(2) Revalue remaining assets to current market values, result is "Adjusted Operating Assets"

(3) Subtract from (2) all non-interest bearing liabilities, result is "Adjusted Net Operating Assets"

(4) Apply Cumulative Excess Earnings method to discover some Intangible Assets in the Nature of Goodwill & add to Adjusted Net Operating Assets for Total ANOA

(5) Subtract Total Debt from Total Adjusted Net Operating Assets , result is "Market Value of Equity"

**Adjustments to Assets**

(A) Inventory & PP&E adjusted up to current market values. Assumption is that the owner leveraged his extensive business network to obtain below-market prices

(B) Accounts Receivable was adjusted down Assumption is a lack of allowance for doubtful accounts. Normally just writes it off if missed collections.

(C) Cash & Security Deposit left unadjusted

**Balance Sheet (Pre-Cumulative Earnings)**

| **Assets** | **Original** | **Adjusted** | **Adjustments** | **Adjusted Liabilities & Equity** | **Adjusted** |
|---|---|---|---|---|---|
| Cash | $266,507 | $266,507 | Same | Accounts Payable | $12,819 |
| Accounts Receivable | $163,053 | $146,748 | 10% Down | Current Portion of Long-Term Debt | $56,893 |
| Inventory | $20,173 | $25,216 | 25% Up | Long-Term Debt | $426,995 |
| Security Deposit | $20,000 | $20,000 | Same | Owners' Equity | $939,743 |
| PP&E | $814,982 | $977,979 | 20% Up | | |
| Total | $1,284,715 | $1,436,449 | | Total | $1,436,449 |

| **Adjusted Net Operating Assets** | | **Required Earnings** | |
|---|---|---|---|
| Adjusted Operating Assets | $1,436,449 | Adjusted Net Operating Assets | $1,423,630 |
| Non-Financial Liabilities | ($12,819) | WACC | 7.66% |
| Adjusted Net Operating Assets | $1,423,630 | Required Earnings | $109,062 |

| **Excess Earnings** | | **Cumulative Excess Earnings** | |
|---|---|---|---|
| Next Year's EBIT | $613,765 | Excess Earnings | $504,703 |
| Required Earnings | ($109,062) | WACC | 7.66% |
| Excess Earnings | $504,703 | Cumulative Excess Earnings | $6,588,095 |
| **Total Adjusted Net Operating Assets** | | **MV of Equity (Post-Cumulative)** | |
| Adjusted Net Operating Assets | $1,423,630 | Total Adj. Net Op. Assets | $8,011,726 |
| Cumulative Excess Earnings | $6,588,095 | BV(Debt) | ($483,888) |
| Total Adj. Net Op. Assets | $8,011,726 | MV(Equity) | $7,527,838 |

Recall that the Asset Approach involves adjusting the firm's book value Balance Sheet (on an asset-by-asset and liability-by-liability basis) to current market values, and then computing the Excess Earnings, which is the difference between next year's forecasted EBIT and the firm's WACC times its Adjusted Net Assets. We then assume that these Excess Earnings occur in perpetuity and take their present value to compute the Cumulative Excess Earnings. Cumulative Excess Earnings is a measure of whether there is any value hidden off-balance sheet in the Intangible Value in the Nature of Goodwill. We then add these Cumulative Excess earnings to the Adjusted Equity in order to obtain an estimate of the market value of AB's equity.

## *Valuing Alpha Brewing Company*

To bring this chapter to a close, we present a football field for the valuation of Alpha Brewing and use this to arrive at a final point estimate. To this end, we employ three valuation approaches: an income approach, a market approach, and the asset-based approach. We include a sensitivity analysis for each of the valuation approaches to get a better sense of the precision of our estimates and to create the range of valuations that will be mapped onto the football field. Lastly, we examine the resulting football field to arrive at a final, defensible point estimate.

We begin with the income approach. The calculations behind the valuation here can be found in the Alpha Brewing example that we presented in Chapter 9. Since the brewery was created with the intent of paying steady and reliable dividend to its owners (this is basically going to be their retirement cash generator), it is an excellent candidate for the direct method of equity valuation. It isn't often the case that the dividend discount (direct) method is preferable to the indirect approach, so we thought that this would be a great opportunity for you to see an example when it works well. As in Chapter 9, we use the base case of 3.50% for the terminal growth rate for our dividends. We conduct a sensitivity analysis around our terminal growth rate assumption and, accordingly, allow the terminal dividend growth rate to move up or down 25 basis points; in other words, the range would be from 3.25% to 3.75%. We feel that this range is reasonable and appropriate given our knowledge of the brewery's product market and our discussion with the management team and the owners. So based on our modeling, we found that the expected value would be \$8.1MM, with the pessimistic case at \$7.5MM and the optimistic case at \$8.3MM. This gives us a range of \$0.5MM.

Next, we use the market approach. Here we use the comparable market valuation taken from the Alpha Brewing example presented in Chapter 10. Specifically, we use the EV/EBITDA multiple because we believe that this would likely be the multiple that would be used if we were to sell this business today. We begin with a base case EV/EBITDA multiple of 13.62x, and then conduct a sensitivity analysis by allowing the multiple to move between the range of 13x and 14x EBITDA. Again, we believe this range is reasonable given our understanding of the comparable firms in the market. The base case valuation is \$8.1MM, with the sensitivity analysis ranging from a downside valuation of \$7.7MM and an upside valuation of \$8.3MM.

The third valuation involves the asset-based approach. Here we rely on the asset-based valuation of Alpha Brewing that we presented back in Chapter 11. If you recall, the base case EBIT was \$613k and it yielded an equity valuation of \$7.5MM. We conduct a sensitivity analysis around this EBIT forecast by allowing it to vary by ±5%. The sensitivity analysis yields a range between \$7.1MM and \$7.9MM. The following three tables provide a summary of our sensitivity analysis results.

| **Income Approach** | **Growth Rate** | **Equity Value** |
|---|---|---|
| Worst | 3.25 | 7,806,967 |
| Best | 3.75 | 8,307,367 |
| Base | 3.50 | 8,047,111 |

| Market Approach | EV/EBITDA | Equity Value |
|---|---|---|
| Worst | 13 | 7,731,769 |
| Best | 14 | 8,343,242 |
| Base | 13.62 | 8,110,882 |

| Asset Approach | EBIT | Equity Value |
|---|---|---|
| Worst (EBIT – 5%) | 583,077 | 7,127,259 |
| Best (EBIT + 5%) | 644,453 | 7,928,425 |
| EBIT Base Case | 613,765 | 7,527,838 |

Once we have these three valuations and their associated sensitivity analyses, we can then build a football field and arrive at a reasonable and defensible point estimate. See the following figure for the football field:

***Football field for Alpha Brewing Company***

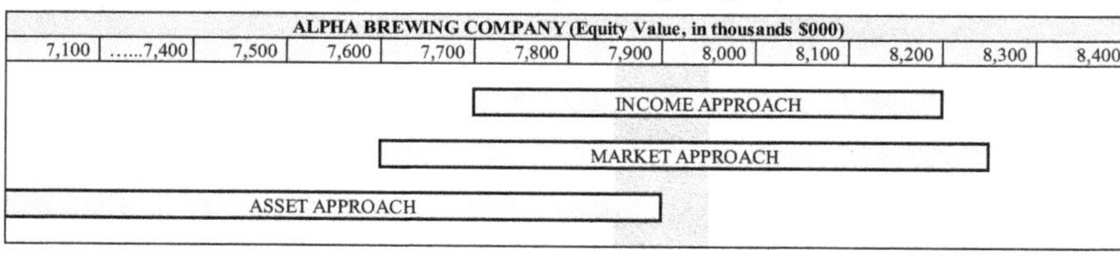


As can be seen from this figure, the sensitivity analysis ranges of the three approaches overlap each other significantly. There is a region of intersection among the three approaches (between $7.7MM and $8.0MM). This is a good sign: it means that our valuation of Alpha Brewing is relatively robust to our choice of valuation methodology.

Of the three approaches, we believe that the market approach is probably the most accurate with respect to getting a fair market value, given that it uses actual market prices when getting the comparable EV/EBITDA ratios, and would likely be the approach that would be used if we were to sell the brewery on the open market. Consequently, we give the market approach more influence in our decision-making process. We have highlighted the area (in blue) where we believe the value of Alpha

Brewing should likely reside. We would be very confident of a valuation that is somewhere in the area of $7.95MM and $8.1MM. If we were to choose a solid, defensible point estimate, it would be right at $8.00MM.

The analysis is done, now all we need to do is negotiate the transaction and convince our counterparty that our valuation is on the money.

## Key Takeaways

- The mean and the median (the 50th percentile, where half of the possible outcomes are higher than the median, and the other half are lower than it) are identical when a distribution is symmetrical.
- Sensitivity analysis forces you to challenge the key assumptions that drive the valuation.
- The most common assumptions challenged are the growth rate in revenues, especially the terminal growth rate and the Weighted Average Cost of Capital (WACC).
- The closer the terminal growth rate is to WACC, the more sensitive the terminal value is to small errors in the growth rate.
- Typically, the sensitivity analysis for the market approach has only two inputs: the multiple and the cash flow.

# Chapter 15

# Appendix: Alpha Brewing Company Financials

ALPHA BREWING COMPANY

*Annual Income Statement, 2017–2024E*

| | | HISTORICAL | HISTORICAL | HISTORICAL | *PROFORMA* | *PROJECTED* | *PROJECTED* | *PROJECTED* | *PROJECTED* |
|---|---|---|---|---|---|---|---|---|---|
| **YEAR** | | **2017** | **2018** | **2019** | **2020** | **2021** | **2022** | **2023** | **2024** |
| Total Revenues | | 1,209,600 | 1,663,200 | 1,829,520 | 1,957,586 | 2,055,466 | 2,122,268 | 2,191,242 | 2,262,457 |
| *Revenue growth rate* | | *N/A* | *37.5%* | *10.0%* | *7.0%* | *5.0%* | *3.25%* | *3.25%* | *3.25%* |
| Total Excise and Sales Tax | | 85,365 | 117,376 | 129,114 | 137,994 | 144,686 | 149,322 | 154,107 | 159,047 |
| Net Revenues | | 1,124,235 | 1,545,824 | 1,700,406 | 1,819,593 | 1,910,780 | 1,972,946 | 2,037,135 | 2,103,411 |
| Cost of Goods Sold (COGS) | | 166,320 | 199,584 | 172,553 | 181,181 | 185,710 | 190,353 | 195,112 | 199,990 |
| Gross Profit | | 957,915 | 1,346,240 | 1,527,853 | 1,638,412 | 1,725,070 | 1,782,593 | 1,842,023 | 1,903,421 |
| Selling, General and Administrative Expenses | | 771,494 | 893,223 | 916,380 | 939,641 | 986,624 | 1,018,689 | 1,051,796 | 1,085,980 |
| Depreciation & Amortization | | 74,506 | 74,506 | 85,006 | 85,006 | 85,006 | 24,806 | 24,806 | 17,949 |
| Operating Income | | 111,916 | 378,510 | 526,467 | 613,765 | 653,440 | 739,099 | 765,421 | 799,493 |
| Interest Expense | | 38,336 | 35,300 | 32,070 | 28,632 | 24,972 | 21,077 | 16,932 | 12,520 |
| Earnings Before Taxes | | 73,580 | 343,210 | 494,397 | 585,133 | 628,468 | 718,021 | 748,489 | 786,973 |
| Income Taxes | 21.0% | 15,452 | 72,074 | 103,823 | 122,878 | 131,978 | 150,784 | 157,183 | 165,264 |
| **Net Income** | | **58,129** | **271,136** | **390,574** | **462,255** | **496,490** | **567,237** | **591,306** | **621,709** |
| *Net Income growth rate* | | | *366.4%* | *44.1%* | *18.4%* | *7.4%* | *14.2%* | *4.2%* | *5.1%* |

ALPHA BREWING COMPANY

*Annual Balance Sheet, 2017–2024E*

| | HISTORICAL | HISTORICAL | HISTORICAL | PROFORMA | PROJECTED | PROJECTED | PROJECTED | PROJECTED |
|---|---|---|---|---|---|---|---|---|
| **YEAR** | **2017** | **2018** | **2019** | **2020** | **2021** | **2022** | **2023** | **2024** |
| **ASSETS** | | | | | | | | |
| Cash | 93,466 | 213,709 | 266,507 | 50,000 | 50,000 | 50,000 | 50,000 | 50,000 |
| Accounts Receivable | 21,602 | 98,485 | 163,053 | 174,481 | 183,225 | 189,187 | 195,342 | 201,697 |
| Inventory | 15,632 | 17,843 | 20,173 | 17,253 | 17,687 | 18,129 | 18,582 | 19,047 |
| Total Current Assets | 130,700 | 330,037 | 449,733 | 241,735 | 250,912 | 257,315 | 263,924 | 270,744 |
| Security Deposit | 20,000 | 20,000 | 20,000 | 20,000 | 20,000 | 20,000 | 20,000 | 20,000 |
| PP&E, net | 921,994 | 847,488 | 814,982 | 729,977 | 644,971 | 620,165 | 595,359 | 577,410 |
| **Total Assets** | **1,072,694** | **1,197,526** | **1,284,715** | **991,711** | **915,883** | **897,480** | **879,283** | **868,154** |
| **Liabilities & Owners' Equity** | | | | | | | | |
| A/P — Ingredient Suppliers | 3,829 | 7,749 | 12,819 | 14,892 | 15,264 | 15,645 | 16,037 | 16,437 |
| Current Portion Long-Term Debt | 50,224 | 53,455 | 56,893 | 60,552 | 64,447 | 68,592 | 73,004 | 77,700 |
| Total Current Liabilities | 54,053 | 61,204 | 69,712 | 75,444 | 79,711 | 84,238 | 89,041 | 94,138 |
| Long-Term Debt | 537,342 | 483,888 | 426,995 | 366,442 | 301,995 | 233,403 | 160,398 | 82,698 |
| Total Liabilities | 591,395 | 545,091 | 496,707 | 441,886 | 381,706 | 317,641 | 249,439 | 176,836 |
| Owners' Units — par value | 1,000 | 1,000 | 1,000 | 1,000 | 1,000 | 1,000 | 1,000 | 1,000 |
| Owners' Units — add'l paid-in capital | 422,170 | 422,170 | 422,170 | 422,170 | 422,170 | 422,170 | 422,170 | 422,170 |

(*Continued*)

| | HISTORICAL | HISTORICAL | HISTORICAL | PROFORMA | PROJECTED | PROJECTED | PROJECTED | PROJECTED |
|---|---|---|---|---|---|---|---|---|
| **YEAR** | **2017** | **2018** | **2019** | **2020** | **2021** | **2022** | **2023** | **2024** |
| Retained Earnings | 58,129 | 229,264 | 364,838 | 126,655 | 111,007 | 156,670 | 206,673 | 268,148 |
| Total Owners' Equity | 481,299 | 652,434 | 788,008 | 549,825 | 534,177 | 579,840 | 629,843 | 691,318 |
| **Total Liabilities & Owners' Equity** | **1,072,694** | **1,197,526** | **1,284,715** | **991,711** | **915,883** | **897,480** | **879,283** | **868,154** |
| *Check* | — | — | — | — | — | — | — | — |
| Net Working Capital (NWC) | 33,045 | 108,579 | 170,407 | 176,843 | 185,648 | 191,670 | 197,887 | 204,306 |
| Net Increase/(Decrease) in NWC | 33,045 | 75,174 | 61,828 | 6,436 | 8,805 | 6,022 | 6,217 | 6,419 |

ALPHA BREWING COMPANY

*Annual Cash Flow Statement, 2017–2024E*

| | HISTORICAL | HISTORICAL | HISTORICAL | PROFORMA | PROJECTED | PROJECTED | PROJECTED | PROJECTED |
|---|---|---|---|---|---|---|---|---|
| **YEAR** | **2017** | **2018** | **2019** | **2020** | **2021** | **2022** | **2023** | **2024** |
| CASH AND CASH EQUIVALENTS, BEGINNING OF PERIOD | — | 93,466 | 213,709 | 266,507 | 50,000 | 50,000 | 50,000 | 50,000 |
| OPERATING ACTIVITIES: | | | | | | | | |
| Net income | 58,129 | 271,136 | 390,574 | 462,255 | 496,490 | 567,237 | 591,306 | 621,709 |
| Adjustments to reconcile net income to net cash from operating activities: | | | | | | | | |
| Depreciation | 74,506 | 74,506 | 85,006 | 85,006 | 85,006 | 24,806 | 24,806 | 17,949 |
| Changes in working capital: | | | | | | | | |
| Accounts receivable | (21,602) | (76,883) | (64,568) | (11,428) | (8,744) | (5,961) | (6,155) | (6,355) |
| Inventories | (15,632) | (2,211) | (2,330) | 2,920 | (433) | (442) | (453) | (465) |
| Security Deposit | (20,000) | — | — | — | – | — | — | — |
| Accounts Payable | 3,829 | 3,920 | 5,070 | 2,073 | 372 | 382 | 391 | 401 |
| Current Portion of Long-Term Debt | 47,189 | 3,035 | 3,231 | 3,438 | 3,659 | 3,895 | 4,145 | 4,412 |
| Net cash provided by (used in) operating activities | 79,229 | 270,468 | 413,752 | 540,825 | 572,691 | 586,021 | 609,895 | 633,239 |

*(Continued)*

| | HISTORICAL | HISTORICAL | HISTORICAL | PROFORMA | PROJECTED | PROJECTED | PROJECTED | PROJECTED |
|---|---|---|---|---|---|---|---|---|
| **YEAR** | **2017** | **2018** | **2019** | **2020** | **2021** | **2022** | **2023** | **2024** |
| INVESTING ACTIVITIES: | | | | | | | | |
| Capital Expenditures | (996,500) | — | (52,500) | — | — | — | — | — |
| Net cash provided by (used in) investing activities | (996,500) | — | (52,500) | — | — | — | — | — |
| Cash Available for Debt Repayment | (917,271) | 363,933 | 574,961 | 807,331 | 622,691 | 636,021 | 659,895 | 683,239 |
| FINANCING ACTIVITIES: | | | | | | | | |
| Equity Investment from Founders | 423,170 | — | — | — | — | — | — | — |
| Long-Term Debt | 634,755 | — | — | — | — | — | — | — |
| Long-Term Debt - proceeds principle repayment | (47,189) | (50,224) | (53,455) | (56,893) | (60,552) | (64,447) | (68,592) | (73,004) |
| Dividends | — | (100,000) | (255,000) | (700,438) | (512,138) | (521,574) | (541,303) | (560,234) |
| Net cash provided by (used in) financing activities | 1,010,736 | (150,224) | (308,455) | (757,331) | (572,691) | (586,021) | (609,895) | (633,239) |
| *Dividend growth rate* | | | *155.0%* | *174.7%* | *–26.9%* | *1.8%* | *3.8%* | *3.5%* |
| Net increase/ (decrease) in cash and cash equivalents | 93,466 | 120,244 | 52,797 | (216,507) | 0 | (0) | 0 | 0 |
| **CASH AND CASH EQUIVALENTS, END OF PERIOD** | **93,466** | **213,709** | **266,507** | **50,000** | **50,000** | **50,000** | **50,000** | **50,000** |

# Index

www.ingramcontent.com/pod-product-compliance
Lightning Source LLC
LaVergne TN
LVHW011809200926
848484LV00005B/1121